Also available at all good book stores

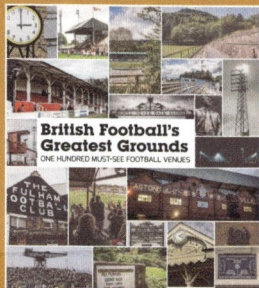

9781785316470

9781785313929

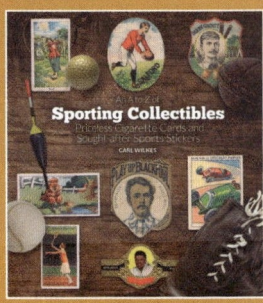

9781785316739

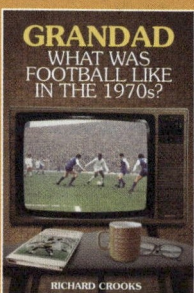

9781785312632

9781785316845

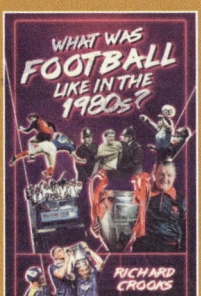

9781785315534

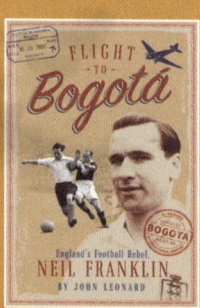

9781785316548

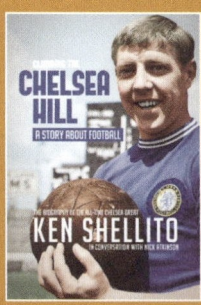

9781785316807

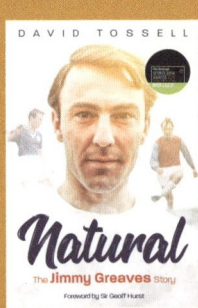

9781785314902

THE
HISTORY OF
FOOTBALL
IN 90 MINUTES
(PLUS EXTRA TIME)

BEN JONES AND GARETH THOMAS
THE FOOTBALL HISTORY BOYS

First published by Pitch Publishing, 2021

Pitch Publishing
A2 Yeoman Gate
Yeoman Way
Worthing
Sussex
BN13 3QZ
www.pitchpublishing.co.uk
info@pitchpublishing.co.uk

ISBN 978 1 78531 839 9

Typesetting and origination by Pitch Publishing
Printed and bound in India by Replika Press Pvt. Ltd.

Contents

Introduction 12

1. Nándor Hidegkuti opens the scoring at Wembley (1953) 17
2. Dennis Viollet puts Manchester United ahead in
   Belgrade (1958) 20
3. Gaztelu help brings Basque back to life (1976) 22
4. Wayne Rooney scores early against Iceland (2016) 24
5. Brian Deane scores the Premier League's first goal (1992) 27
6. The FA Cup semi-final is abandoned at
   Hillsborough (1989) 30
7. Cristiano Ronaldo completes a full 90 (2014) 33
8. Christine Sinclair opens her international account (2000). .35
9. Play is stopped in Nantes to pay tribute to Emiliano
   Sala (2019) 38
10. Xavi sets in motion one of football's greatest team
    performances (2010) 40
11. Roger Hunt begins the goal-rush on *Match of the
    Day* (1964) 42
12. Ted Drake makes it 3-0 to England at the Battle of
    Highbury (1934) .45
13. Trevor Brooking wins it for the underdogs (1980) 48
14. Alfredo Di Stéfano scores for Real Madrid in the first
    European Cup Final (1956). 50
15. The first FA Cup Final goal (1872) 52
16. Carli Lloyd completes a World Cup Final hat-trick from
    the halfway line (2015) 55
17. The first goal scored in the Champions League (1992). .57
18. Helmut Rahn equalises for West Germany in the
    Miracle of Bern (1954) 60
19. Lucien Laurent scores the first World Cup goal (1930). .63
20. Michelle Akers opens the scoring in the first Women's
    World Cup Final (1991). 65
21. Roberto Carlos's banana goal (1997) 67
22. Mario Balotelli asks, 'Why Always Me?' (2011) 69
23. Johan Cruyff turns the footballing world inside
    out (1974) 72

24. Just Fontaine's first of 13 in Sweden (1958). 74
25. The end of Ronaldo's final, but not the end for
    Portugal (2016) 76
26. Kevin-Prince Boateng takes a stand against racism (2013) 78
27. David Beckham scores his first US goal (2007) 80
28. Nigel de Jong kung fu kicks Xabi Alonso (2010) 82
29. Germany score their fifth in the 7-1 Mineirazo defeat
    of Brazil (2014) 85
30. Ada Hegerberg nets her Champions League Final hat-
    trick (2019) 87
31. Pelé scores his first of five v Eusébio's Benfica (1962). . .89
32. Katie Chapman helps make it four in a row for
    Arsenal (2009) 91
33. Australia's 13th in a record-breaking 31-0 win (2001) . .93
34. Ivan Perišić's handball leads to history-making VAR
    penalty (2018). 95
35. Gino Colaussi helps Italy to back-to-back World
    Cups (1938). 97
36. Jimmy Simmons opens the scoring in the Khaki Cup
    Final (1915) 100
37. Lawrie Sanchez helps the Crazy Gang lift the FA
    Cup (1988) 103
38. Joe Gaetjens's 'Miracle on Grass' (1950) 106
39. The world sees Frank Lampard's 'goal' cross the
    line (2010). 109
40. The Valley Parade fire begins in Bradford (1985). . . . 112
41. Mario David's 'worst tackle in history' (1962) 115
42. North Korea stun Italy (1966) 117
43. Gerd Müller's World Cup winner (1974) 120
44. Robin van Persie's flying header (2014). 123
45. Britain's first £1m player helps pay back his fee (1979) . 125

Half-Time. 128

46. Steven Gerrard sees red against Manchester
    United (2015) 131
47. David Beckham kicks out at Diego Simeone (1998) . . 133
48. Eric Cantona is sent off and goes berserk at Crystal
    Palace (1995) 136

49. The El Clásico stranglehold on Spanish football is finally broken by Atlético (2014) 138

50. David Seaman is lobbed by Ronaldinho at the World Cup (2002) 141

51. 'A little with the hand of God and a little with the head of Maradona' (1986) 144

52. Robert Lewandowski makes it two out of five (2015) . 146

53. Lionel Messi's 400th goal in La Liga (2019) 148

54. 'Hello, hello … here we go' – The Miracle of Istanbul (2005) 151

55. Hal Robson-Kanu turns into Johan Cruyff (2016) . . . 154

56. Gini Wijnaldum equalises in the Miracle of Anfield (2019). 157

57. Angelos Charisteas shocks Portugal to win the Euros (2004) 160

58. Michel Platini wins the European Cup which should never have been played (1985) 163

59. The Copa del Generalísimo begins in Barcelona (1939) 166

60. Future full time? (2017). 169

61. Alan Shearer sets a seemingly unbreakable record (2006) 172

62. Tommy Gemmell equalises in Lisbon (1967). 174

63. Khalid Boulahrouz sees red in the Battle of Nuremberg (2006) 176

64. Gareth Bale's Champions League overhead brilliance (2018). 179

65. Megan Rapinoe stands tall for women's football (2019) 181

66. Welsh hearts broken by 17-year-old Pelé (1958). 184

67. Redemption for Ronaldo (2002) 187

68. Falcão equalises for Brazil in Barcelona (1982) 190

69. Benfica's final European triumph before the Curse of Béla Guttmann (1962) 193

70. Sammy Thomson completes English football's first double (1889) 197

71. Lars Ricken lobs Dortmund to the Champions League (1997). 200

72. Luís Figo welcomed back to the Camp Nou with a pig's head (2002) 202

73. Bert Trautmann breaks his neck (1956) 205
74. Hughie Ferguson wins the FA Cup for Cardiff
    City (1927) 208
75. José Mourinho self-proclaimed Special One after
    Champions League victory (2004) 211
76. Wolves equalise before becoming 'champions of the
    world' (1954) 213
77. Jürgen Sparwasser's winner as East meets West (1974) . 216
78. Handball! But was it a Welsh or a Scottish hand? (1977) 219
79. Alcides Ghiggia scores the winner in Maracanazo (1950) 222
80. Number eight Jimmy Dunn scores Everton's third in
    the FA Cup Final (1933) 225
81. Alejandro Villanueva scores for Peru at the 1936
    Olympics (1936) 228
82. Robert Ullathorne's injury ends the Battle of Bramall
    Lane (2002). 231
83. Dixie Dean scores 60 in a season (1928) 234
84. Super-sub David Fairclough makes the Kop go
    wild (1977) 237
85. The final Premier League goal before COVID-19
    suspends play (2020) 239
86. Carlos Alberto scores *that* goal for Brazil (1970) 242
87. Lionel Messi makes fools of Real Madrid in El
    Clásico (2011). 244
88. Hosts South Korea equalise in one of the game's most
    controversial matches (2002) 247
89. An epic comeback for Turkey at Euro 2008 (2008) . . 250
90. 'Dennis Bergkamp! Dennis Bergkamp! Dennis
    Bergkamp!' (1998) 253

When The Clock Passes 90. 256

91. 'It's up for grabs now!' – Michael Thomas's title
    winner (1989) 262
92. Bill Perry wins the Matthews Final (1953) 264
93. 'And Solskjær has won it!' – Manchester United seal
    the treble (1999). 267
94. 'Agüerooooooo' – Manchester City snatch the title (2012) 270
95. Oliver Bierhoff's golden goal wins Euro 96 (1996) . . . 273

96. Ajax stunned by Lucas Moura's last-gasp winner (2019) 276
97. Troy Deeney punishes Anthony Knockaert's penalty miss (2013) 279
98. Germany's golden goal snatches the Women's World Cup (2003) 281
99. Bobby Charlton completes United's remarkable journey back from the brink (1968). 283
100. Shannon MacMillan's Olympic golden goal sends USA to the final (1996). 285
101. Pipo Rodríguez's winner sparks the Football War (1969) 288
102. Injuries take their toll in 'the most brutal game in English football history' (1970) 290
103. Thierry Henry's handball sets it up for William Gallas (2009) 293
104. Henri Camara wins the 'best golden goal period ever' (2002) 295
105. Traianos Dellas scores football's only 'silver goal' (2004). 298
106. Roger Milla dances around the corner flag (1990) . . . 300
107. Blackburn Olympic provides football's early rebirth (1883) 303
108. Klaus Fischer equalises for West Germany against France (1982) 306
109. Substitute Ryan Giggs weaves through the entire Arsenal defence (1999) 309
110. Zinedine Zidane headbutts his way into retirement (2006) 311
111. The 'Game of the Century' is settled by Gianni Rivera (1970) 314
112. Johan Cruyff's Dream Team completes the set (1992) . 317
113. The Soviet Union win the first European Championships (1960) 320
114. Laurent Blanc's golden goal puts the Rainbow Team on course for victory (1998). 323
115. Argentina win the most controversial tournament in history (1978) 326
116. Andrés Iniesta wins the World Cup for Spain (2010) . 329

117. Homare Sawa equalises for Japan in the World Cup
      Final (2011) 332
118. Marcelo helps seal La Décima for Real Madrid (2014) . 335
119. Fabio Grosso's late strike decides one of football's
      greatest ever matches (2006) 338
120. 'They think it's all over... it is now!' – England win
      the World Cup (1966) 341

Penalties. 344

Epilogue 351

Bibliography 354

Dedication

We would like to thank our friends and family as well as those who have supported *The Football History Boys* for the last eight years.

And a special thank you to those who inspired our love for both sport and history at school and university:

Mr K. Morgan
Mrs S. Osmolska
Mrs C. Lamrick
(Bishop of Llandaff CiW High
School, Cardiff)

Mr T. Wallace
Mrs S. Hall
(Whitchurch High School, Cardiff)

Professor Martin Johnes
(Swansea University).

Introduction

'The first 90 minutes of a match
are the most important.' [1]

A LOT can happen in 90 minutes. In the past 160 years, key moments from thousands of matches have left remarkable legacies still felt strongly to this day. When football is offered into a conversation, replies will often consist of certain instances which have left a lasting impact on the game. 'The hand of God', 'Zidane's headbutt' and 'Gazza's tears' are just a few common responses among football fans around the world. Prior to a match starting, no one could predict these events or the minute they would materialise in, but they have been endlessly dissected and scrutinised almost every day since. Upon their occurrence, in different minutes, it gives further proof to the old notion that every minute in football is as important as the next.

Football stands alone in its present format with most team sports favouring 60- to 80-minute matches. Understandably, most football histories make little reference to the longevity of a single game, but its individuality makes it stand out. Despite being essential to the modern game, football has not always been played over 90 minutes, even since its codification in 1863. The length of a game was not written into the first set of rules adopted after the initial meeting of the Football Association

1   Famously said by Sir Bobby Robson, BBC, 'Robson in his own words', BBC Sport, 30 August 2004 http://news.bbc.co.uk/sport1/hi/funny_old_game/3612008.stm

with laws initially focused on alleviating potential disagreements on the pitch. In general, matches were to last longer than an hour however, usually with a break halfway through.

Despite the formation of the FA in 1863, its future was less than certain in the immediate years after. Other codes of the game were just as prevalent during this time. The lack of willingness of many clubs to initially join the association offers a suggestion as to why a definitive duration wasn't immediately agreed upon. References to the length of a game are difficult to find and our research into newspaper archives led us to the 1860s for the first real mentions of an 'hour and a half'. Our first such find was in 1865, when Charterhouse met Westminster in which an 'hour and a half of vigorous play' was recorded.[2] Charterhouse had infamously chosen not to join the FA at the Freemason's Tavern in 1863, preferring a more progressive style of play focused on passing the ball forwards.

Further evidence for a 90-minute game came in 1866 from a match between Sheffield and Nottingham (played under 'Sheffield rules'). It was recorded as having two halves each consisting of 'three quarters of an hour'.[3] Although seemingly a suitable length of time, it wasn't definitive. Just a month earlier, the two sides had played for a period double the length.

In 1869, a series of matches between different sides were recorded by *The Field* with alternative time limits. Although not conclusive whether each were playing 'association rules', it reports that Lilliputians and Mr Broughton's Team played for 75 minutes; Royal Engineers and Ravenscourt Park played for 90 and other matches from the same year were recorded as lasting up to two hours.[4] It is important to note that many of the early games, particularly among those outside of the FA, offered fluctuating rules (if agreed upon by the opposing

---

2   *Morning Post*, 24 November 1865

3   *Nottinghamshire Guardian*, 23 March 1866 – Bad weather played a major part in the decision to play 90 minutes. The paper reports that it rained and snowed 'incessantly' and created a 'swampy and ridgy' pitch

4   *The Field*, 16 January 1869

sides). Fixtures would often see uneven numbers of players on the respective teams.

The introduction of the FA Cup would be essential to the sport's agreement on 90 minutes of play. Just weeks before the competition began in November 1871, *The Sportsman* reported on a match between the Wanderers and Civil Service lasting only an hour.[5] Although not officially included in the association rules, the inaugural FA Cup season would use 90 minutes as its definitive time limit. The *Morning Post* wrote that the Football Association was 'assimilating' the rules of the popular Rugby Football Union.[6] Although true to some extent, football's simplistic nature and relatively few rules were in stark comparison to rugby's 59 laws. The adoption of 45-minute halves was also seen in the international game when Scotland entertained England in 1872. It seemed for the first time that a definitive duration had been decided.

It is generally agreed that the duration of 90 minutes finally reached a consensus around 1877. The change goes a long way to explaining why the earliest FA Cup Finals have no accurate records of the minutes in which the goals were scored. Relying solely on the post-match newspaper reports and their less than reliable time-keeping, many of the defining fixtures in the game's infancy were difficult to include in this book. Referees still had the power to change the length of a game, with poor weather or lack of players often leading to early finishes. The most notable use of this rule came in 1879 in the first tie between England and Wales at the Kennington Oval.[7] Ninety minutes was eventually written into the game's official rules and confirmed by the International Football Association Board (IFAB) in 1897.[8]

* * *

5   *The Sportsman*, 18 October 1871

6   *Morning Post*, 11 March 1872

7   *The Field*, 25 January 1879

8   'Minutes of Annual General Meeting', *International Football Association Board (IFAB)*, 1897, Available at: https://theifab.com/home

Football, as the old cliché suggests, is a game of two halves and in this book, we have separated the first 45 from the second. The first half typically sets the tone for the rest of the game and the opening section features a number of significant goals, challenges and bookings. From Nándor Hidegkuti's first-minute opener in the 'Match of the Century' to Trevor Francis's repayment of his £1m transfer in the 1979 European Cup Final, it has provided incredible passages of play to rival the second period of a match. Upon researching the moments we have chosen to represent these minutes, it has become evidently clear that they reveal stories that go far deeper than just a ball crossing the goal line or a player's studs being planted into their opponent's chest.

The second half is generally regarded as football's most entertaining and pivotal to defining decades of history. The first half, no matter how bad it may have gone for a side, can always be rectified if the team in question has the hunger and togetherness for victory. As the game reaches its often-dramatic climax the tension inside and outside the stadium heightens. This of course leads to the later minutes becoming the most shocking, the most heartbreaking and the most euphoric.

In total, there are 130 different moments covered throughout the book as we couldn't leave out the incredible drama often found in periods of extra time. Remarkably, the extra 30 minutes needed if a game ends in a draw has been a key element in football since its earliest days. The 1875 FA Cup Final was one of the first to feature an additional period and ever since, its presence has been altered and edited to suit the setting in which it is played. The introduction of the 'Golden Goal' was meant to initiate attacking play in the 1990s and remove the fear of losing. Despite leaving some of the sport's most joyous yet heart-breaking minutes of play, its initial aim was ultimately flawed. Its successor, the 'Silver Goal', didn't last long and yet its single use in a major tournament features later in this book.

Penalty shootouts have arguably provided football's most dramatic moments. They are a relatively new innovation in the game, only being used since 1970, but the sense of theatre they bring is unrivalled in wider sport. In comparison to other sports, the rarity of a shootout is perhaps what makes it so special. Despite the fact the clock has stopped and the minutes in which a penalty is scored or saved aren't recorded, it would be foolish to leave them out.

The earliest moment recorded in this list comes from 1872 with the first FA Cup Final goal. Upon its scoring, it brought almost ten years of Football Association uncertainty to a conclusion and set in stone a competition we still play today. The minutes also include an incredibly modern moment, which at the time of its occurrence held little initial relevance but in the subsequent weeks has led to arguably the biggest news story since the end of World War Two. An 85th-minute goal from Leicester's Harvey Barnes against Aston Villa was indeed the last scored in the Premier League before the suspension of the game due to the coronavirus pandemic.

Matthew Taylor writes that football provides a sanctuary with which we can escape from real life, even if just for 90 minutes.[9] For the next 90 minutes (plus extra time) we hope you enjoy your journey through the unrivalled history of football as much as we have enjoyed writing about it.

1

Nándor Hidegkuti opens the scoring at Wembley (1953)

'KEEP IT tight early on, give nothing silly away!'

Often, that is the instruction given by managers at the start of football matches across the world. However, on 23 November 1953, Hungary had no such plans to keep it tight as within the first minute they took the lead at Wembley Stadium versus their hosts, England. The game that would take place is commonly labelled the 'Match of the Century' – a fixture which is etched into football history.

Hungary came to Wembley as reigning Olympic gold medallists and on an unbeaten run of 24 matches. England, though, had never lost on home soil to a side from outside the British Isles. This would be a fascinating clash, but as over 105,000 fans packed into the national stadium there was no genuine belief they were about to witness a shock.

Hungary's XI contained the likes of Ferenc Puskás, Sándor Kocsis and Zoltán Czibor and they were led by their innovative coach Gusztáv Sebes. England would line up in their usual WM formation, while Hungary's inventive 2-3-3-2 formation (played like a 4-2-4), would allow for József Bozsik, 'one of the finest playmakers in European soccer history',[10] to pull the strings creatively alongside deep-lying centre-forward Nándor

10   Dave Thompson, *Football FAQ* (Milwaukee: Backbeat Books, 2015) p 151

Hidegkuti. This allowed goal machines Puskás and Kocsis the opportunity to relentlessly attack the opposing defence, as England were about to find out.

England's side, featuring some all-time greats like Stanley Matthews, Stan Mortensen and Alf Ramsey, were overwhelmed in the first minute. Hidegkuti found space in the inside-right channel and blasted a shot past goalkeeper Gil Merrick. Despite Jackie Sewell levelling for England in the 13th minute, just seven minutes later Hidegkuti had a second. Puskás got in on the act with a brace of his own, the first a glorious drag-back. Puskás, on the right side of the six-yard box, saw England captain Billy Wright ready to come flying in to make a tackle. Dragging the ball back with his heel, Wright was sent sliding away as the Galloping Major smashed the ball home. Puskás described the 'instinctive' move as 'my favourite goal of all time'[11] – and he had a lot to choose from.

Despite Mortensen pulling England back to 4-2 behind at the interval, Hungary continued the rout in the second half. Bozsik added a fifth before Hidegkuti completed his hat-trick in the 53rd minute. Ramsey's penalty notched a third for England but when the final whistle blew, the score read England 3 Hungary 6. The thumping was resounding, and the *Daily Mirror* waxed lyrical about the Hungarians in its match report the next day, crediting them as 'masters of the ball, of position, of movement'.[12]

England wanted revenge so in May 1954 they would travel to Hungary to right the wrongs of Wembley. Puskás (who scored 84 international goals in 85 appearances), Kocsis (75 in 68) and Hidegkuti (39 in 69) once more tore England apart. The Hungarians decimated England again, this time 7-1, and centre-half Syd Owen described the experience as 'like playing people from outer space'.[13]

11   *The Guardian*, 19 November 2006

12   *Daily Mirror*, 26 November 1953

13   Jonathan Wilson, *Inverting the Pyramid: The History of Football Tactics* (London: Orion, 2010) p.90

England, the self-proclaimed creators of the beautiful game, had been destroyed at home and away by the Mighty, Magical Magyars. Along with their 1950 World Cup humiliation (Minute 38), the 1950s provided a wake-up call to the British nations. They were, in fact, not as good as they thought they were.

2

Dennis Viollet puts Manchester United ahead in Belgrade (1958)

WHEN INSIDE-FORWARD Dennis Viollet netted in the second minute, little did he and all the watching spectators know that this goal would not be remembered for what it should be – a vital European Cup quarter-final second leg strike. Violett was part of the famous Busby Babes, the legendary Manchester United side led by manager Matt Busby, brought together by scout Joe Armstrong and trained by assistant manager Jimmy Murphy. The day after this European clash, the majority of this side would be killed in the terrible Munich air disaster.

The Busby Babes were reigning English First Division champions, having won the title in 1955/56 and defended their crown in 1956/57. A European Cup was the ultimate goal for the side with an average age of just 21 years old. Their 1957/58 run had seen them dismantle Irish team Shamrock Rovers, before comfortably dispatching Czechoslovakia's Dukla Prague. This set up a tie with Red Star Belgrade of Yugoslavia in January and February of 1958.

United had a 2-1 lead to take to Belgrade from the home leg at Old Trafford. Avoiding defeat on the night (5 February) would set up a potential semi-final clash with AC Milan. Viollet's opener was added to by a brace from Bobby Charlton in a fine United first-half performance. This meant even a second-half treble from Red Star was not enough to overturn the 5-4 aggregate scoreline. The Busby Babes were into the semi-final.

Following the game, United's journey home involved a refuelling stop at Munich-Riem airport in West Germany. The snowy weather had seen their British Airways plane abandon two take-off attempts, but the pilot insisted on one more try before giving in and having to stay the night. Flight 609 once more failed to take to the air, this time with tragic consequences. The plane skidded on the icy slush of the runway and hit a fence then a house. The destruction was enormous, with 23 of 38 passengers losing their lives.

Matt Busby's dream team was torn apart as Geoff Bent (25), Roger Byrne (28), Eddie Colman (21), Duncan Edwards (21), Mark Jones (24), David Pegg (22), Tommy Taylor (26) and Billy Whelan (22) all died. Two others would never play the game again (Jackie Blanchflower, 24, and Johnny Berry, 31). Additionally three club staff, eight journalists and two other passengers succumbed to their injuries in Munich.[14] The side that promised so much would have to be 'virtually rebuilt'.[15]

Unbelievably, chairman Harold Hardman vowed to finish the 1957/58 campaign. He defiantly promised, 'We carry on. Even if it means being heavily defeated, we shall fulfil the season's programme. We have a duty to the public and a duty to football to carry out.'[16] Hardman fulfilled his proclamation, United playing again as early as 13 days after Munich. With a side containing two survivors (Harry Gregg and Bill Foulkes) and the rest made up of youth and reserve players, a 3-0 win showed extraordinary resilience in the midst of grief.

Matt Busby remained at the helm of United until 1969, significantly achieving his goal ten years on from Munich. In May 1968, Manchester United finally lifted the European Cup, this time at Wembley as they defeated Portuguese side Benfica 4-1 (Minute 99). Redemption was complete, but the Munich air disaster is a moment that shall never be forgotten.

14   Ben Jones and Gareth Thomas, *Football's 50 Most Important Moments* (Worthing: Pitch Publishing, 2020) p.84
15   *Birmingham Daily Post*, 7 February 1958
16   *Daily Mirror*, 8 February 1958

3

Gaztelu help brings Basque back to life (1976)

THE BASQUE derby between Real Sociedad and Athletic Bilbao is perhaps not the most glamorous tie in the beautiful game. However, on 5 December 1976, a particular derby day would go down in Basque history. It would not be remembered for Sociedad's thumping 5-0 victory, nor for midfielder Gaztelu's third-minute strike to give his side the lead. A year after the death of Franco, this derby brought with it the rebirth of cultural identities across Spain.

General Francisco Franco ruled Spain from 1 October 1936 until his death on 20 November 1975. Franco ruled as Caudillo, his fascist state closely aligned with Benito Mussolini's Italy and Adolf Hitler's Nazi Germany. Franco's authoritarian ruling of Spain saw the Catalan and Basque peoples (to name but a few) pushed to the margins and their cultures criminalised. Franco's politics were based around his people fearing and/or respecting him and the discourse from the dictatorship was that 'any foreign declarations against Franco were the design of communists or other hostile politicians'.[17]

Barcelona's Camp Nou became a safe haven for those seeking to speak Catalan whereas the Basque football clubs of Athletic Bilbao and Real Sociedad quietly (but with defiance) represented

---

17 Antonio Cazorla Sánchez, *Fear and Progress: Ordinary Lives in Franco's Spain, 1939–1975* (Chichester: John Wiley & Sons Ltd., 2010) p.25.

their culture. After decades of repression, Franco's death in 1975 offered the opportunity for a new Spain, triggering a resurgence in Spanish provincial identity.

In the derbies following El Caudillo's death, Athletic Bilbao recorded a 2-0 home win thanks to Dani and Javier Irureta, while a superb Ricardo Muruzábal hat-trick at Sociedad's Atocha Stadium gave the home side a 3-2 win. In December 1976 though, the derby would take a political turn as 'ardent Basque nationalist' yet Sociedad bit-part player,[18] Josean de la Hoz Uranga, came up with the idea of parading the banned Ikurriña flag around the pitch before the winter derby.

The flag had been hidden inside Uranga's kitbag. Uranga was lucky to avoid detection from the regular searches players were subject to and a possible prison sentence was the risk for possessing the contraband.[19] Both captains agreed to the deed before leading out their sides at Atocha. Sociedad skipper Inaxio Kortabarria and Bilbao captain José Ángel Iribar would walk on to the field proudly displaying the Ikurriña flag. It was a significant moment as the Basque people stuck their fists up at decades of Francoist rule, and it became a derby that would never be forgotten.

Gaztelu would open the scoring after just three minutes of the most famous Basque derby of all time. His double (the second in the 88th minute), would be added to by a brace from Jesús María Satrústegui (27 and 31) and a Jesús María Zamora strike (72).

The wider importance of this game would be celebrated on 19 January 1997, as the Basque flag was legalised in Spain.[20] The famous 5-0 of 1976 would not be forgotten. It was a moment when the Basque people pushed back, and where the Ikurriña made a triumphant and defiant reappearance.

18   Euan McTear, 'How a Basque Derby brought about the legalisation of the Basque flag', *These Football Times*, 19 February 2016 https://thesefootballtimes.co/2016/02/19/how-a-basque-derby-brought-about-the-legalisation-of-the-basque-flag/
19   Ibid
20   Real Sociedad club website, 'The Ikurriña derby', *Real Sociedad*, 19 July 2013 https://www.realsociedad.eus/en/news/details/the-ikurrina-derby

4

Wayne Rooney scores early
against Iceland (2016)

WHETHER IT is the English media, the English fans or even the players themselves, whenever England go to an international tournament, the intention is to win it and end the wait stretching back to 1966 (Minute 120). UEFA Euro 2016 was no different – the hopes of a nation rested upon the shoulders of the squad of 23 and their coach, Roy Hodgson. In the round of 16, England were presented with a seemingly favourable tie against relative 'minnows' Iceland.[21] When Wayne Rooney gave them a fourth-minute lead, it seemed as though progression to the last eight was assured.

England waltzed through qualifying for Euro 2016 with a perfect ten wins from ten matches, scoring 31 goals and conceding just three. The Three Lions were drawn in a group for the tournament proper alongside Russia, Slovakia and historic rivals Wales. While Wales were appearing in their first tournament finals since the 1958 FIFA World Cup, England were one of the favourites to lift the title on 10 July.

Wales were victorious against Slovakia in their opener while England were denied a win by Russia's equaliser in the 92nd minute. The rivals then clashed in Lens, a match that would potentially decide who would top Group B, and England

21   *Daily Mail*, 27 June 2016

secured an injury-time victory with Daniel Sturridge breaking the hearts of the Welsh fans. Wales would now require a win versus Russia to have a hope of finishing top of the group, with England sure to beat Slovakia and secure top spot themselves. Wales put Russia to the sword 3-0 but England meanwhile laboured to a 0-0 draw with the Slovakians, giving them second place and a knockout game against Iceland.

Iceland, like Wales, were making their European Championship debut and had narrowly missed out on topping their own group. An opening draw against Portugal was followed by another draw with Hungary to leave Iceland needing a final win to progress. Against Austria, Jón Daði Böðvarsson gave his nation the lead before the opposition levelled in the 60th minute. An injury-time strike by Arnór Ingvi Traustason sent Strákarnir Okkar into the knockout phase.

England were delighted to have landed a seemingly straightforward fixture, especially after missing out on winning the group. Pundit Paul Merson commented pre-game, 'We couldn't have wished for a better draw,' and added, 'If we don't win this, then it would surely be the biggest shock in the history of the European Championship.'[22] Iceland, though, had won many fans beyond their shores with their performances so far and the 'thunderclap' celebration bringing supporters and players together. Iceland, with a population of around 330,000 (less than the city of Cardiff, and significantly dwarfed by the population of London), were intent on causing a major upset.

Led by their captain, Aron Gunnarsson, Iceland were unflinching in their resolve against the Three Lions on 27 June. Even after Rooney opened the scoring, Iceland did not shrink and just two minutes later Ragnar Sigurðsson equalised. Iceland continued to shock the watching world and in the 18th minute, Kolbeinn Sigþórsson netted for the underdogs. Try as

22   Lewis Dean, 'England v Iceland preview: Roy Hodgson to ring changes', *Sky Sports*, 27 June 2016 https://www.skysports.com/football/england-vs-iceland/preview/353099

England might, the score remained 2-1 at full time – Iceland had dumped the English out.

The reaction was brutal, with *Match of the Day* host and former England goalscoring hero Gary Lineker labelling the result as 'the worst defeat in our [England's] history'.[23] Fans at the stadium hounded the players with chants of 'you're not fit to wear the shirt' and Hodgson stepped down minutes after the final whistle.[24] Iceland's underdog story grabbed the hearts of spectators throughout Europe, just not in England.

23 *The Independent*, 28 June 2016
24 *The Guardian*, 27 June 2016

5

Brian Deane scores the Premier League's first goal (1992)

THE PREMIER League era had begun. By 1992, English football had found itself in a state of flux. Previous decades had been blighted by hooliganism, tragedy and social angst. Attendances at matches had dropped significantly and only the positive English performance at the World Cup, two years earlier, gave a reason for celebration. Football was attempting to shake off the image of 'a slum sport, played in slum stadiums, increasingly watched by slum people who deter decent folk from turning up'.[25]

Few could predict the magnitude of Sheffield United striker Brian Deane's early goal to open the scoring against eventual champions Manchester United. Not even the man himself could really comprehend it after the game.[26]

The goal itself was a close-range header following a long throw-in and a timely flick-on. Having headed past Danish Euro 92 winner Peter Schmeichel, it is only now that Deane appreciates the poignancy of the goal, 'For as long as the league has the format, I'll always be the first person. Some people can

---

25 *Sunday Times*, 19 May 1985

26 Greg Whelan, 'Brian Deane: The story of the first Premier League goal', *Sky Sports*, 23 November 2019
https://www.skysports.com/football/news/11095/11867410/brian-deane-the-story-of-the-first-premier-league-goal

get sick of it, but most players would like to have been the first to score.'[27]

The Premier League was initially met with a mixed reaction. Despite most top-flight clubs being fairly adamant in their desire for a new league driven by financial profit through television deals, supporters were generally ambivalent. Many feared that such impetus on television would lead to most fans abandoning the terraces for the comfort of their own homes. What the investment would do was quite the opposite.

The final season of the old First Division saw average attendance figures at just over 21,500 fans per game. This number was considerably lower than those at the start of the previous decade (26,327). Even the figures in 1980 were signifying a sharp downwards trend from those ten years before (32,113). Alongside new all-seater stadiums, in place after the *Taylor Report* (Minute 6), supporters once again felt safe in the football environment. Armchair fans, encouraged by the new image and the improved quality of the players on display, returned to the stadiums and revitalised fanbases once more.

Of course, the change has not been to everyone's taste. More recently, the astronomical transfer fees and the constant high-profile battles involving television rights have left many thinking back to the 'good old days'. But what does this really mean? The increase in financial motivation, often at the expense of supporters, is worrying for the purity of the sport but football in its modern form has seen an improvement in the standard of play and is far safer for the spectator. Perhaps the positives of the 1992 rebranding of the Football League into the Premier League outweigh the negatives.

So why was the moment so iconic? Its relevance is in what happened in the resulting 28 years. It infuriates many football fans in the modern day that media outlets tend to neglect football's 160-year history. Instead, any 'best of' or 'history' pieces only stretch back as far as 1992. The formation of the

27 *Shropshire Star*, 9 August 2017

Premier League is the start of the true modern era of football. It is Brian Deane's goal that cemented the legacy which was to come. It marked the end of the 'good old days' and the start of a 'whole new ball game'.

6

The FA Cup semi-final is abandoned at Hillsborough (1989)

THE SIXTH minute of the 1989 FA Cup semi-final between Liverpool and Nottingham Forest is perhaps one of the longest minutes in this book. In just 60 seconds it thrust decades of negligence and incompetence into the forefront of discussion. Furthermore, upon the game's abandonment, it introduced over 30 years of struggle and wider mistrust for police, football authorities and the mass media. The Hillsborough tragedy is one which shakes people to the very core, as much today as it did in the late 1980s.

Liverpool had been the dominant team domestically and across the continent throughout the 1970s and 1980s. Under the stewardship of former player Kenny Dalglish, the side had retained their form until the end of the decade and were chasing a second double in four seasons. On the continent, Liverpool had not been able to compete following the aftermath of the Heysel disaster in 1985 (Minute 58). Despite this, Dalglish's men, spearheaded by the attacking prowess of Ian Rush and John Barnes, had proven too good for most British sides.

The decision to play the FA Cup semi-final at Hillsborough had caused resentment from both Liverpool and their opponents Nottingham Forest. The Leppings Lane End in particular had been the scene of multiple crushes throughout the decade, due in part to the draconian steel fences separating supporters from the pitch. In the 1981 semi-final between Tottenham and Wolves, serious overcrowding had led to injuries to over 30 people and in 1987 and 1988 almost identical situations arose. The latter of those even featured Dalglish's Liverpool.[28]

The 1989 fixture was immensely popular with fans. Two of the nation's most successful sides were meeting for a chance to compete for the FA Cup at Wembley. With a large number of supporters expected, it came as a shock to commentators who had noted the lack of spectators in the stands just ten minutes before kick-off. Indeed, the limited amount of ticket inspection posts (mainly due to the perceived threat of hooliganism and to limit the spread of fans around the stadium) had slowed the movement of supporters into the ground.

Fearing a delay to the kick-off, police ordered the opening of an exit gate to allow the fans still outside the Leppings Lane End with the opportunity to freely enter the stand. The limited space inside quickly ran out and fans at the front were pressed and crushed against the steel fences. With the match under way, the watching audiences on TV were horrified as the gruesome nature of the disaster unfolded. Fans eventually spilled on to the pitch as the sheer weight of the crush broke the fences. Amidst the chaos and confusion, the game was brought to an immediate stop.[29]

'There are tragedies that happen in your life which you never forget. All these years on the memories of Hillsborough remain so horrific I find it very difficult to talk about them,' Dalglish later said.[30]

Dalglish still deeply feels the trauma of the tragedy to this day, commenting that the events truly changed him and played a major role in his resignation two years later.[31] The

28   Ben Jones and Gareth Thomas, *Football's Fifty Most Important Moments* (Worthing: Pitch Publishing, 2020) p.131

29   Phil Scraton, *Hillsborough: The Truth* (London: Mainstream, 2016) p.105

30   Ian Rush, *Rush: The Autobiography* (London: Ebury, 2008) pp.322-23

31   Kenny Dalglish, *My Liverpool Home: Dyed-in-the-Wool Red* (London: Hodder and Stoughton, 2010)

coverage by the mass media, in particular that of *The Sun*, shamefully attempted to pin the blame on Liverpool supporters. Blatantly disregarding the facts of the matter and adhering to the stereotype of badly behaved football fans, fabricated stories were published with the intent of selling copies rather than reporting the truth. The newspaper has been widely boycotted on Merseyside ever since and its belated apology in 2011 came too late for most to accept.

Remarkably, the tragedy at Hillsborough is still yet to be fully closed. The past 30 years have seen the families of the victims continue their fight for justice. The resulting 96 deaths have yet to be attributed to the decisions of certain individuals, leading to widespread mistrust and animosity towards authorities across the footballing world. It is a tragedy in itself that such a disaster still causes those who have suffered so much pain further torment and anguish. We hope that justice will arrive soon.

7

Cristiano Ronaldo
completes a full 90 (2014)

THE LAST 15 years have been dominated by two professional players – Lionel Messi and Cristiano Ronaldo. Ronaldo has often been described as the world's 'best second-best player' ever.[32] It is a crying shame that any mention of one means the other name is never far from the discussion. Incredibly, their respective names have almost become synonymous with each other. Every element of both Ronaldo and Messi's games have been endlessly scrutinised and analysed since their club debuts, with many believing theirs is a rivalry on a par with the game's great derbies.[33]

Public opinion is generally swayed in Messi's favour, but Ronaldo still boasts an incredibly strong and loyal fanbase. Since making his club debut in 2002, the player himself has won five Ballons d'Or and scored over 700 goals. It seems unfair that Ronaldo's incredible career will always be remembered in comparison to Messi. The biggest difference between the two is the journeys both have taken to get to this point. Unlike one-club man Messi, Ronaldo has played for a wealth of great sides since his professional debut. Sporting Lisbon, Manchester United, Real Madrid and now Juventus have all benefited

---

32   Jonathan Stevenson, *Twitter*, 11 April 2012
33   Luca Caliono, *Messi vs Ronaldo 2018: The Greatest Rivalry* (London: Icon Books Ltd., 2017)

from the forward's goals and incredible consistency. His list of honours highlights his importance.

What sets him apart from his Argentine rival, however, is that he has scored in each and every minute of a regulation 90-minute match. The goal to complete the set was against Atlético Madrid at the Vicente Calderón in 2014. A seventh-minute penalty was enough for the Portuguese forward to make football history. It was at Atlético's city rivals, Real Madrid, that Ronaldo scored most of his career goals. His eventual record of 450 in 438 games will take some beating.

'Cristiano is simply amazing. This man is surely the best. He is both a goal machine and an incredible player. There will never be another Cristiano Ronaldo,' claimed José Mourinho.[34]

The 2013/14 season would lead to one of Madrid's finest achievements – La Decima (Minute 118). Ronaldo had played a key role in the side's journey to the Champions League Final in Lisbon. The Portuguese number seven had scored a single-season Champions League record 17 goals, including one in the final itself – remarkably, it was another penalty against Atlético. Real's mid-2010s revival can look to Ronaldo's influence as a key component of their future dominance, winning three Champions League titles in four years and becoming the first side to defend the crown since the new format began in 1992 when retaining it in 2017 against Juventus, having again beaten Atlético in 2016. For good measure, they made it three in a row by beating Liverpool in 2018.

Seven domestic league titles and five Champions Leagues prove Ronaldo's worth and, in the seasons following his completion of a full 90, he has almost completed his second. Just the first and 46th minutes are needed for history to repeat itself. Messi, on the other hand, is still looking to join Ronaldo and Swedish striker Zlatan Ibrahimović for this remarkable honour. This is not the last time Ronaldo (or indeed Messi) will feature in this book as the Portuguese's incredible career continues to make history with every minute he plays.

34   Jose Mourinho in *Irish Independent*, 15 January 2015

8

Christine Sinclair opens her international account (2000)

INTERNATIONAL FOOTBALL boasts some of the game's most prestigious records. For appearances and goals, the crowns both belong to women's football. In terms of caps for their country, Kristine Lilly's 354 for the US demonstrates an incredible commitment to her national team. Alongside this achievement, Lilly also holds fourth spot on the list of all-time international goals (130) behind former team-mates Mia Hamm (158) and Abby Wambach (184). Until very recently, Wambach's remarkable total was yet to be beaten, but following a first-half brace against minnows St Kitts and Nevis, Canada's Christine Sinclair has made genuine football history.

Incredibly, Sinclair's record stretches back two decades to the turn of the millennium. In the year 2000, she was only 16 years old as she made her national team debut. Her first appearance came at the 2000 Algarve Cup as Canada faced off against some of the world's mightiest international sides including the 1999 World Cup winners, the USA, and runners-up China.

China would be the first test for Canada and Sinclair. A performance inspired by Sun Wen saw the Chinese emerge as 4-0 winners. It was not the desired opening for Canada, but the side coached by Even Pellerud saw a chance to upset the odds when they met 1995 World Cup winners Norway in Albufeira. After just eight minutes, the 16-year-old Sinclair scored to put

Canada into the lead. Despite the Norwegians replying with two goals either side of half-time to eventually win the game, Sinclair had left her first mark of many on women's football.

A 2-1 defeat was surprisingly welcome to the Canadian women's team as at the World Cup a year earlier, the same fixture had seen them beaten 7-1. Sinclair would go on to score twice more in the Algarve Cup and her international side would eventually finish fifth. Remarkably, at the time of the tournament, Sinclair was yet to join a club. Indeed, her talent had been spotted while playing for her high school in Burnaby South. Her performance at the Algarve Cup had earned her praise from across the women's game.

Following the moderate success in Portugal, the Canadian authorities would promote football to the country's youth. A runners-up finish at the 2002 FIFA Under-19 Women's World Cup, held in Canada, highlighted the game to new supporters and young women (Sinclair won the Golden Ball). The extensive media coverage, heightened by Sinclair's performances, saw matches broadcast live on Canadian TV. Despite being a 'hockey nation', female participation in 'soccer' boomed in the late 1990s and early 2000s.[35]

After international success, Sinclair's career has seen her play college and later professional club football. She has performed for some of the game's greatest clubs and continues to regularly feature for her national team. A recent CONCACAF Olympic qualifier against St Kitts and Nevis saw her score her 184th and 185th goals for Canada to make history. The striker later tweeted that she had been 'overwhelmed' by the praise given by ex-professionals and supporters. Even Canadian Prime Minister Justin Trudeau offered his admiration for the achievement.[36]

35 Fan Hong, *Soccer, Women, Sexual Liberation: Kicking Off a New Era* (London: Frank Cass, 2004) p.30

36 George Ramsey, 'Christine Sinclair breaks all-time international goalscoring record', *CNN*, 30 January 2020 https://edition.cnn.com/2020/01/30/football/christine-sinclair-goal-record-canada-football-spt-intl/index.html

He wrote, 'She did it Christine Sinclair is now international soccer's all-time leading goal scorer. Congratulations, @sincy12 – you rock!'[37]

What Christine Sinclair has done for the women's game should not be understated. Indeed, her goalscoring exploits and leadership skills have helped the game to thrive in North America and have highlighted the skill and dedication needed to see the sport continuously disseminated. The first of a number of women's football moments in this book – it seems apt that the first should be dedicated to its most recent record-breaker.

---

37   Justin Trudeau, Twitter, 30 January 2020

9

Play is stopped in Nantes to pay tribute to Emiliano Sala (2019)

FOOTBALL IS a game of emotions. You cheer wildly when your team scores, you boo loudly when the referee gives a decision against your side, and some even weep openly when a vital match is lost. However, perhaps the biggest emotion fans feel is the connection with a player who has pulled on the club's jersey loyally to represent them. Emiliano Sala and FC Nantes had that connection and in 2019, tragedy struck to break the hearts of Les Canaris's fans. In the ninth minute of their game on 30 January 2019, the action was halted to honour that bond.

Emiliano Sala was born in Cululú, Santa Fe, Argentina, where his love for football developed. Sala played for Argentinean sides San Martín de Progreso and Proyecto Crecer, before being spotted for a move to Europe. A short spell in Portugal with FC Crato was followed by a move to French Ligue 1 club Bordeaux. His time there was fairly uninspiring, but some successful loan spells at third-tier US Orléans, Ligue 2 team Niort and fellow Ligue 1 outfit Caen had seen FC Nantes willing to take a punt on the striker.

Sala joined FC Nantes in July 2015 for €1m, and in the seasons that followed he more than paid back that transfer fee. The centre-forward was a regular goalscorer, netting 42 times in 120 Ligue 1 fixtures, and so by 2018/19 he had attracted the interest of Premier League clubs. Newly promoted Cardiff

City led the way with manager Neil Warnock seeing Sala as the perfect target man to keep the team in the top flight. After being scouted and touted for a number of weeks, Cardiff finally announced the club-record deal for £15m on 19 January 2019.[38]

Sala was allowed to return to Nantes in the following days to bid goodbye to team-mates, but it was when returning to south Wales that disaster struck. On 21 January, at 7.15pm, Sala's plane took off bound for Cardiff airport. The plane would never arrive, sparking fears it had gone missing en route. That morning, police confirmed the Piper PA-46 Malibu, a single-engine aircraft, and its two passengers, had indeed gone missing over the English Channel in bad light and bad weather.[39]

On 30 January, after the news of his disappearance had devastated fans in France and Wales, Nantes and St Etienne joined together to pay tribute to their number nine. In the ninth minute of their Ligue 1 clash, the match was stopped as both sets of players and all fans in attendance chanted for, and applauded, their beloved former striker. Manager Vahid Halilhodžić was in tears, along with hundreds of supporters too. Meanwhile at the Emirates Stadium in London, Cardiff also paid tribute to their new signing at their away tie with Arsenal, flowers being laid to pay homage to a striker they never saw pull on a Bluebirds shirt.

On 3 February 2019, it was announced an underwater search had found the downed plane, and on 7 February a body was recovered – that of the 28-year-old. Sadly, the body of his pilot, 59-year-old David Ibbotson, has still not been found. In the months that followed, legal wrangling would bitterly ensue as both Nantes and Cardiff disputed the £15m transfer debt and the legitimacy of Sala's contract. This moment produced one of football's more unsavoury juxtapositions, the bond between player and fans often being overshadowed by the business and money running the sport.

38 Cardiff City club website, 'Record signing | Emiliano Sala is a Bluebird', 19 January 2019 https://www.cardiffcityfc.co.uk/news/2019/january/record-signing – emiliano-sala-is-a-bluebird

39 *The Telegraph*, 25 January 2019

10

Xavi sets in motion one of football's greatest team performances (2010)

THE BARCELONA side which dominated European football between 2008 and 2012 is arguably the greatest club team of all time. The squad, spearheaded by the goals and talent of Lionel Messi, came to prominence under innovative manager Pep Guardiola. Throughout his tenure, Guardiola had promoted the irresistible style of football named 'tiki-taka'. The tactics were based on short, intricate passing, shown most clearly through their main creative duo – Xavi and Andrés Iniesta.

Xavi set in motion one of the game's finest team performances in late 2010. Arriving at the Camp Nou were Barcelona's bitter rivals Real Madrid, under their new manager José Mourinho. Just six months earlier, Mourinho's Inter Milan side had beaten Barca in a hotly-contested two-legged Champions League semi-final. Upon sealing the victory, he had celebrated wildly on the turf of the Camp Nou, much to the annoyance and irritation of the Catalan club's faithful.

AlthoughEl Clásico was kicked off by Karim Benzema and Mesut Özil, it would take just ten minutes for Barcelona to assert their authority. Iniesta threaded a ball through the Madrid defence and past the outstretched leg of Marcelo before Xavi controlled and then volleyed into the net. The goal scored by the Spanish central midfielder was testament to the tiki-taka mentality instilled at the club. The following goal, scored by

Pedro, came after a 20-pass move. For many commentators, beating Real Madrid in a distinctly 'Barcelona way' was what really made *this* victory stand above all others.[40] David Villa added a second-half brace to put the result beyond doubt with youngster Jeffrén scoring the fifth in stoppage time. The humiliation, despite Mourinho's vehement denial,[41] was seen etched on the faces of Madrid's XI. Los Blancos were eventually reduced to ten after Sergio Ramos saw red following a mass fracas near the centre circle.

As soon as the final whistle blew, the global media had a field day as they purred over the Barcelona side. Some went as far as describing Guardiola's men as the 'orgasm team', one step beyond even the Dream Team of Johan Cruyff.[42] Perhaps fortunately, this name has not stuck in modern-day conversation. Messi took most of the plaudits with his two assists for Villa, but the impact of Iniesta and Xavi shouldn't be forgotten. Even Messi himself had the highest of praise for the latter, 'He is the best player in the history of Spanish football.'[43]

These words say it all. Xavi's talent deserves to be revered among the best in football history. On three consecutive occasions, from 2009 to 2011, he finished third in the Ballon d'Or voting. Two of those were behind only behind Lionel Messi and Cristiano Ronaldo, and in 2010 Messi came out top with Xavi's midfield partner Iniesta in second.

Were it not for the innovation and technical brilliance of Xavi, tiki-taka would not have been possible. There is little doubt that in future histories of football, Xavi will play a leading role.

40   Sid Lowe, *Fear and Loathing in La Liga: Barcelona vs Real Madrid*, (London: Yellow Jersey, 2013) p.386

41   Jose Mourinho post-match interview, 29 November 2010

42   Sid Lowe, *Fear and Loathing in La Liga*, p.386

43   Lionel Messi on Xavi in 2015: Joshua Hayward, 'Lionel Messi: Xavi is the best player in the history of Spanish football', *Eurosport*, 2 June 2015 https://www.eurosport.co.uk/football/liga/2014-2015/lionel-messi-xavi-is-the-best-player-in-the-history-of-spanish-football_sto4764080/story.shtml

11

Roger Hunt begins the goal-rush on *Match of the Day* (1964)

FOOTBALL SHARES a wonderfully intricate relationship with television. Watching *Match of the Day* has been a regular feature in British football supporters' weekly routines. For over 50 years it has provided fans with the chance of seeing all of the weekend's goals. From the school playground to the office photocopier, it has helped to kick-start debates across the nation. When Roger Hunt opened the scoring against Arsenal at Anfield in 1964, few could imagine that upon hitting the back of the Anfield Road net, the goal would leave a lasting legacy still felt strongly today.

Liverpool would go on to win the game 3-2 after a late winner from Scotsman Gordon Wallace. The tie was the only one featured on the fledgling show that week as the BBC planned on providing highlights of a solitary match each episode. The fixture truly was the match of the day. Around 20,000 people tuned in to watch the new programme as Liverpool (in unfamiliar red with white shorts) and Arsenal delighted the crowd.[44]

Such numbers in today's thinking are relatively low, but as part of a trial run for the 1966 World Cup, *Match of the Day* proved immediately popular, even if not among the league's

---

44   John Motson on BBC documentary, *Match of the Day at 50* (2014)

top clubs. Fearing its broadcasting would negatively impact gate receipts, they would try in vain to have it removed from the TV schedule.[45]

The 1960s was a decade of change both on and off the field as popular culture developed and sport became increasingly open to the mainstream. The Beatles track 'She Loves You' could be heard over presenter Ken Wolstenholme as he opened the show, highlighting a new age of broadcasting.

By 1969, Liverpool would once more provide a *Match of the Day* first. Their 2-0 victory over West Ham was the first episode broadcast in colour. The BBC would dominate coverage of British sport and throughout the next two decades, new programmes would begin to appear in order to break the stranglehold. *The Big Match* became a weekly feature on ITV from 1968 and before long, the first major battles of broadcasting rights took centre stage. In 1978, ITV had managed to win the right to show highlights from Saturday fixtures, with *Match of the Day* demoted to Sunday afternoons from 1980.

Despite ongoing arguments between the nation's two major broadcasters, the standard of programming, helped in part by the expert analysis from ex-professionals like Jimmy Hill, was excellent. For some, it was one of television's only 'redeeming features' as the quality of other shows generally dropped.[46] An increase in football coverage meant that the more successful sides grew their already fanatical fan bases far beyond the reach of their localities. Such numbers created an opportunity for immense commercial revenue.

This will not be the last time the relationship between football and television appears in this book. Indeed, in just the first 11 minutes we have already seen how much it has impacted the modern game (Minute 5). Arguments will always be found

45 Nick Constable, *Match of the Day 50 Years: Players, Goals, Matches and Memories* (London: BBC Books, 2014) p.8

46 Jay Scherer and David Rowe, 'Sport, Public Service Media and Cultural Citizenship' in *Sport, Public Broadcasting and Cultural Citizenship: Signal Lost?* (London: Routledge, 2013) p.9

to support and discourage the use of television in the beautiful game. For many, its use has helped to promote, raise the profile and even add to the excitement of football.[47] For others, it has created a new game in which profit stands above all else. One thing is for sure – Roger Hunt's 11th-minute strike in 1964 was more than just a goal.

47   Raymond Boyle and Richard Haynes, 'Football and Television' in *Football in the New Media Age* (London: Routledge, 2004) p.15

12

Ted Drake makes it 3-0 to England at the Battle of Highbury (1934)

ON 10 June 1934, Italy lifted the second FIFA World Cup. On home soil, at Stadio Nazionale PNF in Rome, the Azzurri beat Czechoslovakia 2-1 (after extra time) to record a first World Cup for their country. However, England and the fellow home nations refused to enter and so on 14 November 1934, a different 'World Cup Final' would take place. The Battle of Highbury was a fundamental moment in international football in the 1930s, and in the 12th minute England's Ted Drake made the score 3-0.

Benito Mussolini took control of Italy in 1922 as Prime Minister and by 1925, he established a fascist dictatorship. Mussolini was known as Il Duce, and the 'cult of the Duce' played a prominent role in Italian society. A major role in this cult was sport, Mussolini seeing it as expressing fascism's demand for 'individual dedication to the greater collective need'.[48] The success at the 1934 World Cup had given Mussolini great pleasure, fulfilling his order that was given to all sports competitors, 'Remember… When you compete abroad, the honour and sporting prestige of the nation is entrusted to your muscles and above all your spirit.'[49]

48 Simon Martin, *Sport Italia: The Italian Love Affair with Sport* (London: I.B. Tauris, 2011) p. 55
49 Ibid, p. 57

Therefore, when England agreed to host the Italian national team in November 1934, the game was significantly built up as a massive clash. England's captain that day, Eddie Hapgood, recalled how it was billed as the 'most important match that has been played anywhere in the world since the Great War [World War One]'.[50] With England's rejection of the World Cup outright and FA chairman Charles Sutcliffe branding the tournament a 'joke',[51] the prospect of unofficially taking the crown from Mussolini's champions was tantalising.

England included seven Arsenal players in their starting XI. Herbert Chapman's side had proven to be the dominant domestic force in the 1930s. Italy, meanwhile, included nine of their World Cup Final starters. While their tournament top scorer, Angelo Schiavio, missed out, stars such as Internazionale's Giuseppe Meazza and Juventus's Mumo Orsi did take to the field at Arsenal's Highbury stadium in front of over 50,000 spectators.

Within minutes the tone of the game was set, Hapgood calling it 'the dirtiest football match I have ever played in'.[52] Centre-half Luis Monti broke his foot just two minutes in and with no substitutes permitted, he bravely played on for quarter of an hour. His decision to continue potentially damaged his side though; Eric Brook headed in after three minutes before adding his second, a free kick, after ten minutes. In the 12th minute, Drake had surely won the game as he scored at the second time of asking following 'incessant pressure' from the hosts.[53]

The half-time 3-0 lead was too much for the Italian visitors to overcome. Adapting to playing with ten men due to the loss of Monti, they were able to show their credentials as world

50   Eddie Hapgood, *Football Ambassador* (Norfolk: GCR Books Limited, 2009) p.36

51   Matthew Taylor, *The Leaguers: The making of professional football in England, 1900–1939* (Liverpool: Liverpool University Press, 2005) p. 217

52   Eddie Hapgood, *Football Ambassador*, p. 37

53   *Hartlepool Northern Daily Mail*, 14 November 1934

champions, fighting back 'splendidly'.[54] Centre-forward Meazza scored a brace (58 and 62) but it was not enough to topple the English and a significant victory was recorded with a final score of 3-2.

Both sides were left counting the cost of injuries. Hapgood (broken nose), Drake (shoulder and leg), Cliff Bastin (elbow), Ray Bowden (ankle) and Wilf Copping (thigh) were a few of the players who missed some time after the gruelling match.[55]

The wider importance of the Battle of Highbury was *this* game's impact on the attitude of the home nations to join the FIFA World Cup. If the current title holders could be dispatched, then why did England need to bother with the risk of letting their self-proclaimed crown slip every four years at the 'so-called'[56] world championships?

54 Ibid
55 *Nottingham Journal*, 16 November 1934
56 *Hartlepool Northern Daily Mail*, 14 November 1934

13

Trevor Brooking wins it for the underdogs (1980)

IF THE FA Cup is famous for one thing, it is probably its ability to help lower league teams play out of their skin and upset the 'bigger' clubs. For as long as it has existed, so too has the famous 'cupset'. The word provokes memories of Ronnie Radford's strike for Hereford against Newcastle in 1972 and Wrexham's Mickey Thomas shocking Arsenal 20 years later. In 1980, arriving at Wembley to face Arsenal were Second Division side West Ham. The Irons had been in decline at the start of the decade, with memories of their 1960s dream team becoming increasingly distant.

Despite their status, the side still featured a number of quality individuals. Trevor Brooking, Frank Lampard (Senior) and David Cross at least offered a glimmer of hope against the Gunners. Arsenal, on the other hand, were playing in a third successive final having won the tournament the year before. The odds, it seemed, were rightly stacked in favour of the north London side.

It took just 13 minutes for the game to see its only goal. With the ball initially blocked by a staunch Arsenal defence, Stuart Pearson struck it across the face of the goal. Stooping low to make a good connection, Brooking headed past Pat Jennings and into the net. What made the moment even sweeter for Brooking was that he was not known for his heading ability.

Living up to their favourites tag, Arsenal dominated the rest of the game. With increasing possession, the final became a battle between attack and defence. West Ham would prevail and defeat their London counterparts 1-0 to send the claret and blue half of Wembley wild. With 'I'm Forever Blowing Bubbles' playing over the stadium's speakers, the match would never be forgotten by West Ham's fans. Perhaps the memory is made stronger by the fact the club has only reached one final since, in 2006.

'We didn't really go into the game thinking we were underdogs because, although we were a second division side, we had a lot of very good players in that team,' said captain Billy Bonds.[57]

The rise of the underdog is a theme we will see frequently in this book. The David and Goliath battles are often those that leave the most powerful messages. It provides the favourites with a cautionary tale of arrogance and assumption and the underdog with hope. In football, nothing is ever clear-cut. From the grassroots level clashes to Champions League finals (Minute 54), there is always a chance to emerge victorious. Like no other sport, football is truly a game for everyone.

---

57 West Ham United club website, 'In their words: The 1980 FA Cup winners', 13 December 2019 https://www.whufc.com/news/articles/2017/december/13-december/their-words-1980-fa-cup-winners

14

Alfredo Di Stéfano scores for Real Madrid in the first European Cup Final (1956)

THE 1950S is one of football's finest decades, with many great domestic and international moments to reminisce upon. The birth of the European Cup, though, is arguably one of the greatest legacies of that fine period. In the first final in 1956, Real Madrid quickly fell 2-0 behind to France's Stade Reims, until Alfredo Di Stéfano pulled back the first goal in the 14th minute during Real's comeback 4-3 victory.

In 1954, the mighty Hungarian side Honvéd visited England to play Wolverhampton Wanderers in a floodlit friendly (Minute 76). Wolves' 3-2 win saw national media, such as the *Birmingham Daily Gazette*, declare them the 'club champions of the world'.[58] This so enraged the rest of Europe that the editor of French newspaper *L'Equipe*, Gabriel Hanot, challenged, 'Before we declare that Wolverhampton Wanderers are invincible, let them go to Moscow and Budapest. And then there are other internationally renowned clubs: Milan and Real Madrid… A club world championship, or at least a European one… should be launched.'[59]

---

58 *Birmingham Daily Gazette*, 14 December 1954
59 Edward Couzens-Lake, *Mapping the Pitch: Football Coaches, Players and Formations Through The Ages* (Maidenhead: Meyer and Meyer Sport Ltd., 2015) p.161

The 1955/56 season saw the first European Cup introduced. Sixteen teams from 16 nations united in a straight knockout tournament stretching from September 1955 to June 1956. Scotland sent their league champions, Hibernian, but the Football Association refused to allow First Division champions Chelsea to join. The Blues agreed with the FA, as they commented that the 'League programme does not allow for "six or eight" visitors from abroad.'[60]

Spaniards Real Madrid started well, putting out Swiss side Servette and then Yugoslavia's FK Partizan to set up a semi-final with AC Milan of Italy. Stade Reims meanwhile saw off Danes Aarhus and Hungarians Vörös Lobogó to earn a semi-final against Hibernian. Madrid emerged victorious in a rip-roaring 5-4 aggregate battle with Milan to make the Parc des Princes final in Paris. For Hibs, their run came to an end, losing 3-0 over two legs. Reims would earn their final place for 10 June 1956.

Reims took the lead through midfielder Michel Leblond after just six minutes. The score was doubled four minutes later as forward Jean Templin netted, and Madrid looked in trouble. However, future club icon Di Stéfano would get Los Blancos back into the tie in the 14th minute, connecting with Miguel Muñoz's sumptuous through ball.[61] Héctor Rial then levelled the scores, making it 2-2 at half-time.

Reims once more took the lead after the interval but Real yet again levelled in the 67th minute before Rial secured the winner in the 79th, poking the ball inside goalkeeper René-Jean Jacquet's far post. Real hung on at 4-3 and were crowned Europe's first official football champions, but this title was just the start of a glorious five-time consecutive winning run for Los Blancos.

---

60   *West London Observer*, 29 July 1955

61   UEFA website, 'Madrid bounce back to start era of dominance', 1 September 2014 https://www.uefa.com/uefachampionsleague/news/ newsid=2155985.html?iv=true

15

The first FA Cup Final goal (1872)

STILL PLAYED today, the FA Cup is football's oldest competition and for almost 150 years, it has provided a wealth of stories. From the victories of the underdog (Minute 13) to extraordinary exhibitions of football (Minute 92), it remains one of the game's greatest institutions. Its creation, in the autumn of 1871, provided the fledgling sport with an opportunity to grow in size and status.

Following the emergence of rugby as a genuine competitor to football in 1870, the FA needed something radical in order to compete. Since its formation in 1863, the association had struggled to attract new clubs and numbers were often decreasing. Rugby's move into the international game in March 1871 provided FA secretary Charles Alcock with the impetus to respond.

The first edition of the FA Cup was only moderately successful and not quite as ground-breaking as some modern commentators will have us believe. Fifteen teams entered the tournament with the Wanderers and Royal Engineers battling it out in the final at The Oval.

With 2,000 spectators in attendance, there was indeed great scope for the competition to grow and expand in the coming years.

It was the Wanderers who would win the tie with midfielder Morton Betts (also known as A.H. Chequer) scoring the only goal in the 15th minute. Betts, a former public schoolboy at

Harrow, was one of the side's more colourful characters.[62] The goal itself saw the ball 'worked well down to the front' before the chance was taken.[63] Interestingly, the article continues to praise the use of 'scrimmage'. This style of play would eventually be phased out with the passing or 'combination' game becoming more popular.

With his early goal, Betts had set in motion a true dominance of the FA Cup by the Wanderers. The side was even described as the 'crème de la crème' of the footballing world prior to their first triumph[64] and by their fifth in 1878 (once more at the expense of the Royal Engineers) they were offered the trophy for good.

Following the climax of the first FA Cup Final, the tournament would become an annual feature in the British sporting calendar. Indeed, by 1880 over 50 teams were competing for the trophy and even sides from Wales began to enter. Perhaps even more notable was that the later 1870s also saw clubs that are instantly recognisable today. These included Blackburn Rovers, Nottingham Forest and Aston Villa.

Although seemingly innocent additions to the competition, in 1880 they were greeted with suspicion. The dissemination of the game had meant northern industrial towns were also being bitten by the football bug. As more working-class sides developed and progressed in the cup, questions would be asked about how the players could fund their love of the game alongside their working commitments. It would later emerge that these sides were in fact receiving payments to play, much to the dismay and irritation of upper-class southern amateurs.

The FA Cup would only last a short while in its amateur status and clubs like the Wanderers would eventually succumb to the growth of the game. Football was now about so much more than playing for the sake of playing, with the FA Cup

62   Rob Cavallini, *The Wanderers: Five Times FA Cup Winners* (Surrey: Dog and Duck, 2005) p.82

63   *Derbyshire Courier*, 23 March 1872

64   *Morning Post*, 16 March 1872

becoming a breeding ground for new talent and new clubs. Each year from its humble beginnings, the tournament grew and grew, eventually seeing over 700 entrants in the 2007/08 season. The FA Cup is a competition embedded in stunning moments which have shaped football's incredible history and there are more to come.

16

Carli Lloyd completes a World Cup Final hat-trick from the halfway line (2015)

THE US Women's National Team (USWNT) has been blessed with some of the finest players to have ever played the game. When the international side is mentioned, it immediately conjures up images of Mia Hamm, Kristine Lilly and Abby Wambach, to name but three. In 2015 Wambach was playing in her final tournament for the side, having scored over 180 international goals in a remarkable career. Despite her impending retirement, the USWNT could still rely on other players to take over the mantle and lead the side to glory once again. Alongside the goalscoring talent of Alex Morgan was the effervescent Carli Lloyd, a deeper-lying striker who would score goals for fun.

Three of these would come in the 2015 World Cup Final in Canada. In front of 53,341 spectators, Lloyd would captain her side to a commanding 4-0 lead after just 16 minutes. Their opponents at BC Place were the 2011 world champions, Japan, who had stunned the footballing community just four years earlier with a miraculous victory over the US (Minute 117).

The US looked to start the game quickly and after Lloyd's initial two goals in the first five minutes, Tobin Heath thumped in a blistering volley. The game was as good as over but the US would not take their foot off the gas. Picking the ball up in her own half, Lloyd would take two touches before attempting the impossible. Striking the ball just inside the Japanese half, her shot would travel over the head of goalkeeper Ayumi Kaihori and into the net. Cue pandemonium.

'It was instinct. Every single game I play I'm always checking to see where the goalkeeper is. She was really off her line. When the ball left my foot, I knew that I couldn't have hit it any more perfect. It was like I was playing in the park with my friends and I just happened to go for it at that moment,' Lloyd said.[65]

Alongside winning the tournament, the strike was made even more significant due to Lloyd's completion of a remarkable hat-trick. The forward had delivered the first three-goal performance in a World Cup final since Geoff Hurst in 1966 (Minute 120). Lloyd has helped the women's game hit new heights over the last decade and the success of her international side would be replicated at the 2019 World Cup in France.

Led by the inspirational Megan Rapinoe (Minute 65), Lloyd would be limited to being a bit-part player. Despite this, Lloyd's presence in the squad helped her team to win and the tournament to have another instantly recognisable name on its roster. With over one million spectators, the 2019 competition highlighted that for the women's game, the only way is up.

---

65   FIFA website, 'Lloyd's audacious halfway strike stuns the watching world', 20 April 2019 https://www.fifa.com/womensworldcup/news/lloyd-s-audacious-halfway-strike-stuns-the-watching-world

17

The first goal scored in the
Champions League (1992)

THE EUROPEAN Cup has grown considerably since its start in 1955 and is now the continent's most prestigious and beloved competition. Nevertheless, in 1992, similar to the Premier League, the tournament needed a rebrand. The 1990s had promised something of a revolution in football as it attempted to shake off its worrying image of hooliganism and negative play, and 1992 had almost become a fresh start for football and a chance for the game as a whole to reinvent itself. The removal of the back-pass rule and the wider use of three points for a win had created a game based primarily on attacking play.

With television rights driving its rebrand, the European Cup became known as the Champions League. Contrary to the current format, the inaugural season of the competition only saw the 'league' introduced after an initial two knockout rounds. Two groups would consist of four teams, each playing each other home and away. The two group winners would then face off in the final at the end of the season. With only 11 games needed in order to win the competition, it boasts a remarkably streamlined version compared to what we are used to today.

The first goal of the rebranded tournament was scored by Daniel Amokachi of Club Brugge. In the 17th minute of their opening tie against CSKA Moscow, he latched on to a through ball and slotted it past CSKA's Dmitri Kharine. Amokachi's goal had helped to propel the centre-forward into the spotlight and eventually earn him a move to Premier League side Everton.

Highly competitive and increasingly lucrative, the first season of the rebranded European Cup was a success. Given its achievements, it is surprising to find that little is written about it, in comparison to the birth of the Premier League that very same year. Perhaps the controversy surrounding eventual winners Marseille masks what should be regarded as a definitive moment in football history. The French club would later be stripped of their domestic league title for match-fixing. Arguably, their Champions League crown should have followed.

The Champions League has since grown into one of sport's most lucrative competitions and caters for the world's biggest clubs and best players. Following the 1992/93 season, the tournament would continue to prove successful commercially. As the decade progressed, it expanded from eight teams to 32. The early knockout rounds were abandoned and moved to later in the competition. The rise of large sponsorship deals from beer companies, games manufacturers and even suppliers of natural gas has caused revenue to sky-rocket.

With the promotion of attacking football and featuring the best players on the planet, the Champions League is only really rivalled by the World Cup in terms of prestige. The 2018/19 season was regarded by many as the finest tournament in football history.[66]

That being said, the competition still has its critics, most notably those who raise concerns as to the financial fair play involved. Furthermore, the television rights money given to the 'bigger' European clubs has helped them increase revenue at the expense of the smaller sides. Some commentators have dubbed the current competition a somewhat 'quasi-closed' league in which most editions feature the same sides despite the fact that

66   Emlyn Begley, 'Champions League 2018-19: The Greatest Tournament Ever?', BBC Sport, 2 June 2019 https://www.bbc.co.uk/sport/football/48354681

theoretically 'anyone can enter'.[67] The Champions League is writing new chapters into the history of football with every minute played. In this book, there are many more of its pivotal moments covered.

67   Wladimir Andreff, 'Sports events, economic impact and regulation', in Michel Desbordes and André Richelieu, (eds), *Global Sport Marketing: Contemporary Issues and Practice* (London: Routledge, 2012) p.91

18

Helmut Rahn equalises for West Germany in the Miracle of Bern (1954)

THE HUNGARIAN side of the 1950s, known as the Mighty Magyars, are arguably the best international side never to win a World Cup. In the years leading up to the 1954 FIFA tournament in Switzerland, Hungary were the team to beat. An Olympic gold medal in Finland against Yugoslavia in 1952 helped the squad to develop and was part of a wider unbeaten run that stretched from May 1950 to 1954. This run also included two big victories against England, 6-3 away and 7-1 at home (Minute 1). In the 1954 World Cup Final, after just eight minutes, it looked like the Hungarians would have their trophy with the side leading 2-0. However, by the 18th minute, West Germany were level through Helmut Rahn.

The 1954 World Cup saw 16 teams make their way to Switzerland hoping to lift the trophy in the competition's fifth edition. Brazil were desperate to right the wrongs of their defeat on home soil four years previously, while defending champions Uruguay hoped to make it a third success. West Germany, meanwhile, were welcomed into their first tournament since World War Two and were drawn against Europe's hottest team.

The Hungarians, boasting the likes of Ferenc Puskás, Sándor Kocsis, József Bozsik and Nándor Hidegkuti, were full of goals. They decimated South Korea 9-0 in their opener, before an 8-3 thrashing of West Germany, courtesy of four from Kocsis, saw them top Group Two. West Germany required a play-off win against Turkey to keep their place in the competition, winning that game in style, 7-2. Brazil were Hungary's next opponents and the infamous Battle of Bern ensued. The violent clash was labelled a 'disgrace' by English referee Arthur Ellis.[68] Even injured talisman Puskás lashed out at Brazilian defender Pinheiro with a bottle to the face.[69]

Uruguay, who had put out England, took Hungary to extra time after a 2-2 draw in 90 minutes. Kocsis scored yet again, his brace taking his tally to 11 for the tournament and delivering Uruguay their first World Cup loss. West Germany's victories over Yugoslavia and local rivals Austria, saw them earn a place in the final for 4 July 1954.

Hungary were described as 'hot favourites' to win the final, especially having brushed aside the well-fancied Uruguayans and Brazilians. While it was noted West Germany had 'improved considerably' from their 'trouncing' earlier in the World Cup, there was little doubt that Hungary were set to lift the trophy at the Wankdorf Stadium, Bern.[70]

Puskás and Zoltán Czibor gave the Magyars a stunning 2-0 lead after just eight minutes but the Germans fought back quickly. The first came through top scorer Max Morlock in the tenth minute, and the vital equaliser, netted by Rot-Weiss Essen's Rahn in the 18th minute. Then, just six minutes from time, Hans Schäfer robbed Bozsik of the ball before Ottmar Walter's header fell to Rahn. The 'well-directed' shot was placed past Gyula Grosics in the Hungarian goal and the West Germans had a winner – the Miracle of Bern had occurred and 'women wept as Hungary fell'.[71]

The defeat is still a sore point for Hungary, a missed opportunity and perhaps the 'greatest disappointment Hungarian

68   *The Independent*, 9 June 1998

69   Alex Bellos, *Futebol: The Brazilian Way of Life* (London: Bloomsbury, 2002) p.100

70   *Shields Daily News*, 3 July 1954

71   *Belfast Telegraph*, 5 July 1954

sport has known'.[72] For the West Germans though, Franz Beckenbauer would sum up the importance, 'For anybody who grew up in the misery of the post-war years, Bern was an extraordinary inspiration. The entire country regained its self-esteem.'[73]

72   Jonathan Wilson, *The Names Heard Long Ago* (New York: Bold Type Books, 2019) p. 346

73   Ibid

19

Lucien Laurent scores the first
World Cup goal (1930)

THE MODERN-DAY World Cup is the game's greatest and most renowned tournament. Arguably, it is the pinnacle of competitive sport as a whole, with the one exception being the Olympic Games. Indeed, it is with the Olympics and its successful football tournaments in 1924 and 1928 that the promotion of a World Cup was first introduced. Following Uruguay's victories in Paris (1924) and Amsterdam (1928), which at times were over 'superior' European opposition, the questions over who the greatest footballing nation on Earth was were introduced with growing vigour and enthusiasm.

International football had proven immensely popular before 1930, particularly in the UK. England and Scotland had battled out annual contests since 1871, with Wales and later Ireland also establishing football associations in the following years. With the expansion of the British empire and the success of the first modern Olympics in 1896, football and indeed wider sport was brought to nations around the world.

In South America, the popularity of the game in Brazil, Argentina, Uruguay and Chile had led to the introduction of the Campeonato Sudamericano de Fútbol (now Copa América) in 1916.[74] The first international tournament outside of the British

74   *The Guardian*, 17 June 2015

Isles, it would grow to include Peru, Bolivia and Paraguay during the following decade. The emergence of South American football was clear at the 1924 and 1928 Olympics when the Uruguayan side defeated their European counterparts to win consecutive gold medals.

It was in Uruguay where the first tournament was to be held. An unpopular decision in Europe, primarily due to the restrictions on travel, meant that only three European sides participated. France, Belgium and Yugoslavia would make the long journey across the Atlantic to face the challenge of South and North America. It would be France who claimed the credit for the first World Cup goal, scored by inside-right Lucien Laurent against Mexico in Montevideo.

In the 19th minute, Laurent volleyed in from 12 yards after a cross from right-winger Ernest Libérati. The goal itself was barely reported back home in France and Laurent's celebration was muted. Instead, after putting Les Bleus 1-0 up, he turned and walked back to the halfway line. Perhaps even more bizarre was the fact snow was falling at the Estadio Pocitos.[75] With modern-day images of the World Cup being drenched in sunlight, this is a somewhat alien thought.

The goal itself was not seen with any particular importance. Indeed, its place in history has become more significant from the subsequent 2,547 goals scored at World Cups. The tournament has grown into the biggest single sport competition on Earth in terms of support and status and Laurent's opener was the first in a series of memorable goals at World Cups. Playing at the tournament is often perceived as the pinnacle of many players' careers but scoring takes personal achievement to a whole new level.

75   Callum Rice-Coates, 'Lucien Laurent: France's forgotten World Cup pioneer', Tifo Football, 4 June 2018 https://www.tifofootball.com/features/lucien-laurent-frances-forgotten-world-cup-pioneer/

20

Michelle Akers opens the scoring in the first Women's World Cup Final (1991)

FOLLOWING DECADES of struggle and fight for the freedom to play, women's football would see a major milestone in 1991. As the game began to grow around the world, FIFA would organise the first Women's World Cup in China. The FIFA website describes the tournament as a 'coming of age' and a resounding success. Brought to life by then-president João Havelange, the competition saw 12 nations competing for what would become the biggest prize available.

Women's football had started to see genuine global growth in the 1980s and the FIFA Invitational Tournament arranged by the federation in 1988 had tested the feasibility of a women's World Cup.[76] Won by Norway and hosted in China, it featured 16 of the best sides the game had to offer. The final between Norway and Sweden had even attracted 35,000 spectators, a large number that perhaps even the most ardent of supporters would not have expected. The success of the invitational and indeed China as the host would lead to the Asian country providing the venue for the first women's World Cup.

After two weeks of intense competition, it would be the US who would emerge victorious. A dream team featuring the mercurial talents of Mia Hamm, Michelle Akers and Carin

Jennings would defeat Scandinavian nation Norway in front of a raucous 65,000 in Guangzhou. Jennings and Akers were joined by captain April Heinrichs to form the famous 'triple-edged sword' in attack for the US. Amazingly, the trio managed to score 20 of the side's 25 goals in China.

In the final, it would be Akers who opened the scoring in the 20th minute as she powerfully headed Shannon Higgins's free kick past Norwegian keeper Reidun Seth. Following a quick equaliser, Akers won the game for the US late in the second half and created history. Lifting the cup in front of the capacity crowd, the side had achieved something the men's side had not. Women's football was here to stay.

For Jennings, the affinity and togetherness of the squad was something she hadn't witnessed on such a level before. The family atmosphere among competing nations would be a sign of things to come in the women's game.

Jennings said, 'What I remember most is the friendship of the players on the team... We all played for the love of the game and for our team-mates.'[77]

The heroics of Akers in China should not be understated. The performances, particularly in the final, helped the game to boom in the 1990s across the US. The tournament as a whole was relatively modest in terms of coverage and was even officially named the '1st FIFA World Championship for Women's Football for the M&M's Cup'. It can be argued that the football world's governing body was reluctant to initially name it a 'World Cup' in case it failed to gain support. Despite such misogynistic concerns, its success in China paved the way for an official 'Women's World Cup' in 1995 and female participation in Olympic football.[78]

---

77   Carin Jennings in, 'USA's triple-edged sword sets China PR 1991 ablaze', FIFA, 16 July 2016 https://www.fifa.com/about-fifa/who-we-are/news/usa-s-triple-edged-sword-sets-china-pr-1991-ablaze-2812104

78   Kieran Theivam and Jeff Kassouf, *The Making of the Women's World Cup: Defining Stories from a Sport's Coming of Age* (London: Robinson, 2019)

21

Roberto Carlos's banana goal (1997)

IN 1997, Brazil were world champions and developing a side capable of creating a new footballing dynasty well into the next decade. From defence to attack, the team was full of undeniable talent. Ronaldo led the line alongside Romário, with the stalwart full-backs Cafu and Roberto Carlos supplying an endless amount of energy down the right and left wings, respectively.

It was Carlos who would emerge as one the game's great attacking full-backs in 1997. Signing for Real Madrid in the summer of 1996, he finished second behind Ronaldo in the following year's FIFA World Player of the Year voting. Integral to his success was his ability over free kicks. Using the outside of the boot, he would often lash the ball into the net before the goalkeepers could even react.

With the World Cup due to take place in France in 1998, the host nation decided to hold a warm-up tournament the year before, named Le Tournoi de France. Alongside favourites Brazil were France, 1966 world champions England and three-time World Cup winners Italy.

It took just 21 minutes to see Le Tournoi's first goal and it came from Carlos. Around 35 yards from goal, the Brazilian left-back placed the ball down for a free kick and took several steps backwards – surely it was too far out? As he hit the ball with his trademark outside-of-the-boot technique, it seemed to be heading out for a goal kick. With French keeper Fabien

Barthez rooted to his line, the ball then swung viciously towards the goal and into the net off the post.

'I'll always remember the advertising behind the goal. I was aiming for the "A" in La Poste, but when I hit the shot it was miles away from that – going towards a different advert! The ball boy was diving out of the way of the shot, too. He should have had more confidence in me!' Carlos later said.[79]

Such was the global astonishment after the goal was scored, some even turned to science to explain it. *The Science of Soccer* by John Wesson even devotes an entire chapter to explaining the phenomenon of the 'banana shot'.[80]

Brazil would go on to finish second in the tournament behind England. Their runners-up spot perhaps foreshadowed events the following year when they were defeated in the World Cup Final by hosts France.

Carlos had cemented his legacy as one of football's greatest ever left-backs and began to completely reinvent the position. In fact, the position of full-back has generally been seen as the least glamorous position in football. The words of Jamie Carragher seem to highlight this, 'No one grows up wanting to be a Gary Neville.'[81] But Carlos made it sexy. Combining attacking flair with defensive solidity created a new breed of full-backs like Jordi Alba, Dani Alves and more recently Trent Alexander-Arnold.

79   Roberto Carlos in Andrew Murray, 'Roberto on THAT goal in 1997', *FourFourTwo*, 10 April 2018 https://www.fourfourtwo.com/features/roberto-carlos-goal-1997-i-was-aiming-a-la-poste-it-went-miles-away

80   John Wesson, *The Science of Soccer* (Bristol: Institute of Physics, 2002) pp.43–69

81   Jamie Carragher on *Monday Night Football*, Sky Sports, 18 August 2014

22

Mario Balotelli asks, 'Why Always Me?' (2011)

THERE IS no one quite like Mario Balotelli. When the Italian forward joined Manchester City from Inter Milan on 12 August 2010, he already had a reputation for his attitude and love for controversy. Balotelli has spent most of his career as a love him/ loathe him figure, but on 23 October 2011 in the 22nd minute, he truly grabbed the attention of the football world.

Balotelli came to Britain as a divisive figure and immediately stories began following the youngster around in the media. Stories started after he was reportedly found with £5,000 cash on the front seat of his car after a crash just a week after his debut, to which he replied, 'It is because I am rich.'[82] Perhaps it was the story about him being found wandering an Italian women's prison to 'have a look round',[83] the club investigation into him throwing darts at youth team players from the academy balcony window,[84] or the gifting of £1,000 to a homeless man after a casino win,[85] but fans were gripped by his adventures.

On the pitch, Balotelli was part of a Manchester City side who were desperate to catch up and overtake long-term rivals

82   *Daily Mirror*, 5 September 2010
83   *The Telegraph*, 25 July 2011
84   *The Independent*, 28 March 2011
85   *Metro*, 20 April 2011

Manchester United. City had started the season in imperious form, winning seven of their eight league matches and drawing the other one. Then a trip to Old Trafford awaited and a chance for City to truly show their title credentials against United, the defending champions. Strikers Sergio Agüero and Edin Džeko had found fine form but Mario Balotelli still had a key role to play for the Citizens.

However, less than 48 hours before the massive derby clash, firefighters were called to Mario's house at 1am. The remarkable character had some friends around and the group decided to set off fireworks from the bathroom window. The story was reported that bathroom towels were set alight and the 'blaze spread'.[86] The headlines attracted vast media attention, not the ideal build-up to the crunch derby fixture.

Come game day and City boss Roberto Mancini elected to start Mario ahead of Džeko, backing his fellow countryman. Twenty-two minutes into the crucial tie, the risk paid off as Balotelli stroked the ball into the bottom corner of the United goal to give City the lead. In recognition of a chaotic week for the 21-year-old, Balotelli celebrated by lifting his shirt and revealing a pre-printed top that read 'Why Always Me?', taking a swipe at the tabloid attention he had been attracting.

Balotelli's goal was the difference at half-time but after United defender Jonny Evans was shown a red card minutes into the second period, the game was firmly in City's favour. Balotelli netted his second in the 60th minute before Agüero (69), Džeko (89 and 90+3) and Silva (90+1) helped make the final score Manchester United 1 Manchester City 6. It was a staggering performance. The result was United's worst home defeat since February 1955, the first time United had conceded six at home since 1930 and the heaviest defeat in their Premier League history.[87] This was quite some day for the blue half of Manchester.

86   *The Guardian*, 22 October 2011

87   Phil McNulty, 'Man Utd 1 – 6 Man City', BBC Sport, 23 October 2011
     https://www.bbc.co.uk/sport/football/15325536

Mario Balotelli's time in the north-west finished in 2013 and the maverick has been branded 'unmanageable'[88] by José Mourinho after his time as his coach at Inter Milan. For Mario though, despite all the fun and games, he has often stood firm in the face of racism. His career has been sadly blighted by racial abuse aimed towards him from spectators in stadiums across the world.

Football has certainly benefited from the character of the striker; we have also been privileged to see his stand against those who seek to target players simply because of the colour of their skin ...

88 *The Telegraph*, 8 April 2012

23

Johan Cruyff turns the footballing world inside out (1974)

THIS BOOK is rightly made up of fine goals, major sendings off, terrible tragedies and footballing funnies. This moment though, is probably the most replicated in the modern game and was first produced by the Dutch master Johan Cruyff. As *The Independent* noted, 'Few players do something so original and so brilliant…that a trick is named after them.'[89] In the 23rd minute of the 1974 World Cup clash between Netherlands and Sweden, Cruyff made the magic happen.

The Dutch side of 1974 has gone down in footballing history with its glorious style of play under manager Rinus Michels, named 'Total Football'. This demanding, high-press system required 'players of exceptional quality to interchange positions…and for all outfield players to be able to participate in attacks…even a "flying" goalkeeper was encouraged to take part in the passage of play'.[90] Total Football helped the Netherlands waltz through the World Cup with six goals in their first three games, followed by victories over Argentina (4-0), East Germany (2-0) and Brazil (2-0) to set up a final against West Germany.

89   *The Independent*, 24 March 2016

90   Berend Scholten, 'Michels – a total footballing legend', UEFA, 3 March 2005 https://www.uefa.com/insideuefa/about-uefa/history/obituaries/newsid=285010.html?redirectFromOrg=true

It was in their second match, however, that Cruyff would turn in such a way that the world would never forget it. The fixture, a 0-0 draw with Sweden, followed a 2-0 win over Uruguay in their opener. Despite a goalless tie, the *Daily Mirror* reported, 'This was a match where one man stamped his authority on the game right from the start – and that man was Cruyff.'[91]

In the 23rd minute, Cruyff received the ball from team-mate Arie Haan on the left-hand side of the penalty area, just outside the box. Cruyff was closely marked by Swedish defender Jan Olsson who had handled the Dutch talisman expertly thus far. This time, Cruyff found a way to beat his man. Pulling his foot back as though going to play the ball back upfield, Cruyff instead dummied Olsson by stepping over the ball and drawing it back behind his standing left leg. Cruyff then spun his whole body 180 degrees to take control of the ball again, while Olsson, completely sold by the feint, made to follow Cruyff up the pitch in the original direction. The defender lost several yards on Cruyff and the attacking midfielder seized the advantage, now through on goal.

Sadly for football, this move did not lead to a Netherlands goal, and perhaps the breakdown of play could have undermined the moment. Nevertheless, Cruyff recalled how the move was immediately remembered, 'Everyone was talking about the feint that I'd done, the so-called "Cruyff Turn".'[92] The question was, did he mean it? According to the great man himself, he'd never practised it beforehand, stating, 'The idea came to me in a flash, because at that particular moment it was the best solution for the situation I was in.'[93]

The Dutch would fail to beat West Germany in the final of the 1974 World Cup, losing 2-1. In spite of this, Total Football would provide a lasting legacy to the beautiful game, as would the Cruyff Turn – a skill taught to children across the world as soon as they are able to kick a ball.

91   *Daily Mirror*, 20 June 1974
92   Johan Cruyff, *My Turn* (London: Pan Macmillan, 2016) p. 56
93   Ibid

24

Just Fontaine's first of 13 in Sweden (1958)

THE 1958 World Cup is renowned for introducing a 17-year-old Pelé to the global stage. Helping his national team, Brazil, to their first title, it would be easy to suggest that the youngster was indeed the tournament's finest player that year. Held in Sweden, the competition saw the South Americans dominate, but the exploits of a French individual truly shone in this remarkable edition of football's most prestigious trophy.

The man in question is France's Moroccan-born forward Just Fontaine. Fontaine made international football history at the tournament with a staggering 13 goals in just six games. At the start of it he had been playing for post-war sensations Stade de Reims. Reims had won three French titles in the immediate aftermath of World War Two, establishing themselves as arguably the nation's finest team. The signing of Fontaine in 1956 from domestic rivals Nice meant that the side had become feared, not just in France but across the continent.

The French national team was also benefiting from a highly competitive domestic Ligue 1. An impressive qualification campaign for the World Cup had seen the side score an outstanding 19 goals in only four games. Remarkably, Fontaine didn't feature for Les Bleus in their qualification journey and the World Cup's opener against Paraguay was only his sixth cap. Despite making his debut in 1953, Fontaine would have to wait for his time on the centre stage. When it came, he certainly didn't look back.

It took 24 minutes for Fontaine to score his first goal of the tournament. Beating the offside trap set by the Paraguayan defence, he latched on to a long ball and smashed his shot right-footed past the keeper and into the net. The goal equalised for France and after an eventful 90 minutes, they had defeated the South Americans 7-3. Fontaine had scored a hat-trick and truly introduced himself to the watching world.

In total, the French forward scored six goals in the group stage to help his nation to reach the knockout rounds. Fontaine was the 'athletic heart of the team' and scored twice more to down the Northern Irish challenge in Norrköping.[94] With eight goals to his name, he was comfortably the tournament's top scorer and despite adding another in the semi-finals against Brazil, it was a mere consolation as the Seleção won 5-2.

An incredible tournament for the French had one final match to play. The third-place play-off saw a meeting against arch-rivals West Germany in Gothenburg. Just 13 years after World War Two, a match 'rife with symbolism' and often violent challenges again brought Fontaine to the fore as[95] four superb goals helped Les Bleus to record a 6-3 victory. The third-place finish would be met with critical acclaim in France, throwing Fontaine firmly into the limelight.

94   Lindsay Sarah Krasnoff, *The Making of Les Bleus: Sport in France 1958–2000* (Plymouth: Lexington, 2013)

95   Ibid

25

The end of Ronaldo's final, but not the end for Portugal (2016)

IN THE opening 25 minutes of this book, Cristiano Ronaldo has already featured twice. The Portuguese forward has helped shape the modern game alongside his rival Lionel Messi. Domestically, the two players are relatively evenly matched. In terms of Champions Leagues, Ronaldo boasts five titles to Messi's four, yet the diminutive Argentine is by far and away ahead when it comes to domestic leagues and cups.[96] For their respective international sides, however, the argument from some critics has always been that neither can be regarded as the greatest until they have achieved global success. In 2016 Cristiano Ronaldo was able to put his side of the argument to rest.

The European Championships of 2016 has split opinion. For all those who criticised the 'lack of quality', there is a balance of supporters quick to give it praise.[97] [98] The main positive was that it was truly a tournament for the underdog. In spite of claims that allowing 24 teams to qualify would lessen the standard, it

96 As of the end of the 2019/20 season.

97 Phil McNulty, 'Euro 2016: England Disappoint, Iceland Impress, Portugal Come Good', *BBC Sport*, 12 July 2016 https://www.bbc.co.uk/sport/football/36763052

98 Tom Adams, 'Best and Worst of Euro 2016: The tournament in review', *Eurosport*, 11 July 2016 https://www.eurosport.co.uk/football/euro-2016/2016/best-and-worst-of-euro-2016-the-tournament-in-review_sto5683581/story.shtml

saw heroic runs to the latter stages by Iceland (Minute 4) and Wales (Minute 55). Likewise, Ronaldo's Portugal were largely un-fancied before the competition began and a run of three draws from their group stage fixtures did little to change people's opinions. Captain Ronaldo had scored a brace in the final match against surprise group winners Hungary to draw 3-3.

Portugal had scraped through in third place. The revised format of 24 teams in 2016 gave four of the best third-place sides an opportunity in the knockout rounds. After overcoming the Croatian challenge after extra time in Lens, Poland would also be defeated, this time on penalties. Incredibly, Ronaldo had skippered his side to the semi-finals without a single win in normal time. The impressive Wales, minus the influential Aaron Ramsey and Ben Davies, were seen off in the semi-finals, leading to a final showdown with France.

This was truly Ronaldo's time to shine. For all of France's home advantage, Portugal had Ronaldo. What a final it would be. And 25 minutes in, Ronaldo was injured.

Even the most hardened football fan felt their heart sink as injury forced the then world's best player into an early substitution in the moth-infested Stade de France. The weeping attacker was stretchered from the field, taking a seat on the Portuguese bench. Ronaldo could have been forgiven for fearing the worst for his nation but his response was quite the opposite. Indeed, for the remainder of the final and especially in extra time, the captain almost became a second manager, beckoning his team on while supporting an ice pack around his injured leg.

The only goal of the game from Eder came with 11 minutes left of extra time. At the final whistle, Ronaldo would hobble on to the pitch and join in the celebrations. Portugal had erased decades of near-misses and finally put their name on one of football's finest international trophies. For BBC Sport's Phil McNulty, Ronaldo could 'now be regarded with the true greats of the game'.[99]

99   Phil McNulty, Euro 2016: Cristiano Ronaldo becomes true great with Portugal win, *BBC Sport*, 11 July 2016 https://www.bbc.co.uk/sport/football/36761007

26

Kevin-Prince Boateng takes a stand against racism (2013)

KEVIN-PRINCE BOATENG has had a varied, colourful, love him/loathe him career. In 2013, however, while playing for Italian giants AC Milan, Boateng took a stand against racial abuse he was receiving and found the support of the footballing world. Very sadly, this is not a moment that ends here, and the racial abuse of footballers continues to this day.

Milan were playing against fourth-tier club Pro Patria in a friendly match. The Ghanaian international had been subjected to racial abuse by a section of Pro Patria supporters. Kevin-Prince, in the 26th minute, rightly upset and angered by the disgusting behaviour of the 'fans', reacted by kicking the ball at the crowd in the stands. Boateng then proceeded to leave the pitch, tearing his shirt as he left and refusing to continue playing.

Pro Patria defender Dario Polverini attempted to keep Boateng on the field, but the 25-year-old was supported by his captain, Massimo Ambrosini. Ambrosini led the Milan players to the dressing room, as I Rossoneri later stated that more players of colour had also been abused, including Urby Emanuelson, Sulley Muntari and M'Baye Niang.[100] The game was abandoned and the president of the Italian FA, Giancarlo Abete, promised,

100 *The Guardian*, 3 January 2013

'We must react with force and without silence to isolate the few criminals that transformed a friendly match into an uproar that offends all of Italian football.'[101]

Sadly, football has not been able to rid itself of racism across the world. Too often there are stories of mindless fools who continue to target players based on the colour of their skin and it is undoubtedly a scourge of the modern game. In November 2019, Boateng was forced to declare that 'nothing has changed' after striker Mario Balotelli was abused playing for Italian side Brescia, away at Hellas Verona.[102] This incident was then followed by a minority of Lazio fans also insulting Balotelli later that month.

The problem is also not just limited to countries such as Italy either, with England's black players being on the receiving end of chants that saw a stadium ban imposed after an away match with Bulgaria in October 2019. English football too has had its fair share of disgraceful incidents in recent seasons – both Bournemouth and Chelsea 'fans' (to name but a few) have been handed lifetime bans following racism aimed at England winger Raheem Sterling.

The case remains that while footballing authorities and confederations hand out paltry fines and stadium bans (€75,000 and two games behind closed doors to Bulgaria in 2019[103], Lazio – €20,000 and no ban[104]), there is unlikely to be a cessation of all forms of discrimination. The beautiful game is being muddied by the continuation of these criminal activities. Let us hope that the 2020s puts an end to them for good.

101 Ibid
102 *Daily Mail*, 4 November 2019
103 *Metro*, 29 October 2019
104 *The Guardian*, 8 January 2020

27

David Beckham scores his first US goal (2007)

YOUR TEAM has a free kick, 30 yards from goal, and David Beckham is in your squad. You would be right to feel pretty confident that the midfielder is going to score. In 2007, LA Galaxy fans were treated to their first Beckham free kick masterclass as he opened the scoring in the 27th minute versus DC United. 'Golden Balls' had made his way 'across the pond' in July 2007, and in August he opened his account with the West Coast side.

London-born Beckham was part of Manchester United's renowned 'Class of 92' youth crop. The group of players were developed by prolific academy coach Eric Harrison and became part of the backbone of Sir Alex Ferguson's phenomenally successful Manchester United team. At United, Beckham won six Premier Leagues, two FA Cups, two Charity Shields and a UEFA Champions League, playing a role in the Red Devils' stunning treble season of 1998/99 too. Wider than this, David Beckham found celebrity fame after marrying Victoria Adams, of pop group the Spice Girls, catapulting his status across the world.

In 2003 Beckham's career was furthered still by a move to Real Madrid, becoming part of their Galácticos era. Beckham added a La Liga title and Supercopa de España to his personal trophy cabinet, but his eventual move to MLS team LA Galaxy is the focus of this moment. His move would earn him £128m when the transfer was confirmed, a staggering £25.6m per season.[105] As part of this deal Beckham was also offered the future opportunity to bring his own cut-priced franchise to the MLS, an option that was brought to fruition in 2020 as he launched his Florida-based club, Inter Miami.

Beckham was not the first footballing superstar to make his way to the USA, former Florida side Fort Lauderdale Strikers having hosted players including Gordon Banks, Gerd Müller and George Best; while Brazilian legend Pelé turned out for New York Cosmos in the 1970s. Beckham, though, indicated a new generation of excitement for MLS fans and his signing saw a reported 11,000 extra Galaxy season tickets sold, along with a host of mega-bucks luxury suites and a major new sponsorship deal for the club.[106]

Beckham's Galaxy career was initially stunted by an ongoing injury, featuring off the bench in a friendly game against Chelsea in July 2007. Golden Balls then missed a number of weeks to fully recover from injury before making his league debut away to DC United on 9 August. The next week, Galaxy would face DC United again in the North American SuperLiga semi-final. In the 27th minute, Galaxy won a free kick and their new talisman stepped up. Beckham's trademark set-piece strike found the back of the net and the watching crowd were sent into a 'frenzy';[107] the moment they had dreamed of had arrived.

Beckham would net 20 times in his Galaxy career, winning two MLS Cups and topping the Western Conference three times. Beyond this, Beckham's move paved the way for further icons of the game to move stateside as Zlatan Ibrahimović, Steven Gerrard, Frank Lampard, Wayne Rooney, Kaká, Thierry Henry, Didier Drogba and Andrea Pirlo all took their shot at American glitz and glamour.

105 *The Guardian*, 11 January 2007

106 Grant Wahl, *The Beckham Experiment* (New York: Three Rivers Press, 2010) p. 44

107 *The Telegraph*, 16 August 2007

28

Nigel de Jong kung fu kicks
Xabi Alonso (2010)

IF THE Dutch national team is known for one thing, it is Total Football. Introduced to the game as early as the 1930s, it was developed into a seemingly unbeatable brand of attacking play in the 1970s (Minute 23). Its very utterance is synonymous with the Netherlands and their mercurial number 14 – Johan Cruyff. Therefore, it came as a surprise for millions watching around the globe as the Dutch seemingly abandoned all ties with the system at the 2010 World Cup.

In the 28th minute of the World Cup Final, played at Johannesburg's Soccer City, central midfielder Nigel de Jong produced a 'tackle' sure to be regarded in future football histories as one of the worst ever seen. De Jong and his midfield partner Marc van Bommel had utilised their bruising tactics throughout the tournament as the Dutch saw off favourites Brazil and a talented Uruguay featuring a front three of Diego Forlán, Edinson Cavani and Luis Suárez.

Despite the combative style of play, the earlier performances of the Dutch had generally drawn praise from commentators and journalists. A pragmatic approach to the game could indeed have seen the country win the World Cup for the first time. Sky Sports had praised their 'fighting spirit',[108] with the BBC

108 James Riach, 'Dutch courage stuns Brazil', *SkySports*, 2 July 2010 https://www.skysports.com/football/netherlands-vs-brazil/report/218453

complimenting their defensive discipline.[109] Nevertheless, it wasn't to everyone's taste with *The Guardian* making note of the 'spiteful' nature of the physical confrontation with Brazil.[110]

Meeting the Netherlands in the final were Spain. Throughout the tournament, La Roja had impressed spectators with their tiki-taka brand of football. Intricate passing, instigated by the Barcelona trio of Sergio Busquets, Andrés Iniesta and Xavi (Minute 10), had mesmerised viewers and players alike leading to many commentating that this was indeed the best international side in football history. Surely the final would produce a different approach from Bert Van Marwijk's Dutch XI?

Not so. In total, referee Howard Webb distributed 14 yellow cards and eventually a red for Oranje defender Johnny Heitinga in extra time. The worst offence, however, came in the 28th minute as the ill-disciplined de Jong challenged Xabi Alonso for the ball. Raising his boot high with his studs showing, he caught the Spanish playmaker in the middle of his chest and sent him crashing to the turf. Spain were incensed and immediately surrounded Webb (admittedly, this had become a regular feature in Spanish matches). It seemed to the whole world that a red card had to be shown, yet somehow the English referee only brandished a yellow.

In his autobiography, Webb would later explain that his positioning (behind Alonso) meant he did not get a proper view of the challenge. Knowing it was reckless, but not knowing the extent, he was 100 per cent certain it was only worth a yellow. It would only be at half-time that Webb would realise how poor de Jong's challenge was.[111] Alonso was clear in his thoughts a number of years later, claiming that he felt his body

109   Chris Bevan, 'Netherlands 2-1 Brazil', *BBC Sport*, 2 July 2010 http://news.bbc.co.uk/sport1/hi/football/world_cup_2010/matches/match_57/default.stm

110   *The Guardian*, 2 July 2010

111   Howard Webb, *The Man in the Middle* (London: Simon and Schuster, 2016)

had been 'torn apart'. De Jong, on the other hand, hoped to see the funny side and even joked about having a beer with his Spanish counterpart in the future.[112] For all of de Jong's joviality, Dutch football's legacy of entertaining football and attractive styles of play will forever be tarnished by *that* tackle on football's biggest stage.

112 *FourFourTwo* website, 'De Jong: I hope to have a beer and laugh about "that" tackle with Alonso one day', 6 June 2018 https://www. fourfourtwo.com/features/de-jong-i-hope-have-a-beer-and-laugh-about-tackle-alonso-one-day

29

Germany score their fifth in the 7-1 Mineirazo defeat of Brazil (2014)

THE FIFA 2014 World Cup was hosted by five-time winners Brazil. Despite all of the Seleção's victories, the only previous time they had hosted the tournament – 1950 – had ended in the devastating Maracanazo (Agony of Maracanã) defeat to Uruguay (Minute 79). In the 29th minute of their 2014 semi-final, however, fans were witnessing a decimation that would soon be known as Mineirazo (Agony of Mineirão), as Germany scored their fifth within half an hour.

Nike's famous advertising slogan says 'Joga bonito', 'play beautifully', which sums up the Brazilian principles of playing football. As they headed into the 2014 edition of the tournament, the hopes of the whole, passionate nation rested upon the shoulders of the squad of 23, the Seleção. At just 22 years old, Neymar was the competition's poster boy and had an opportunity to write his name into the history books forever. The World Cup lived up to the hype with 171 goals in just 64 matches (2.67 per game). It gripped watching spectators, earning its place in the discussion as one of the 'greatest tournaments' ever.[113]

Brazil topped Group A, winning twice and drawing once to set up a South American clash with Chile in the last 16.

---

113 *The Telegraph*, 12 July 2014

A 1-1 draw after extra time led to a penalty shootout with Neymar scoring the winning spot kick to earn a quarter-final against fan favourites Colombia. Brazil would have their centre-halves to thank for this victory, David Luiz and captain Thiago Silva netting either side of half-time to secure a 2-1 win and a semi-final against Germany. Could the Seleção banish the demons of 1950?

Manager Luiz Felipe Scolari was dealt a major blow before the semi-final as Neymar was ruled out for the rest of the tournament. Seemingly targeted by heavy Colombian challenges, a broken vertebra was confirmed. Neymar later labelled this as 'the most painful' moment of his career, noting, 'It was my childhood dream to become world champion on home soil, but it all went wrong because of an injury that could have forced me to leave football altogether.'[114]

On 8 July, Brazil hosted Germany with a place in the final at stake. The game started poorly for Brazil, Thomas Müller netting his fifth of the competition in the 11th minute, before Miroslav Klose made it 2-0 in the 23rd minute. This started a crazy six-minute spell, Toni Kroos adding a brace (24 and 26), while Sami Khedira made it 5-0 after just 29 minutes. The watching world was stunned.

Haunting images of crying fans, young and old, are etched into the memories of those who witnessed the massacre. The second half did not show any Brazilian improvement either, as André Schürrle added two more (69 and 79). Only Oscar scoring a single goal in injury time gave the Brazilians something very minor to cheer, but in truth it was a rout. The seismic result spurred Germany on to beat Argentina in the final to lift the World Cup but for Brazil this moment is 'a ghost that still haunts the Seleção'.[115]

114 *Daily Mail*, 12 July 2016
115 *The Independent*, 27 March 2018

30

Ada Hegerberg nets her Champions League Final hat-trick (2019)

OLYMPIQUE LYONNAIS Féminin won the UEFA Women's Champions League six times in the 2010s, a staggering run of success that included four in a row between 2016 and 2019. The 2018/19 final was hosted at the Groupama Arena in Budapest as Barcelona Femení attempted to knock Lyon off their perch. Striker Ada Hegerberg had a different idea – she struck a hat-trick within the first 30 minutes to give her side a 4-0 lead.

Hegerberg joined in 2014 from German team Turbine Potsdam and immediately the goals flowed for her new team; 34 in 32 games were netted in the 19-year-old's first campaign with the French giants and she added to that with 54 in 35 in her second season. With a French league title in each of those campaigns, two more would follow in 2016/17 and 2017/18. The latter would result in her biggest personal achievement to date, the first Ballon d'Or Féminin.

The Ballon d'Or has awarded a peer-voted trophy to the best male player in the game ever since Stanley Matthews's crowning in 1956. However, in 2018, the women's game would finally be recognised and Hegerberg would beat Dane Pernille Harder into second place. Sadly, the Norwegian would have her big moment spoiled, as host and DJ Martin Solveig asked the striker if she 'knew how to twerk' (shake her rear) on stage. Solveig later apologised, but it saw many public figures, including British tennis star Andy Murray, jump in to criticise yet 'another example of the ridiculous sexism in sport'.[116]

Hegerberg's reign as Ballon d'Or Féminin saw Lyon win yet another league title and reach yet another Champions League final. Lyon would use two-legged ties to put away Norwegian side Avaldsnes 7-0, Dutch team Ajax 13-0 and Germans Wolfsburg 6-3 en route to the final where Barcelona awaited. The Spaniards started as underdogs on 18 May 2019, and that would be where they would remain – 23-year-old Hegerberg putting Blaugranes to the sword in style.

Just five minutes into the final, Dzsenifer Marozsán gave Lyon the lead before Hegerberg made it 2-0 nine minutes later. Amel Majri then set up Hegerberg in the 19th minute for her second, and she had her hat-trick after connecting with England's Lucy Bronze's cross on the half-hour mark. The 4-0 lead would not be conceded, even with Asisat Oshoala getting one back for Barcelona. Lyon were 'stronger, faster, smarter and more clinical' than their opponents and lifted the continental honour once again.[117]

In late October 2019, Hegerberg became the fastest player, male or female, to reach 50 European goals (in 49 games). She surpassed former Manchester United striker Ruud van Nistelrooy who took 62 matches and waltzed past both Lionel Messi and Cristiano Ronaldo, who needed 66 and 91 games respectively.[118] Hegerberg is still young enough to achieve many more great things in her career, and the footballing world is sure to benefit.

116 *The Guardian*, 4 December 2018

117 *Daily Mail*, 18 May 2019

118 Emma Sanders, 'Ada Hegerberg: Lyon striker breaks Women's Champions League goalscoring record', BBC Sport, 30 October 2019 https://www.bbc.co.uk/sport/football/49746194

31

Pelé scores his first of five v Eusébio's Benfica (1962)

PELÉ AND Eusébio are two of those players who modern fans of the beautiful game wish they could've seen play live. Portugal international Eusébio was born in Mozambique and became Africa's first footballing superstar, possessing 'one of the most fearsome shots to have graced the planet'.[119] Pelé, meanwhile, shot to fame at the 1958 World Cup, the 17-year-old Brazilian netting six in the tournament to help his country lift their first title (Minute 66). In 1962, Brazil retained the trophy in Chile, but Pelé had the opportunity for more club success with Santos as they faced Eusébio's Benfica in the Intercontinental Cup.

The Intercontinental Cup was first contested in 1960, between the winners of the European Cup (founded in 1955) and the winners of the newly-formed South American version, the Copa Libertadores.[120] Both confederations, UEFA (Europe) and CONMEBOL (South America), endorsed the tournament but FIFA (the game's governing body) did not. Nevertheless, in 1960 Real Madrid would beat the Copa Libertadores's first champions, Uruguayan side Peñarol, over two legs. The following season saw Peñarol reach the cup again, this time facing off against Béla Guttmann's Benfica side who had won

119 Richard Witzig, *The Global Art of Soccer* (New Orleans: CusiBoy Publishing, 2006) p. 171
120 *Daily Mail*, 18 December 2019

the European Cup against Barcelona (Minute 69). Peñarol were victorious following a play-off decider in Montevideo and the two continents were level at 1-1.

The 1962 Intercontinental Cup saw a mouth-watering tie drawn. Pelé's Santos earned their place in the competition with their Copa Libertadores success over Peñarol (who were denied a third straight appearance), while Eusébio's Benfica featured again after an impressive 5-3 European Cup Final win over a Real Madrid side who boasted the likes of Ferenc Puskás, Francisco Gento and Alfredo Di Stéfano.

The first leg was hosted at the Maracanã Stadium, Brazil, in September 1962. After 31 minutes Pelé opened the scoring for Santos, giving the home team the advantage. Coutinho would add a second after half-time, before Pelé popped up again five minutes from time to secure a 3-2 'shock' victory for the Santásticos.[121] A month later, Santos would travel to Portugal for the return fixture, needing only a draw to win the Intercontinental Cup (the competition being decided on points rather than aggregate score). Some 73,000 supporters filled Estádio da Luz in Lisbon, expecting Benfica to force a play-off.

Just 15 minutes in, Pelé scored once more as he diverted home a ball fired across the box. Ten minutes later, he had his second after producing 'a hypnotising feint' to beat one opponent, before 'skipping past' two more, and smashing a 'stinging left-foot drive' into the Benfica net.[122] Pelé would complete a stunning hat-trick after the break, a mazy run that included a nutmeg of Eusébio to leave even the home fans 'applauding' him.[123] The magician had five over two matches, and while Eusébio managed a consolation goal before the end, it was only enough for a 5-2 defeat. Santos were Intercontinental Cup champions for the first time, and it was done in magnificent style.

121 *Coventry Evening Telegraph*, 20 September 1962

122 FIFA, 'Extraordinary Pele crowns Santos in Lisbon', 11 October 2012 https://www.fifa.com/news/extraordinary-pele-crowns-santos-lisbon-1782903

123 Ibid

32

Katie Chapman helps make it four in a row for Arsenal (2009)

IF, IN the 1990s and 2000s, Manchester United dominated men's football, then Arsenal would certainly conquer all before them in the women's game. Under the stewardship of one of football's greatest coaches, Vic Akers, the north London outfit would truly revolutionise the sport in Britain, promoting participation and many of its players into genuine idols for thousands of young girls around the country.

With sustained success both domestically and on the continent, Arsenal's fortunes in the late 1990s and 2000s saw the women's game reach new levels. Akers, and his promotion of a scintillating brand of attacking football, had seen the establishment of a true footballing dynasty as good as anything the men's game had seen. Perhaps only rivalled by the victories of the Doncaster Belles in the 1980s, no team can boast a greater influence in shaping modern women's sport in the UK.

The FA Cup became Arsenal Ladies' most coveted trophy and by winning ten between 1993 and 2009, they truly dominated. Their greatest spell came towards the end of this period when they achieved an incredible 51 consecutive victories in the league – something which led some journalists to believe that their dominance should surely be regarded above even the men's invincible season of 2003/04.[124] By 2009 they would

124 *The Guardian*, 4 May 2008

continue to set records with every goal scored and became the first side in football history to win four consecutive FA Cups (men's and women's).

The opening goal in the 2009 final against Sunderland came in the 32nd minute. After goalkeeper Helen Alderson failed to hold on to Gemma Davison's vicious long-range strike, Katie Chapman pounced on the mistake. Scottish forward Kim Little sealed the win in the final minute before Sunderland replied with a consolation goal. Lifting the cup to an impressive 23,291 supporters, the successes of Akers's side was clear. Just a decade earlier the cup final had only welcomed 6,000 fans and ten years before that failed to even attract 1,000.

Arsenal Ladies' 2000s roll of honour reads like a Hall of Fame of the women's game. Forward Kelly Smith netted 73 times in 66 league appearances for the club in the 2000s, right-back Alex Scott and centre-back Faye White are rightly regarded as two of England's finest ever defenders and winger Rachel Yankey is a legend in her own right. It wasn't just English talent though as Scotland's Julie Fleeting was the hat-trick hero in the 2004 Women's FA Cup Final while Jayne Ludlow, future Wales Women manager, was an influential midfielder for the Gunners during the decade.

Arsenal Ladies are one of British football's greatest sides. Their trophy cabinet is good enough to rival any club in both the men's and women's games. They helped to put women's football on the map in Britain and inspired thousands of young girls to take up playing[125]. The late 2000s became a pivotal period for the sport as participation levels rose and calls for a rebranding of the national women's league grew, eventually culminating in the successful Women's Super League (WSL) in 2010.

---

125 Women's Sport and Fitness Foundation, 'Football Factsheet', Sport England, March 2011, Available at: https://sportengland-production-files.s3.eu-west-2.amazonaws.com/s3fs-public/case-study-female-team-v-individual-sports.pdf

33

Australia's 13th in a record-breaking 31-0 win (2001)

AUSTRALIA ARE regulars at the World Cup and since 2006 they have qualified for each edition of the quadrennial tournament. In 2001 however, qualification was often a futile effort with a lack of representation given to the Oceania Football Confederation (OFC). Winning the qualification group would only lead to a continental play-off, often against a strong side from South America. The Socceroos had lost in the 1994 and 1998 qualification campaigns at the last hurdle.

Qualification for the 2002 event saw Australia joined by Fiji, Tonga, Samoa and American Samoa in their group. The gulf in class between the nations was immediately clear as the first round of matches saw Fiji defeat American Samoa 13-0 before Australia went nine better, battering Tonga 22-0 in front of 1,500 spectators in Coffs Harbour. The result had made a mockery of the standard in OFC football and set a wealth of records in the process. John Aloisi had helped himself to six with Damian Mori and Kevin Muscat each scoring four.

Incredibly, the result was only a taste of what was to come. Just two days later, Australia would face continental 'rivals' American Samoa and within 33 minutes they were 13-0 up. David Zdrilic had just scored his fourth goal, comfortably strolling through the Samoan defence and slotting past the helpless goalkeeper. At half-time the game was well and truly over with the scoreboard reading 16-0. The second half continued at the same pace with the Socceroos ruthlessly scoring to goal after goal. Striker Archie Thompson helped himself to a record-breaking 13 in total and put himself firmly at the top of the FIFA qualification goalscoring charts. The final score was 31-0. For a nation which loves their cricket, the scoreline was more reminiscent of an opening batsman's total before lunch.

'The result is still a matter of debate after the initial scoreline of 32-0 was changed,' wrote the BBC.[126]

The quote taken from the corporation's match report says it all. Even the Australian players were in a relatively sombre mood after the victory. For them, playing the fixtures seemed almost pointless and just highlighted the lack of quality in Australasian football.[127] 'It really is a waste of time,' beckoned record-breaker Thompson to international journalists stunned by the result they had just witnessed.

The entire group stage was played over the course of a week at the aforementioned Australian town of Coffs Harbour. In just seven days, Australia had scored 66 goals without reply. After defeating neighbours New Zealand 6-1 on aggregate in the final round, history would unfortunately repeat itself in 2002 with a play-off defeat to Uruguay. The 2002 qualification campaign would be remembered for the serious lack of competition in the OFC and perhaps the final straw for Australia.

Despite qualification being achieved in 2006, after an absence of 32 years, the following World Cup would see Australia enter the qualification stages as part of the Asian Football Confederation (AFC). This would provide the nation with greater competition and a chance to truly test themselves against quality teams for the first time in decades. With subsequent finals appearances between 2010 and 2018, their gamble seems to have paid off …

126 BBC, 'Aussie Footballers Smash World Record', 11 April 2001 http://news.bbc.co.uk/sport1/hi/football/world_cup_2002/1271854.stm

127 *The Guardian*, 12 April 2001

34

Ivan Perišić's handball leads to history-making VAR penalty (2018)

WHETHER IT be the first live radio broadcast of the FA Cup Final (Cardiff City's victory in 1927), the first television broadcast of a World Cup in 1954, the first use of red and yellow cards in the 1970 World Cup or the 2014 World Cup featuring the first use of goal-line technology, football is constantly evolving to meet the needs, demands and desires of the viewing public and the game's power brokers. Such modern clamour would see the 2018 Russian World Cup introducing another development and three distinct letters: VAR, or the Video Assistant Referee.

VAR had been debated for many years. When sides had a seemingly outrageous decision given against them, the calls mounted up about video replays to solve the 'incompetency' of referees. This was added to by the relative success of video referrals in other sports like rugby, cricket and American football. However, many fans noted that football is a more fluid game, with fewer breaks in play to be able to assess and pore over video evidence. The question always arose, 'Would video assistants ruin football?' The 2018 World Cup would have the opportunity to test the viability of VAR, the 32 competing nations subject to its authority.

On a smaller scale, VAR had been tested thoroughly before making its World Cup debut and in 2012 saw its earliest appearance in mock trials in the Dutch Eredivisie. The Australian A-League, America's MLS, Germany's Bundesliga and Italy's Serie A all used the system, as well as the 2017 FIFA Confederations Cup in Russia. Eventually, the International Football Association Board (IFAB) wrote VAR into the official rules of the game in preparation for the showpiece in Russia. In Britain scepticism reigned, as many fans, journalists and ex-pros were united in their pre-judgement of VAR, Alan Shearer lambasting it as a 'shambles' after a trial in an FA Cup game in January 2018.[128]

As expected, VAR played a major role in the tournament. In the group matches alone, VAR checked 335 incidents (nearly seven per game). This led to 14 on-field reviews being made by referees and three reviews made by the VAR team outside the stadium. While it was noted that referees made '95 per cent' of decisions correctly without VAR, the technology 'improved the success rate to 99.3 per cent'.[129] VAR was, on the whole, used quickly, but it did not win all sceptics over during the competition, many worried it would have a lasting impact on the outcome of the tournament. This happened on 15 July at the Luzhniki Stadium, Moscow.

France, chasing a second World Cup, made the final against Croatia who had eliminated England after extra time in the last four. France took an early lead after a Mario Mandžukić own goal before Ivan Perišić leveled the match in the 28th minute. But in the 34th minute Perišić and VAR hit the headlines again as a French corner appeared to strike his arm. Referee Néstor Pitana initially waved away claims, but was advised to consult the video replay, where he changed his mind and awarded a penalty. Four minutes later, Antoine Griezmann stepped up and scored, making history as the first 'VAR influenced' World Cup Final goal. France would win the tie 4-2 and VAR would later be adopted by most top flight leagues across the world. VAR remains controversial but is definitely here to stay.

128 *The Guardian*, 18 January 2018
129 BBC, 'World Cup 2018: VAR system "fine-tuned" after criticism', 29 June 2018 https://www.bbc.co.uk/sport/football/44658757

35

Gino Colaussi helps Italy to back-to-back World Cups (1938)

THE GLOBE was on the brink of World War Two in 1938. Adolf Hitler had assumed power in Germany in 1933 and steadily increased his persecution of the Jewish people and other minority groups. In Italy, Benito Mussolini had taken control in 1922 and under his one-party fascist state, the two dictators had grown closer. Mussolini's regime prioritised sporting success to bring glory to Italy, and the 1934 World Cup was lifted on home soil. In 1938, the World Cup was hosted by France, and with the help of Gino Colaussi, a second successive crown was achieved.

During the 1930s, the watching world had grown concerned by the friendship of Hitler and Mussolini. Newspapers speculated that the pair were 'hatching a plot' and that they should be 'firmly handled' to prevent war.[130] Into this melting pot, the third World Cup was set for France in 1938. The British home nations, however, were still united in their rejection of the international competition. Some believed 'Europe' was hoping for England to be given the right to 'organise the 1942 competition'[131] to bring them into the fold, but for this honour they would have to compete with Nazi Germany and South American countries, should football still be taking place in 1942.

---

130 *Aberdeen Press and Journal*, 10 September 1937
131 *Sunderland Daily Echo and Shipping Gazette*, 9 July 1938

Italy arrived in France as defending champions, led by their coach Vittorio Pozzo. Thus far the World Cup had been won by the hosting nation (Uruguay 1930 and Italy 1934), so France would have been hoping for a similar triumph. Austria were withdrawn from the tournament due to the 1938 'Anschluss' which saw them subsumed into a 'Greater Germany'.[132] Germany therefore forced many Austrians to represent them instead, although Austria's star Matthias Sindelar refused and in January 1939 he was found dead in 'tragic and mysterious' circumstances.[133]

Italy began their tournament to a 'chorus of jeers' following a pre-match fascist salute.[134] Pozzo later wrote that his team's duty that day was 'clear' as the side raised their arms showing 'no fear' and to 'win the battle of intimidation'.[135] They required extra time to put away Norway and set up a quarter-final clash with hosts France. Colaussi and Silvio Piola both netted in the 3-1 victory over the French and a semi-final versus Brazil awaited. Fascist bedfellows Germany, meanwhile, failed in their pursuit of the World Cup. A first-round draw with Switzerland meant a play-off was needed, four second-half Swiss goals earning a 4-2 win and providing Germany with a short trip back across the border.

Pozzo's men continued to face protest wherever they played, and in Marseille, Brazil were defeated 2-1 – Colaussi again and Giuseppe Meazza on the scoresheet. A final lay ahead against Hungary after the Magyars impressively beat Sweden 5-1.

On 19 June, over 45,000 spectators packed into the Stade Olympique de Colombes, Paris. Italy were booed once more, but they put on 'one of the great displays in World Cup history'

---

132 Clemente A. Lisi, *A History of the World Cup: 1930–2010* (Plymouth: Scarecrow Press, Inc., 2011) p.33

133 *The Scotsman*, 24 January 1939

134 Clemente A. Lisi, *A History of the World Cup: 1930–2010*, p.35

135 Vittorio Pozzo, *Campioni del Mondo: Quarant'Anni di Storia del Calcio Italiano* (Rome: Centro Editoriale Nazionale, 1960) p.266

to beat the Hungarians 4-2.[136] Colaussi opened the scoring after just six minutes but Hungary quickly levelled. Piola then gave Italy the lead again, before in the 35th minute Colaussi made it an unassailable 3-1. At full time Vittorio Pozzo would celebrate becoming the first (and only) manager not only to win the trophy twice, but to achieve it back-to-back too.

136 Simon Martin, *Sport Italia: The Italian Love Affair with Sport* (London: I.B. Tauris, 2011) p.71

36

Jimmy Simmons opens the scoring in the Khaki Cup Final (1915)

BY THE summer of 1915, World War One had caused an unthinkable amount of destruction and despair. Despite an initially positive reaction from across Europe, as war was declared, it soon became clear that *this* conflict was different. August 1914 saw the Football League in England continue as usual. After all, it seemed that a war on the continent was no reason to alter daily lives and routines. Football was to remain.

Although initially seen as an important practice in maintaining domestic morale, it wasn't long before calls for the league's suspension became widespread. The *Western Mail* printed an article in January 1915 detailing a protest group which had been formed by Mr F. N. Charrington. Charrington had argued against professional football continuing in wartime and received the support of many leading archbishops and wider clergymen.[137] Further examples from within the press are easy to find as they attempt to undermine the necessity of football in wartime.

Despite what the wartime press would have you believe, by December 1914 football had contributed to the war effort. The famous Football Battalion had been established that Christmas and players were indeed starting to enlist. Despite

---

137 *Western Mail*, 28 January 1915

this sacrifice, the continuation of football meant the FA was 'losing the argument hands down' but was still adamant that the Football League had 'helped to ensure normality and soothe disquiet'.[138] Arguments like this would fall on deaf ears and the *Burnley News* made the position clear in March 1915, 'Never in its history has the game been in such a critical position.'[139]

The eventual fall in attendances across British grounds (which were often used for military drills) meant the writing was on the wall for the Football Association. The game would have to be suspended. In spite of growing agitation among some areas of society (in particular upper-class amateur sportsmen), the FA Cup Final would still go ahead in April. Sheffield United would face Chelsea at Old Trafford in front of a raucous yet underwhelming 49,000 fans.

Sheffield forward Jimmy Simmons would open the scoring nine minutes before half-time. Half-volleying into the back of the net, he invigorated the crowd. After the match's conclusion (a 3-0 victory for Sheffield United), the spectators were the focus of the British press. The *Sussex Agricultural Express* mentioned that 'khaki-clad soldiers [were] very prominent in the crowd'.[140] Their attendance had brought the reality of war into view for all in attendance.

The *Yorkshire Post and Leeds Intelligencer* reported, 'There were so many men in His Majesty's uniform among the crowd on Saturday that one is justified in referring to the match as the "khaki final". More grim as evidence of the dread realities of the war, was the inclusion among the khaki men of numbers of soldiers who had been under the enemy's fire. Bandaged heads, strapped limbs, crutches and here and there the support of a crippled hero on the shoulder of [his] comrades.'[141]

---

138 Matthew Taylor, *The Association Game* (London: Routledge, 2008) pp.120–121
139 *Burnley News*, 27 March 1915
140 *Sussex Agricultural Express*, 30 April 1915
141 *Yorkshire Post and Leeds Intelligencer*, 26 April 1915

Despite many believing that the final had 'disgrace attached to it', the Earl of Derby presented the cup to Sheffield United captain George Utley after the game.[142] Derby used the platform to urge the enlisting of more individuals into the armed forces. The future secretary of state for war would compliment both sides for a great match before adding that he hoped to see them play their part in a greater game for England. Derby was clear in his view that football needed to be suspended.

The 1915 final has since become known as the 'Khaki Cup Final' due to those in attendance. As a game it highlights the impact war can have on ordinary life, right down to something we believe to be sacrosanct – football. In the modern day, it is hard to imagine our current crop of players putting on military uniforms and going off to fight a war but World War One was different. It shook the very fabric of society and caused issues many wouldn't have initially considered in 1914. A greater match was about to begin.

142 *Sheffield Telegraph*, 26 April 1915

37

Lawrie Sanchez helps the Crazy Gang lift the FA Cup (1988)

THE FA Cup is no stranger to an underdog story. Perhaps its greatest example comes from the 1987/88 campaign as Wimbledon upset footballing giants Liverpool at Wembley. Despite losing star striker Ian Rush to Juventus, Liverpool had created one of English football's finest squads under manager Kenny Dalglish. An attacking team featuring the likes of John Barnes, Peter Beardsley and John Aldridge, many had believed it unstoppable. With Liverpool reaching their second final in three seasons, there seemed little chance of Wimbledon's 'Crazy Gang' spoiling the Merseyside party.

Bobby Gould's side had earned their infamous nickname due to their often-questionable playing style and humorous off-the-pitch antics. Just 11 years before the 1988 FA Cup Final the Dons, then managed by Dave Bassett, had been playing in the Southern League, one tier below the Football League. Wimbledon were eventually elected into the Football League in 1977 and began a remarkable journey to the First Division over the following decade.

The eccentricities of the squad, the fans and even chairman Sam Hammam had split public opinion. The players had grown through the divisions together and demonstrated an ethos of fun and a total lack of fear.[143] They were in some ways the antithesis of Liverpool, a team built on enduring success and the height of professionalism. The Merseysiders had played football at its purest and seen many admirers, including members of the Wimbledon side.

Crazy Gang hard man Vinnie Jones described the Reds as a squad of presence and being a team which had swept all before them with a serious sense of swagger and self-belief.[144] However, he continued to note that the Liverpool side had appeared uninterested before the final, maybe assuming that victory was around the corner. For Wimbledon, and Jones, they saw a chance to play up to their reputation and attempt to psych out the opposition. In the tunnel before the match, both Jones and diminutive midfielder Dennis Wise noted how some of their side shouted loudly, perhaps to intimidate the team from Merseyside.

'Liverpool HAD to win. I mean, who wanted to be the team beaten by the biggest underdogs in the history of FA Cup Finals?' wrote Wise.'[145]

After a disallowed goal from Beardsley early in the game, Liverpool had seemed in command despite the decisions of the referee. However, in the 37th minute, Wimbledon were awarded a free kick towards the left touchline. Delivered dangerously by Wise, the ball was flicked by Dons striker Lawrie Sanchez past the stranded Bruce Grobbelaar and into the Wembley net. The looks on both the Wimbledon and Liverpool faces were ones of disbelief. They couldn't, could they?

For Liverpool, this was no reason to stop playing their game and despite the robust challenges from Wise, Jones and striker John Fashanu, they would rally to earn a penalty in the second half. Up stepped Aldridge, fresh from winning the First Division's Golden Boot award. Placing his spot kick at a good

143 Dave Bassett and Wally Downes, *The Crazy Gang* (London, Bantam, 2016) p.15

144 Vinnie Jones, *It's Been Emotional* (London: Simon and Schuster, 2013)

145 Dennis Wise, *The Autobiography* (London: Boxtree, 2012)

height for goalkeeper Dave Beasant, Aldridge watched on as the Crazy Gang stopper kept the penalty out. A massive step had been taken in Wimbledon's search for a first FA Cup and Beasant had made history by becoming the first keeper to save a penalty in a final.

The south London side would hold on until the final whistle and euphoric scenes would follow. As commentator John Motson put it, 'The Crazy Gang have beaten the Culture Club.'

Recent autobiographies from the players and staff from both sides have tried to explain the final. For many, football had been the loser on the day as a 'one-dimensional' Wimbledon had denied Dalglish's men from winning a second double in three seasons. However, Motson disagreed. After all, Gould's side had finished seventh that season and posed the Reds problems both home and away in the league.[146] What the victory did show was that team spirit, togetherness and a unique sense of belief can go a long way, even with the most unlikely of sides.

---

146 John Motson, *Forty Years in the Commentary Box* (London: Virgin, 2009) p.221

38

Joe Gaetjens's 'Miracle on Grass' (1950)

IN 1950, the world was still recovering from the death and destruction of nearly six years of World War Two (1939–45). Sport was a vehicle to rebuild the world, starting with the 1948 'Austerity Olympics', held on a minimal budget in London as countries pulled together to enjoy the festivities once more.[147]

It was football's turn to get back to competing on an international stage, this time in Brazil, as they hosted the fourth edition of the FIFA World Cup. The special tournament is remembered for a number of reasons, one particular gem being Joe Gaetjens's 'Miracle on Grass'.

Of the 16 qualified teams, just 12 would make the journey. Notably for the British home nations, they would finally join the competition. All had refused to play in pre-World War Two tournaments, FA chairman Charles Sutcliffe famously branding the idea a 'joke' in 1934.[148]

Both Scotland and England were eligible to play in Brazil though after FIFA agreed that the top two from the British Home Championships would qualify, but only England would make the journey. The Scottish FA declared they would only attend as victors of the Home Championships, but after coming second they refused to take up their place. Scotland's

147 Janie Hampton, *The Austerity Olympics: When the Games Came to London in 1948* (London: Aurum Press Limited, 2008) p.3

148 Matthew Taylor, *The Leaguers: The making of professional football in England, 1900–1939* (Liverpool: Liverpool University Press, 2005) p. 217

captain George Young reportedly 'begged' the SFA to change their mind, and the plea was even supported by England captain Billy Wright, but secretary George Graham would not budge.[149]

England's first match saw them beat Chile 2-0, Stan Mortensen and Wilf Mannion getting their names on the scoresheet. The challenge, or seeming walkover, of the USA would await. The feelings pre-match were summed up honestly by US coach Bill Jeffrey, the Scottish-born manager having only been appointed two weeks before the World Cup, who said, 'We have no chance... [we are] sheep ready to be slaughtered.'[150] On 29 June, America chose not to send a single journalist to cover the fixture, other than a reporter on holiday, so at Estadio Independencia in Belo Horizonte, Walter Winterbottom's men walked out ready to brush aside the USA.

The 10,000-plus spectators that day saw an England side featuring Tottenham's Alf Ramsey, Wolves's Billy Wright, Preston's Tom Finney, Portsmouth's Jimmy Dickinson and Blackpool's Mortensen. The opponents were inexperienced and filled with part-timers, led by Haitian-born forward Gaetjens (who would finish his international career with just one goal in three appearances). England dominated proceedings as expected, but in the 38th minute, Walter Bahr took a shot from range. Gaetjens connected with his head as the ball flew goalward and the touch was enough to beat Wolves goalkeeper Bert Williams, putting the USA 1-0 up.

Future England manager Ramsey would later claim that Gaetjens's touch was accidental, stating that he 'ducked to avoid the ball'.[151] Accidental or not, it was the only goal of the game. Credit was also given to the USA goalkeeper Frank Borghi,

---

149 *The Guardian*, 7 September 2012

150 Ben Jones and Gareth Thomas, *Football's Fifty Most Important Moments* (Worthing: Pitch Publishing, 2020) p.66

151 Adrian Durham, *Is He All That? Great Footballing Myths Shattered* (London: Simon & Schuster UK Ltd., 2013) p.86

who made a string of 'miraculous' saves.[152] This truly was the Miracle on Grass.

The game stunned the British press, some even printing the score as 10-1, believing the news from across Brazil to be a misprint. The loss to the '500/1 outsiders'[153] was called an 'unbelievable defeat'[154] with the *Birmingham Daily Gazette* marking 'a black day for England'.[155] Things were to get worse just three days later for the English. Another 1-0 loss, this time to Spain, would send England home in shame from their first World Cup.

152 Ibid

153 *Newcastle Journal*, 30 June 1950

154 *Nottingham Evening Post*, 30 June 1950

155 *Birmingham Daily Gazette*, 30 June 1950

39

The world sees Frank Lampard's 'goal' cross the line (2010)

TECHNICALLY THIS 'goal' was scored in the 38th minute of England's 2010 World Cup clash with Germany. However, it was the 39th minute when the watching world saw that England had been robbed of a totally legitimate Frank Lampard beauty. This 'goal' would lead to the goal-line technology we see in football today, perhaps even paving the way for Video Assistant Referees (VAR), as mistakes from officials became more financially costly to sides both domestically and internationally.

England's World Cup in South Africa had not started off perfectly, although their opening game against the USA had seemed straightforward when Steven Gerrard netted after just four minutes. Goalkeeper Rob Green made things trickier though, allowing a Clint Dempsey shot to creep over the line from what should've been a simple save. The 1-1 draw with the USA was followed up with a goalless deadlock with Algeria, meaning England had to beat Slovenia to maintain their World Cup place. Jermain Defoe's 23rd-minute goal was enough to take England through as runners-up behind the Americans. This slip-up gave the English a more difficult second-round match against their old rivals.

England versus Germany has always been a bitter grudge match between the two footballing nations. For many, this stems from two world wars, where the countries 'led' the opposing sides. For others, it dates back to England's World Cup win against West Germany in 1966 (Minute 120). The victory was shrouded in controversy, many claiming Geoff Hurst's second goal (to make the score 3-2 in extra time) did not cross the line. Even newspapers as far away as Bolivia wrote, 'England may now be world champions but it is no longer the country of culture, of education, of gentlemen.'[156] Regardless of where it all began, the last-16 tie on 27 June 2010 was a massive game for both teams.

The match took place at Free State Stadium, Bloemfontein, with over 40,000 packed in for what they expected to be an excellent contest. Germany struck first after 20 minutes, prolific World Cup goalscorer Miroslav Klose then having his goal followed up by a second from Köln's Lukas Podolski and they soon led 2-0. In the 37th minute defender Matthew Upson got one back for the English, before the moment that changed the very future of football.

Less than a minute after Upson's header, Lampard lobbed Manuel Neuer in the German goal. The shot crashed into the underside of the crossbar and down seemingly over the line. Uruguayan referee Jorge Larrionda declared that the ball did not cross the line and play continued, Podolski having an opportunity to score at the other end moments later. While fans and commentators were convinced that the ball had crossed the line, the full horror for England supporters was soon revealed as the television replay clearly showed the ball safely beyond Neuer's line. Two in two minutes would undoubtedly have handed momentum to England, but instead they went on to lose 4-1, a Thomas Müller brace wrapping up the win for Germany.

Understandably the public outcry was sizeable, with linesman Mauricio Espinosa criticised as 'hapless' for not seeing the 'goal'.[157] This incident led to further cries for technological intervention in big matches, with former FIFA president Sepp

---

156 Kevin Moore, *What You Think You Know About Football Is Wrong* (London: Bloomsbury, 2019) p.27.

157 *Daily Mirror*, 28 June 2010

Blatter regarding this as the moment that changed his mind.[158] Eventually the introduction of goal-line technology was seen across the game, and is now accepted as a major benefit to the sport. For Germany, many saw this day as revenge for 1966.

158 *The Telegraph*, 6 July 2012

40

The Valley Parade fire begins in Bradford (1985)

ON 11 May 1985, Bradford City hosted Lincoln City at their home ground, Valley Parade. Bradford were due to be presented with the Third Division trophy at the end of a successful season. In the 40th minute, with the game at 0-0, a major disaster struck. A fan, trying to stub out his smouldering cigarette on the wooden benches of the stand, unfortunately dropped it through a hole in the slats.[159] The cigarette end, mixing with the wood and other years of accumulated rubbish, ignited and the fire instantly took hold. The whole event was captured tragically by television cameras who should have been witnessing a joyous occasion.

Fans were immediately alerted to the situation, but a phone call to the fire brigade was only made three minutes later at 3.43pm. Those three minutes were costly as the fire spread rapidly and fans were forced to rush on to the pitch for safety. The referee blew for the match to be halted and the players rushed away from the emergency. Devastatingly, the evacuation was too late for 56 supporters who lost their lives in the inferno and smoke. A further 265 spectators were injured in the event that shocked the British public and has still not been forgotten to this day.

159 *The Telegraph*, 12 May 2015

Eye-witness accounts of the fire make for grim reading, Detective Michael Blanchfield reporting, 'We were engulfed in thick choking black smoke. Only about four minutes after leaving our seats the place was engulfed in flames.' This is particularly stark compared to his initial sighting of the fire, a 'pale grey wisp or puff of smoke', as he notes, he believed it to be a 'very minor fire'.[160] For commentator John Helm the scenes that day have been too hard to ever watch again. He remembers 'choosing my words very carefully', conscious of the horror unfolding before him but also wishing to 'tell people exactly what was going on'.[161]

The fire was part of a horrendous month for British football. That very same day, 15-year-old fan Ian Hambridge was killed at Birmingham City's St Andrew's. A 12ft wall collapsed on top of the spectator in violent scenes described as the 'Battle of Agincourt'.[162] Then, on 29 May, 39 fans were killed and over 600 injured as Liverpool and Juventus fans clashed at the Heysel Stadium in Belgium (Minute 58).

The latter two incidents were caused by the 'hooliganism' seen regularly in the 1970s and 1980s. *The Times*'s sports editor, Nicholas Keith, wrote, 'If we do not [do something] there is a real danger that football will die for lack of support, because only thugs will go to watch it… Football is sick, it may be terminal.' Sadly this issue hijacked the resulting Popplewell Report, which focused on violence rather than mass improvement to stadium safety, despite not a shred of evidence of hooliganism present at Valley Parade that day. Consequently in the 1980s, 'the image of the football fan was integrally linked' to violence. This superseded those fans whose 'safety needed protecting' and that issue 'remained secondary'.[163]

160 *Reading Evening Post*, 25 July 1985

161 *Yorkshire Post*, 6 May 2015

162 *Birmingham Mail*, 1 May 2015

163 Richard Cox, Dave Russell and Wray Vamplew, (eds), *Encyclopedia of British Football* (Hove: Psychology Press, 2002) pp.84-85

The public did respond to Bradford where authorities did not, an immense outpouring of grief seeing over £3.5m raised. The Bradford Disaster Appeal also drew together the 1966 World Cup Final squads from both England and West Germany, who turned out for a benefit match.[164]

The 1980s were dark times for the British game and Bradford was another blow to the 'terminally ill' sport.

164 *The Guardian*, 29 July 1985

41

Mario David's 'worst tackle in history' (1962)

'The game you are about to see is the most stupid, appalling, disgusting and disgraceful exhibition of football, possibly in the history of the game.'[165]

DAVID COLEMAN'S infamous television rant says it all. The match between Chile and Italy at the 1962 World Cup, now known as the Battle of Santiago, would go down in football history for all the wrong reasons. At the kick-off, tensions between the two nations had been raised by slanderous articles published in the Italian press with most pieces having focused their attention on the suitability of Chile to host such a prestigious and global tournament.

Inflamed, the Chilean population needed little encouragement to rouse their side ready for battle when the game began. Within 14 seconds, the game had its first foul and by the eighth minute its first dismissal had been delivered. A petulant kick-out from Italy's Giorgio Ferrini was enough to warrant a sending-off from English referee Ken Aston. Incensed and citing Chilean provocation, it took ten minutes and armed police to eventually escort the Azzurri's left-winger off the field.

165 David Coleman on *BBC News*, 1962

In the 41st minute the match fully erupted. Italian right-back Mario David, angered after receiving the 'neatest left hook I have ever seen' from Chile's Leonel Sánchez,[166] retaliated with one of the game's worst ever challenges. As the ball was deflected high into the air towards the waiting Sánchez, David caught his Chilean rival in the head with a horrific flying kick. Sánchez dropped to the floor poleaxed as players from both nations surrounded Aston.

'I wasn't reffing a football match, I was acting as an umpire in military manoeuvres,' Aston later recalled.[167]

It comes as little surprise to discover that Aston would later invent red and yellow cards as a way for referees to combat increasingly violent and unpleasant behaviour on the pitch.

The rest of the match saw spitting and spiteful challenges continue before Chile scored twice to win the game. Aston's performance drew questions from the Italian FA, who wanted a full investigation into his refereeing.[168] The official would also pull his Achilles tendon during the battle, as if to add injury to insult.

Post-match conversation, particularly in England, centred on the violence from players. Furthermore, the wider tournament itself was wholly condemned by British journalists. The *Coventry Evening Telegraph* was adamant in its wish for the scandals to 'never be repeated'. Citing the match in Santiago, it described the encounter as the 'worst advertisement for soccer ever presented to the public'.[169] Such was the animosity and vexation felt by Italians after the final result, a police guard was set up around the Chilean embassy in Rome to prevent possible demonstrations.[170]

166 Ibid

167 Kenneth Aston in 'Ken Aston – the inventor of yellow and red cards', FIFA, 15 January 2002 http://www.fifa.com/aboutfifa/developing/ refereeing/news/newsid=80623.html

168 *Liverpool Echo*, 4 June 1962

169 *Coventry Evening Telegraph*, 23 June 1962

170 *Belfast Telegraph*, 5 June 1962

42

North Korea stun Italy (1966)

THE 1966 World Cup is one of the most discussed, dissected and analysed tournaments in the history of sport. A truly 'national experience', it was the first edition of the competition to feature extensive coverage on television and in the wider media.[171] It reflected the changes in wider society and helped to reinvent the image England, and the wider UK, had created for itself. If, for English fans, the tournament holds an incredible reverence, the same can be said for those in North Korea.

North Korea is by no means known for its footballing prowess. Indeed, when Googling the country, the most common searches involve human rights violations, war with South Korea and troubled relations with the West. In 1966, the nation (in its current state) was still in its infancy. A communist dictatorship had emerged following World War Two, with the brutal Korean War splitting the peninsula in two during the early 1950s.

Arriving at the World Cup, the North Korean side was met with immediate suspicion and later criticism, being described by the *Daily Mirror* as 'Mystery Men'.[172] Several further newspaper articles can be found concerning North Korea's anger at the state of their training facilities.[173] In comparison to other competing

171 Ben Jones and Gareth Thomas, *Football's Fifty Most Important Moments* (Worthing: Pitch Publishing, 2020) p.93

172 *Daily Mirror*, 1 July 1966

173 *Aberdeen Press and Journal*, 5 July 1966

nations, North Korea had little to no support following them in England.

The secretive nation had qualified for the tournament after a play-off victory over Australia. Their presence at the finals was helped in part by the widespread boycott of the competition from Africa, Asia) and Oceania. The confederations were frustrated at the lack of representation offered at the Euro/South American-centric World Cup. Nevertheless, drawn against the USSR, Chile and Italy, there seemed little hope of the North Koreans making any significant inroads.

An opening 3-0 defeat to the Soviet Union was followed by a credible draw against Chile at Ayresome Park. The performances of the plucky underdogs led to the local population of Teesside becoming honorary North Korean fans overnight. This was further helped by the fact North Korea played in red kits, similar to those of Middlesbrough.[174] By the time Italy faced the Asian representatives, the Azzurri were met with an almost partisan crowd.

Against all the odds, Pak Doo-Ik's 42nd-minute goal would win the tie for North Korea. It was, at the time, arguably the greatest shock in World Cup history. Described as 'unglamorous, unfancied and unknown', North Korea had delivered at the highest level.[175] The Koreans had won the hearts of the host nation and by the time they met Eusébio's Portugal in the quarter-finals, they were indeed the most supported nation left in the competition (except England of course).

Despite the North Koreans racing to a 3-0 lead, Portugal would come back into the game and eventually triumph 5-3. The influential Eusébio was key to the recovery, scoring four goals at Goodison Park. Although exiting the tournament in the last eight, the North Korean side had done more for its country's global image in four matches than had been achieved through politics in the years before and after the 1966 World

174 John Hughson, *England and the 1966 World Cup* (Manchester: Manchester University, 2016)

175 *Birmingham Daily Post,* 20 July 1966

Cup. It shows the power football can have in changing opinions, opening previously closed minds and bringing people together from every corner of the world.

43

Gerd Müller's World Cup winner (1974)

THE 1974 World Cup was a brilliant one. Hosted by West Germany, it saw some great teams, some great moments and a surprise winner. It may well be remembered for Johan Cruyff's famous turn (Minute 23) or Jürgen Sparwasser's shock goal for East Germany (Minute 77), but in the 43rd minute of the final between Netherlands and West Germany, Gerd Müller struck to sink the Oranje.

The tournament was dominated by the Total Football of Rinus Michels's Netherlands side. 'The General' famously declared that 'football is war'[176] and went about proving it, firstly at Ajax where he won the Eredivisic four times and a European Cup in 1971. Following this, Barcelona came calling, and along with his talisman Cruyff, the two would leave their mark on the beautiful game. In West Germany, the Dutch marched through the tournament and Cruyff was named the competition's best player. For all their success, what the pair could not do was call themselves world champions.

The Netherlands won two and drew their third match in the first group stage of 1974. The tournament, notable for a differing format, then proceeded into a second group stage. Here the Dutch showed their class, beating Argentina (4-0), East Germany (2-0) and Brazil (2-0). As winners of this second group, they earned a place in the final against West Germany.

176 *The Guardian*, 9 June 2010

The West Germans had beaten Chile and Australia in their first two group games but had suffered a demoralising loss to their East German rivals in the third fixture. This result supposedly led to a 'minor meltdown' for manager Helmut Schön, who was East German by birth.[177]

West Germany would recover from the blow in the second group stage, topping this with three wins from three. Their place in the final on 7 July would be in front of over 75,000 spectators on home soil – the Olympiastadion in Munich. The 14 goals scored and just one conceded throughout the competition made the Dutch's Total Football favourites to win a first world title with West Germany seeking the crown for the first time in 20 years.

Just a minute into the final, the Dutch were awarded a penalty. Johan Neeskens dispatched this before the West Germans had even touched the ball. Determined not to surrender, the setback spurred the Germans on. Cruyff was forced to 'retreat' to his own half as Die Mannschaft created more chances.[178] Bernd Hölzenbein won a penalty and Paul Breitner tucked it away to deservedly level the tie after 25 minutes. In the 43rd minute, the game firmly turned in West Germany's favour. Rainer Bonhof, bursting down the right, was able to cut the ball back to Müller, the Bayern Munich front man controlling and finishing past goalkeeper Jan Jongbloed for 2-1.

The *Daily Mirror's* Frank McGhee wrote that the Dutch improvement in the second half was stark, describing it as a 'transformation in mood, style and approach'. He reported that the Germans looked 'swamped by an orange tide' but the Dutch spurned several good chances.[179] Captain Franz Beckenbauer was inspired, with full-backs Breitner and Berti Vogts 'shackling'

177 Scott Murray and Rowan Walker, *Day of the Match: A History of Football in 365 Days* (London: Boxtree, 2008) p.196

178 Clemente A. Lisi, *A History of the World Cup:* 1930-2010 (Plymouth: Scarecrow Press, Inc., 2011) pp.140–142

179 *Daily Mirror*, 8 July 1974

Cruyff despite the 'constant Dutch pressure'.[180] At full time, West Germany could celebrate what had seemed an unlikely home World Cup victory. For the Netherlands, this 1974 side would become perhaps football's greatest ever 'nearly men'.

180 Scott Murray and Rowan Walker, *Day of the Match: A History of Football in 365 Days*, p.196

44

Robin van Persie's flying header (2014)

FOUR YEARS after the heartbreak of the World Cup Final defeat to Spain, the Netherlands were once again drawn against their European rivals. Following on from that 1-0 victory in Johannesburg (Minute 116), the Spanish added the 2012 European Championship to their growing trophy cabinet. Despite their superiority, results before the World Cup had started to decline and the free-flowing tiki-taka was becoming increasingly predictable at club level. The Netherlands, on the other hand, were looking to rebuild following an early exit at Euro 2012.

Remarkably, the fixture between the two sides fell on just the second day of the 2014 World Cup in Brazil. Pre-game, pundits and fans predicted a Spanish victory but knew the gulf between the teams had started to decrease.[181] According to the script, it took just 27 minutes for La Roja to take the lead through a Xabi Alonso penalty. A missed opportunity from the usually dependable David Silva should have put Spain two clear minutes later but he fired straight at Jasper Cillessen.

And in the 44th minute the game changed through a moment of sheer class. Left-back Daley Blind in possession near the halfway line, sprayed a long-ball over the Spanish back four towards Robin van Persie on the edge of the box. Running at speed, van Persie had no other option than to attempt an

181 *The Guardian*, 13 June 2014

audacious diving header. At full stretch, the centre-forward connected perfectly and lobbed the stranded Iker Casillas to score.

Spain were stunned. They had been cruising before van Persie's intervention and in the second half, Arjen Robben scored twice alongside goals from Stefan de Vrij and van Persie once more. Few predicted a Dutch victory, let alone a 5-1 thrashing of the world champions.

Thierry Henry would gleefully comment that Total Football was back and the embarrassment of the violent final four years earlier (Minute 28) was to be eradicated from the memories of neutrals.[182] The result sent shock waves through football and helped heed the notion that you never know what might happen over the course of 90 minutes.

Finding the net just before half-time is often described as a 'good time to score'. Providing it isn't a mere consolation, it can dictate how the second half will progress. A goal as good as van Persie's can take the wind out of the sails of the opposition and ignite a recovery in the next 45. You can be certain that the half-time team talks of both Vicente del Bosque and Louis van Gaal were completely changed as the ball sailed off van Persie's head and into the net in Salvador.

Van Persie's goal did more than just invigorate the Dutch for the remainder of the game – it gave them a spark for the remainder of the tournament. His side finished in a respectable third place and defied the odds set for them at the competition's opening. Spain, on the other hand, crashed out in the group stage. Peculiarly, they helped to continue the trend of early exits for defending champions. From 2002 to 2018, only one holder of the trophy, Brazil in 2006, made it to the knockout rounds.

182 Thierry Henry, in David Ornstein, 'Spain 1-5 Netherlands', BBC Sport, 13 June 2014 https://www.bbc.co.uk/sport/football/25285043

45

Britain's first £1m player helps pay back his fee (1979)

THE FINAL minutes before half-time are vital with sides keeping things tight to make it back to the dressing room with the scores unharmed. However, on 30 May 1979, Britain's first million-pound player would net the winning goal in the European Cup Final in this last minute of the opening half, writing Nottingham Forest's proudest moment in their long history.

On 14 February 1979, a British transfer record was set as Trevor Francis moved from Birmingham City to Forest for a fee worth more than £1m. While the amount Birmingham City received was just shy of £1m at £975,000, with the Football League's fee, VAT and a five per cent cut for Francis himself, the overall outlay was taken to around £1.15m for Forest.[183]

The switch was labelled 'mind-boggling' with the 'most staggering transfer fee the British game has ever known'.[184] This followed on from the world's first million-pound (equivalent) transaction in 1975 when Italian Giuseppe Savoldi moved from Bologna to Napoli for two billion lire (roughly £1.2 million). The Italian press had even given Savoldi the pressuring nickname

183 Richard Cox, Dave Russell and Wray Vamplew, (eds), *Encyclopedia of British Football* (Hove: Psychology Press, 2002) p.256

184 *Birmingham Daily Post*, 8 February 1979

'Mister Two Billion'.[185] Such hyperbole perhaps influenced manager Brian Clough's decision to claim that the deal for Francis was in fact for '£999,999', to protect the player's 'state of mind'.[186]

Francis would begin paying back a chunk of his transfer fee in May 1979 as Nottingham Forest played in their first European Cup Final. Forest had beaten defending double European champions Liverpool in the first round after a 2-0 home win and AEK Athens were next to be defeated, before Swiss side Grasshopper Zürich were put out in the quarter-finals. In their semi-final, FC Köln drew 3-3 at the City Ground in the first leg but Ian Bowyer scored the single goal in Germany to earn Forest their big date in May.

The final itself was against Swedish outfit Malmö, who set up defensively, hoping to frustrate Forest. They were successful in that endeavour until the brink of half-time when John Robertson found space on the left. His pinpoint cross was met by the million-pound man Francis at the back post who beat the resilient goalkeeper Jan Möller to make it 1-0. That was how the score remained, Forest dominating the best of the chances and winning a first European crown.

The legendary Clough called this 'my finest hour' as he described the photograph that was hung on the wall of his study. The picture featured the crosser of the ball, Robertson, and his goalscorer Francis. Robertson, Clough wrote, had been 'nursed, cajoled, sometimes bullied, but mostly encouraged to the top of his profession' and the manager described Francis as 'a thoroughbred'. The image, Clough believed, summed up 'both ends of my managerial spectrum'.[187]

Clough's 'cajoled' project would turn from provider into

185 Simon Winter, 'The story of Giuseppe Savoldi, football's first million pound player', *These Football Times*, 23 February 2016 https://thesefootballtimes.co/2016/02/23/the-story-of-giuseppe-savoldi-footballs-first-million-pound-player

186 *The Telegraph*, 9 February 2009

187 Brian Clough, *Clough: The Autobiography* (London: Corgi Books, 1995) p.205

hero himself the very next season as he scored the only goal in the final, in a 1-0 win over Hamburg at the Santiago Bernabéu Stadium in Madrid. Clough's Forest were back-to-back European champions, a feat not to be forgotten.

Half-Time

ALTHOUGH ONLY lasting for 15 minutes, the decisions made at half-time can leave lasting legacies. As the players from both sides make their way to their respective dressing rooms, the managers and coaches take centre stage. Highlighting the positives and negatives of the first half, a chance is offered to reflect on what went well and what could be done better. For the supporters in the stands, half-time provides ample opportunity to grab a pie, go to the toilet and mull over the finer details of the first period.

Despite an initial focus on socialisation as opposed to revitalisation, the 15-minute interval has developed and evolved into a completely different concept to that in 1860. Tea was more likely to be on the menu than tactics and after almost 160 years, the modern-day boom in advertising, finances and the will to win surely conquers all else.

Here are three of the finest half-time stories:

1. Uruguay's change of football helps to win the first World Cup (1930)

Going in at the break 2-1 down at half-time to neighbours Argentina, defeat would mean that victory in the inaugural World Cup Final had been snatched away from the first host nation. Prior to the match, in a series of arguments which incredibly 'lasted for days', neither side could agree on who would provide the match ball. FIFA eventually stepped in and decided that the ball would be changed at half-time. Argentina would use their ball first with the Uruguayan FA providing it in the second period. The petty squabbling before the game would signify just what the potential of becoming world champions meant for the respective sides.

Now playing with 'their' ball, Uruguay responded in the second half by scoring just 12 minutes after the restart through José Pedro Cea. Roared on by the vociferous and partisan crowd, Uruguay took the lead in the 68th minute as Santos Iriarte's venomous strike from 25 yards flew into the net. The one-armed Héctor Castro would put the tie to bed a minute before the end and spark days of celebration across Uruguay.

2. Phil Brown's on-the-pitch team talk (2008)

Seeing his side slip to a 4-0 deficit to Manchester City after just 36 minutes, it came as little surprise to see Hull City manager Phil Brown angered by the Tigers' first-half performance. As his players made their way off the field, Brown would sternly make his way on to it. Perplexed, those who had failed to perform followed their manager to the goalmouth situated by the Hull supporters. As the XI sat in a circle, a visibly frustrated Brown offered some stern words. Brown was confident that it was the right thing to do and felt that if egos had been bruised then 'so be it'. The talk, remarkably, worked.[188] Eventually losing 5-1, the second-half performance had seen the Tigers at least claw a goal back.

Immediately after the game, former players and pundits were fiercely critical of Brown's actions and found it difficult to believe that his players would ever forgive their manager for such a public dressing-down. In hindsight, most have defended the team talk and don't believe it to have been embarrassing.

A year later, in the same fixture, the exuberant Jimmy Bullard celebrated a penalty with a now infamous re-creation of Brown's discussion. In his post-match interview, Brown

188 *The Guardian*, 28 December 2008

commented, 'It was a fantastic celebration… Great comedy is about timing.'[189]

3. Mainz and Freiburg called back from the changing rooms by VAR (2018)

The controversial nature of VAR has been discussed already in the first half of this book (Minute 34). Prior to the 2018 World Cup it undoubtedly split opinions and its trial use in the German Bundesliga saw several contentious calls from the Video Assistant Referee. In a relegation clash towards the end of the 2017/18 season, a penalty was awarded in what was later regarded as the 'most bizarre use of VAR so far'.[190]

The drama began to unfold on the stroke of half-time as Mainz's Daniel Brosinski's cross appeared to be handled by Marc-Oliver Kempf. Waving away the appeals, referee Guido Winkmann subsequently blew for half-time. As the players walked off and into their respective changing rooms, Winkmann was consulted by the VAR. Clearly seeing that Kempf had deflected the ball with his hand, he had no choice but to call the players back on to the field as Mainz had in fact earned a penalty. Five minutes after the whistle had been blown, the game was restarted, and Pablo de Blasis tucked the spot kick away. Leaving a 'bitter taste' in the mouth of Freiburg sporting director Jochen Saier, the goal would help their opponents to take control of the game in the second half and win.

Mainz's Twitter said it all, 'YESSS! We're confused. But we've scored!'[191]

189 Phil Brown talking to BBC Sport, 28 November 2009, http://news.bbc.co.uk/sport1/hi/football/teams/h/hull_city/8384716.stm

190 BBC, 'Mainz v Freiburg: Hosts awarded penalty on VAR after half-time', BBC Sport, 16 April 2018 https://www.bbc.co.uk/sport/football/43791511

191 Mainz 05 English, Twitter, 16 April 2018

46

Steven Gerrard sees red against Manchester United (2015)

THE START of the second half often sees managers make changes to their starting XI. At times, these decisions work well with the incoming player scoring or inspiring their side into a tactical shift or defensive solidity. However, they can, on occasion, turn out to be a flawed approach with some notable moments failing to inspire. In a heated encounter between arch-rivals Liverpool and Manchester United at Anfield in 2015 it took just 38 seconds for a substitution for the home side to fail dramatically.

Earlier in the season, Liverpool's influential captain Steven Gerrard had announced that he was leaving the club after two decades of service. The emotional strain of his infamous slip against Chelsea during the 2014 Premier League title race had proved pivotal in his decision to move to the MLS at the end of the 2014/15 season. Manchester United had often felt the full force of Gerrard, as his goalscoring record against the Red Devils suggests, and after being sent on by manager Brendan Rodgers at half-time the Liverpool skipper certainly wanted to make an immediate impression.

For Gerrard, there was no more important fixture than against Manchester United, other than the derby against Everton. With his side 1-0 down at the midway point, Gerrard was introduced to rapturous applause from the home support.

Gerrard's most recent autobiography dedicates an entire chapter to this match. Frustrated by the lack of commitment and tepid nature of the challenges offered by Liverpool in the first half, he knew he had to demonstrate what he expected of his side straight after the restart.[192]

Immediately, Gerrard made his first crunching challenge. A forceful but fair tackle on Juan Mata had seemed to ignite the supporters and fellow players. United too were fired up for the physical task and combative midfielder Ander Herrera flew into Gerrard soon afterwards. A late, albeit not too malicious, challenge had left an outstretched leg with which Gerrard admitted 'couldn't stop myself'.[193] In a 'ferocious display of rage' his boot came down hard on to Herrera's shin. Despite him having only being on the field for 38 seconds, referee Martin Atkinson had little option but to show the Liverpool captain a straight red card.

Gerrard was the first to confess his guilt and admits that the occasion had got the better of him. The red card after half-time had been the culmination of a difficult year following the slip and frustrating performances from an under-achieving Liverpool side. Gerrard would find his form again before the end of the season and finish his final campaign on Merseyside with 13 goals.

The bittersweet finish to the 2014/15 season provided a somewhat acrimonious end to one of English football's finest careers. Gerrard had led his side to an incredible comeback in the 2005 Champions League Final (Minute 54) and scored one of the FA Cup's greatest ever strikes against West Ham in 2006. Despite an impressive personal trophy cabinet, the lack of a Premier League title will forever leave a stain on a remarkable career.

Featuring twice in this book, Gerrard is one of the modern game's most intriguing figures.

192 Steven Gerrard, *My Story* (London: Penguin, 2015) pp.382–384
193 Ibid

47

David Beckham kicks out at Diego Simeone (1998)

ENGLAND'S WORLD Cup history has undoubtedly been mixed. Their complete rejection of the competition from 1930 to 1938 saw the tournament branded a 'joke' by FA chairman Charles Sutcliffe.[194] In 1950, they made their debut but were dumped out in the group stages (Minute 38), before in 1966 they would finally lift the trophy (Minute 120). Since 1966, hype has always surrounded England's hopes at the World Cup, but often disappointment follows it. There was another of those setbacks in 1998 as in the 47th minute of their last-16 defeat to Argentina, star midfielder David Beckham kicked out at Diego Simeone and was shown a red card.

England's World Cup in France had not started perfectly, the Three Lions losing their second group late to Romania and ultimately finishing second in the group stages. Argentina, meanwhile, had waltzed past Croatia, Jamaica and Japan with three wins from three to top Group H. This set up a fine clash in the second round.

Argentina versus England had accumulated quite a history, ever since Diego Maradona's 'Hand of God' in 1986 (Minute 51) and the Falklands War of 1982. On 30 June 1998, the rivals

---

194 Matthew Taylor, *The Leaguers: The making of professional football in England, 1900–1939* (Liverpool: Liverpool University Press, 2005) p. 217

would face off once again on the world stage with a place in the quarter-finals at stake.

The first half was a cracker, Gabriel Batistuta netting a penalty for Argentina after just five minutes, while England captain Alan Shearer responded with one of his own in the ninth minute. Seven minutes later, wonderkid Michael Owen scored a beauty. Played in by Beckham, the 18-year-old picked the ball up inside the centre circle and with strength and pace he beat the opposition defence before smashing the ball home. Despite the stunner, Argentina responded on the brink of half-time with Javier Zanetti making it 2-2 to end a breathless first 45.

With manager Glen Hoddle's words still ringing in their ears, Beckham would be harshly challenged by Argentina's Simeone. Beckham, seemingly angered by the tackle, kicked out on the floor at the opposing skipper just yards from the referee Kim Milton Nielsen. Innocuous-looking on first viewing, commentators were surprised as the red card was brandished, but later replays showed Beckham had targeted Simeone purposely. England were down to ten and the game would eventually go to penalties; Beckham would almost certainly have been a taker had he been on the pitch. The 4-3 loss was decided as David Batty missed the final kick and England were going home.

The reaction of the British media was immediate and Beckham took the brunt of the abuse, with one article reading, 'Whether Beckham has the intelligence or backbone to respond [to the backlash] is quite another matter.'[195] The *Liverpool Echo* also joined the criticism of Beckham as it urged him to 'forget the Spice Boy life'. The newspaper believed that his 'immature approach' was 'threatening to undermine his career' and predicted that he would be 'hammered by fans at every ground he visits' in the following season.[196]

The prediction was of course true, Beckham being hounded by fans and press for many months after his split second of

---

195 *Sunday Life*. 5 July 1998
196 *Liverpool Echo*, 2 July 1998

stupidity. The player, though, regards this as one of the defining moments of his career. He recalled how it was 'difficult for me as a player, and as a person' but also how it improved him, enabling him to 'mature very quickly'.[197] Anyone reflecting on Beckham's career must agree that this was most definitely not the end.

197 Freddie Campion, 'David Beckham Picks Infamous World Cup Red Card as One of His "Top Career Moments"', *GQ*, 18 March 2016 https://www.gq.com/story/david-beckham-red-card

48

Eric Cantona is sent off and goes berserk at Crystal Palace (1995)

'I didn't hit the Palace fan strong enough. I should have hit him harder.'[198]

ON 25 January 1995, Eric Cantona made the headlines across the world as he kung fu-kicked Crystal Palace fan Matthew Simmons at Selhurst Park during a Premier League match. Cantona had received rough treatment from Palace centre-back Richard Shaw throughout the first half and eventually lost his cool, getting sent off for retaliating in the 48th minute. Incredibly, on his way to the dressing room, Cantona attacked an abusive spectator who had 'rushed down 11 rows' to 'bid farewell to the United icon'.[199]

The legendary Frenchman had lit up English football since his arrival with Leeds United in January 1992. His excellent finish to that season earned him a £1.2m move to Manchester United in November 1992. In 1992/93 and 1993/94, United lifted the league title, Cantona contributing heavily in both seasons, most notably with 18 league goals in the latter campaign. Cantona's mesmerising style of play, with his collar upturned,

198 Cantona in an interview with Andy Mitten, 'Eric Cantona's kick, 25 years on', *FourFourTwo*, 25 January 2020 https://www.fourfourtwo.com/features/eric-cantona-crystal-palace-fan-i-didnt-punch-strong-enough

199 *The Independent*, 25 January 2020

had won him many admirers, but likewise his temper and talent often made him a target for opposing players.

At Selhurst Park on a cold January night, Palace were doing their best to prevent Alex Ferguson's Red Devils from hitting their full flow. United had just beaten league leaders Blackburn Rovers 1-0 at Old Trafford with Cantona netting the winner. The defending champions were now seeking to follow that with a victory at Palace to keep the pressure on their title rivals.

The referee that day, Alan Wilkie, had come in for criticism from Ferguson for perceived leniency with some of Palace's challenges in the first 45. Cantona took matters into his own hands early in the second half, kicking out at Shaw after he made hefty contact with the Frenchman as he chased keeper Peter Schmeichel's punt upfield. Cantona received his marching orders and significantly turned his collar down, his work over for the day, as kit man Norman Davies escorted him towards the tunnel.

This was until Simmons charged to the front of the stand to abuse the talisman in an expletive-laden outburst. Cantona lost it, launching a 'flying kick' into the crowd followed up by a 'seriously under-rated roundhouse right'.[200] The attack left football in shock as pictures of the incident were beamed around the world.

Cantona was immediately banned for the rest of the season by Manchester United, club director Maurice Watkins officially noting that they 'regret the circumstances which have led to the punishment'.[201] The media unsurprisingly had a field day, some suggesting he had 'finally gone too far' and speculating that it was 'Au Revoir Cantona' after the 'disgraceful incident'.[202] Cantona's ban was eventually extended by the FA to nine months and a £30,000 fine. United retained their man, however, and he returned on 1 October 1995 to score and assist against their historic rivals Liverpool – he was 'back with a bang'.[203]

This moment at Selhurst Park, delivering his own form of justice, added more to Cantona's unique reputation than perhaps any other.

200 *The Guardian*, 25 January 2020

201 *Staffordshire Sentinel*, 27 January 1995

202 *Liverpool Echo*, 26 January 1995

203 *Irish Independent*, 2 October 1995

49

The El Clásico stranglehold on Spanish football is finally broken by Atlético (2014)

THROUGHOUT ITS recent history, the Spanish football league – La Liga – has been dominated by two teams, Real Madrid and Barcelona. In 2014, the two sides had increased their stranglehold over the domestic game and created a seemingly impenetrable duopoly. Barcelona had assembled a new 'dream team' with the likes of Xavi, Andrés Iniesta and of course Lionel Messi. Real Madrid, on the other hand, had gone from strength to strength and boasted the world's most expensive player – Gareth Bale.

Their city rivals, Atlético Madrid, had quietly been creating a strong side under the guidance of maverick manager Diego Simeone. The 2012/13 season had seen Los Colchoneros finish third in La Liga and win the Copa Del Rey following a frenetic and feisty final against Real. Simeone had assembled a squad deemed by some to be 'cast-offs' but one which had been created through sensible financial leadership.[204]

Despite their achievement the previous season, they had ultimately finished 24 points behind winners Barcelona. In spite of unfavourable odds, Simeone had constructed a strong

204 Euan McTear, *Hijacking La Liga: How Atlético Madrid Broke Barcelona and Real Madrid's Duopoly on Spanish Football* (Worthing: Pitch Publishing, 2017)

squad seemingly set to pose a greater challenge to the Spanish giants than in previous years. The team featured a robust spine helped in part by the powerful Diego Godín, young star Koke and controversial forward Diego Costa. Pre-season La Liga previews tended to favour a Real Madrid triumph, helped in part by the multi-million-pound signings of Bale and midfielder Isco. Sid Lowe would go as far as stating that for the rest of La Liga, 'No one is even trying to chase them [Barcelona and Real] anymore.'[205]

Atlético started the season strongly and by Christmas, they had won 15 of their opening 17 fixtures. Unbelievably, this was only good enough to see them in second place as the new year began. Barcelona boasted an identical record but held on to top spot on goal difference. Real, on the other hand, were five points adrift but proving to be excellent in the Champions League. Atlético would remain behind their rivals from Catalonia until February before a poor run of form saw them drift down into third with just 12 games to play.

The 2-2 draw with Real at the Vincente Calderón was heralded as a missed opportunity[206] and saw Los Blancos claim the top spot. For Real, it seemed a first club treble was still well and truly on the cards. With Atlético knocking Barcelona out of the Champions League at the quarter-final stage, it seemed that the Blaugrana would focus their attention solely on the league. It appeared that Atlético's squad was incapable of seriously challenging on two fronts. Defying the odds, a run of nine consecutive victories put Los Colchoneros within three games of the Spanish title.

With one hand on the crown, defeat to Levante and a home draw to Malaga gifted Barcelona with an opportunity to steal the league from under Atlético's nose. Perhaps pre-occupied by their Champions League semi-final triumph over Chelsea, Simeone's side had let their domestic form slip. It all came down to the

205 *The Guardian*, 15 August 2013
206 *The Guardian*, 2 March 2014

final game of the season, which quite incredibly saw Atlético play Barcelona at the Nou Camp. The build-up focused on the 18-year absence of the league title in the Calderón's trophy cabinet but the media were aware that Atlético would 'hold nothing back'.[207]

The opening goal came from Barcelona as Chilean forward Alexis Sánchez thumped a ferocious strike past Atleti keeper Thibaut Courtois and put Tata Martino's men into the driving seat. A win for Barça would see them clinch the league due to their superior head-to-head record. However, just four minutes after the restart Godín headed past Victor Valdes to send the travelling Atlético fans wild.

A staunch rearguard action, which had become synonymous with Simeone's side, then saw Atleti hold out until the final whistle and achieve the unthinkable.

207 *New York Times*, 12 May 2014

50

David Seaman is lobbed by Ronaldinho at the World Cup (2002)

RONALDINHO WAS a man it was seemingly impossible to hate. During the height of his powers, he played every game with a giant smile on his face, improvising and inventing new skills and ways of beating opponents. In the 2002 World Cup, he yet again made an opposition player look a little silly. This time it was England goalkeeper David Seaman who fell victim to 'Dinho's brilliance after he was lobbed from about 35 yards out. The goal spelt the end of another World Cup pursuit for the English and helped lead Brazil on to yet another success.

Ronaldo de Assis Moreira, or Ronaldinho Gaúcho, as he was more commonly known, made his Brazil national team debut in 1999 against Latvia. The attacking midfielder was plying his trade in his native Brazil at this point, with Grêmio, and in 2001, Paris Saint-Germain of Ligue 1 took the opportunity to bring the talent to Europe for around £5m. Comparisons in Brazil were already being made of the 21-year-old, that he was like the legendary Zico – 'explosive, fast, but also very skilful… a creator and a finisher'.[208] Ronaldinho showed the promise he had in his debut campaign, scoring 13 times and creating many for PSG, earning a place in Brazil's squad for the 2002 World Cup in South Korea and Japan.

208 *Dublin Evening Herald*, 17 February 2001

The Brazil side was packed with talent, looking to right the wrongs of 1998 where they lost to hosts France in the final. With Lúcio, Roberto Carlos, Cafu, Rivaldo, Ronaldo and Ronaldinho to name just a few, this Seleção group was surely destined for another shot at glory. They topped their group with three wins from three, Ronaldinho scoring in the win over China. In the last 16, Belgium were brushed aside 2-0 and this set up a tie with England on 21 June 2002.

England themselves had high hopes of banishing the pain of previous tournaments with victory in Asia. They escaped their 'group of death' in second place, then beat Denmark thanks to goals from Rio Ferdinand, Michael Owen and Emile Heskey. For hopeful children across England, the time difference meant many attended school early to catch the big game against Brazil. They would be delighted as Owen gave the Three Lions a 23rd-minute lead. Could England do it?

Just before half-time, Rivaldo levelled the fixture for Brazil, before in the 50th minute, Ronaldinho would have his moment.

Brazil won a free kick about 35 yards from goal on the right, with the attacking players lining up for a cross from Ronaldinho. However, the magician instead saw Seaman off his line in 'no man's land' and hit it at goal. The shot completely caught Seaman out, the keeper scrambling but failing to get back as the ball sailed over his head. Brazil led 2-1 and retained that lead through to full time.

Spectators immediately questioned whether Ronaldinho meant it, but the rest of his career indicates that he probably did. Seaman admitted years later, 'We didn't know how good Ronaldinho was,'noting that England had 'heard about him' but that you needed to see such players on the pitch to 'realise how good they are, and he was good'.[209]

---

209 Seaman in an interview with Joe Moore, 'Former England goalkeeper David Seaman on THAT 2002 World Cup goal', *TalkSport*, 22 February 2019 https://talksport.com/football/497485/we-didnt-know-how-good-ronaldinho-was-former-england-goalkeeper-david-seaman-on-that-2002-world-cup-goal/

Brazil went on to lift the World Cup against Germany, but for Ronaldinho this was only the start of an illustrious career, one where his Barcelona years stood out. He was named FIFA World Player of the Year in 2004 and 2005, to go with a Ballon d'Or also in 2005.

51

'A little with the hand of God and a little with the head of Maradona' (1986)

THIS IS probably the most instantly recognisable moment in this book. Diego Maradona, the hero of Argentina's 1986 World Cup, made headlines across the globe as he scored two goals in four minutes to dump England out of the competition. The Estadio Azteca in Mexico City hosted the quarter-final that would go down in footballing history as in the 51st minute Maradona scored with the 'Hand of God', and in the 55th minute he added the 'Goal of the Century'.

Both teams had made it successfully through the group stages and Argentina then put out fellow South Americans Uruguay 1-0, while England dispatched Paraguay 3-0. This set up a clash at a time of tension between both nations, the Falklands War of 1982 still in recent memory for both governments, squads and fans. Britain had won that war but lost 255 lives in the process, Argentina losing 649 of its troops.

Argentina coach Carlos Bilardo dismissed the political tension, declaring, 'We have come here to play soccer and nothing else.'[210] The first half of the quarter-final saw Argentina dominate the possession and chances, but the score remained 0-0 at the break. Things changed six minutes into the second half as Maradona picked the ball up 40 yards from goal.

210 *Staffordshire Sentinel*, 19 June 1986

Beating three men in front of him, he attempted a one-two with Jorge Valdano but England's Steve Hodge got there first. Hodge's miscued clearance bounced up and allowed the 5ft 4in Maradona to leap up to compete for the ball with goalkeeper Peter Shilton. Maradona seemingly reached the ball first and scored, but it looked like a handball.

The incensed English turned to the officials, but nothing had been spotted, even though television replays showed that Maradona had used his hand to 'punch' the ball into the back of the net.

Understandably there was outrage back in England. Newspapers described how England were 'cheated'[211] by the 'killer punch' of Maradona.[212] The magician was in no mood to apologise post-match, simply telling the media that the 'Hand of God' had helped him beat Shilton.

Minutes later, Maradona scored what became known as the Goal of the Century. There was no doubt about the legitimacy of this one. From collecting the ball in his own half, to finding the back of the net in just ten seconds, this goal showed his genius. Diego beat four men (the unlucky Terry Butcher twice) to then dribble past the stranded Shilton. It was an absolute beauty of a goal to secure the win. A 2-0 lead offered too much for England to respond, even with Gary Lineker scoring a consolation late on.

Maradona then scored another brace in the 2-0 win against Belgium to clinch a spot in the final, where Argentina lifted the World Cup against West Germany 3-2 on 29 June, the number ten's legacy cemented.

There is some debate over that iconic quote from El Diego, which arose immediately after the game itself. Whether the Argentine actually said, 'A little with the hand of Diego and a little with the head of Maradona,' or, 'A little with the hand of God and a little with the head of Maradona,'[213] it is the latter that has stuck.

For such a genius player on the ball, his performance on 22 June 1986 is how he is remembered most significantly.

211 *Staffordshire Sentinel*, 23 June 1986
212 *Sandwell Evening Mail*, 23 June 1986
213 *Dublin Evening Herald*, 23 June 1986

52

Robert Lewandowski makes it two out of five (2015)

TO SCORE five goals in a match is special. To score five in nine minutes is out of this world, yet on 22 September 2015, Bayern Munich striker Robert Lewandowski achieved the feat in style. With his side 1-0 down to Wolfsburg in the Bundesliga, Lewandowski was brought off the bench at half-time. He opened his account just six minutes later and before Bayern's opponents could even adjust, he had his second within a minute. The hat-trick followed in the 55th minute, with four (57) and five (60) quickly completing the glut.

Lewandowski made his professional debut with Polish third-tier team Znicz Pruszków in 2006. His 15 goals in 2006/07 won him the division's Golden Boot and helped win promotion to I liga. Another 21 league strikes would earn him a switch to top-flight Lech Poznań. His fine form at Poznań saw Borussia Dortmund swoop for the talent in 2010, and despite a slow start to Bundesliga life, plenty more goals would follow in the coming seasons.

Speculation long-followed Lewandowski about a big move to Dortmund's German rivals Bayern Munich. This was intensified as Dortmund finished as runners-up to Bayern in an all-German UEFA Champions League Final in 2013. Dortmund resisted the lure of a transfer fee to hold on to Lewandowski for as long as they possibly could. However, 'when Bayern want a player, they usually get him',[214] and at the expiration of his contract the Munich side had their man.

His first season at Bayern proved fruitful with a Bundesliga title (his personal third) to add to his growing personal trophy cabinet.

His five-goal salvo came the following season against Bundesliga runners-up Wolfsburg. Within minutes he had netted his first from close range before 58 seconds later, he showed the scope of his talents by lashing home from 25 yards. His hat-trick came at the third attempt, firstly hitting the post, then forcing keeper Diego Benaglio into a save, before finally finishing and sending the Bayern home crowd into raptures.

Lewandowski's fourth was a smart smash from 12 yards after Douglas Costa's bouncing cross and his fifth, to stun the footballing world, an exquisite volley from just inside the box as he latched on to Mario Götze's ball. Post-match, Lewandowski struggled to sum up his emotions, 'This was just crazy. Five goals, that's just unbelievable.' Manager Pep Guardiola, meanwhile, was lost for words, 'I can't really understand it. Five goals. Neither as a coach nor as a player did I ever experience something like this, and I can't really explain it.'[215]

Poland's all-time record goalscorer's achievement caught the eye of the official Guinness World Records team. They awarded him four records for his feat, 'The most goals scored by a substitute in the Bundesliga (five)'; 'The fastest Bundesliga hat-trick (three minutes and 22 seconds)'; 'The fastest four goals in a Bundesliga match (five minutes and 42 seconds)'; and also 'The fastest five goals in a Bundesliga match (eight minutes and 59 seconds)'.[216]

When you talk of the 2010s, you have to include Robert Lewandowski as one of the decade's greatest goal-getters.

214 *The Independent*, 28 May 2013

215 Taken from the match report: BBC, 'Robert Lewandowski: More goals in nine minutes than Liverpool', BBC Sport, 23 September 2015 https:// www.bbc.co.uk/sport/football/34332408

216 *The Guardian*, 1 December 2015

53

Lionel Messi's 400th goal
in La Liga (2019)

IT COMES as quite a shock to see that it has taken Lionel Messi 53 minutes to appear in this book, or at least in his own specific minute. However, his goal in the 53rd minute of Barcelona's 3-0 win over Eibar on 13 January 2019 marked the major achievement of 400 La Liga goals.

The feat was a long way on from the 17-year-old Messi making his La Liga debut as he replaced Deco with eight minutes left in a 1-0 win over Espanyol. In the following 15 years, Messi has written his name in the history books countless times to be forever considered as one of the greatest footballers to ever lace up a pair of boots.

Lionel Messi was born in Rosario, Argentina, on 24 June 1987. At the age of eight he was signed up by local side Newell's Old Boys to join their academy. As a child, Messi was diagnosed with a hormone deficiency which meant he had a small stature. The deficiency meant regular and costly injections, reportedly at around £1,000 a month. Fortunately, to ease the burden on his family, Newell's offered to help with the payments.[217] At 13, Spanish giants Barcelona took a chance on the slight Leo, moving him from South America to Europe to train at the renowned La Masia academy.

217 *Daily Mail*, 20 March 2018

Successful stints with the Barcelona C and B teams saw him given the opportunity to make his La Liga debut by manager Frank Rijkaard. At 18, Messi signed a professional contract with Barça and from 2005, the Argentine began to establish himself as a first-teamer. His initial role was as a right-winger, in a trio with Ronaldinho and striker Samuel Eto'o. Several fine performances helped to prove his importance to the Blaugrana.

It was under manager Pep Guardiola that Messi would become Barcelona's lynchpin. In May 2009, in a 6-2 El Clásico drubbing of arch-rivals Real Madrid at the Bernabéu, a 21-year-old Messi was used for the first time in a 'false nine' role. This allowed him to drop between the lines, with forwards Eto'o and Thierry Henry running the wings. The move was dubbed 'Guardiola's masterpiece' as Messi scored a brace and Los Blancos were blown away.[218] From this point on, Barcelona would go from strength to strength, with Messi the talisman no matter who played around him.[219]

Messi's greatest goalscoring campaign was 2011/12 with a staggering 50 netted in 37 league matches. This formed part of his record-breaking calendar year of 2012, featuring a mind-blowing 91 goals scored in all competitions. Messi went on to become La Liga's all-time record goalscorer on 22 November 2014. He matched Telmo Zarra's tally of 251 goals for Athletic Bilbao, which had stood since 1955, with a brilliant free kick against Sevilla. He then broke that record in the 72nd minute and extended it in the 78th with his hat-trick during a 5-1 victory over Sevilla.

The goals just kept coming though, and his effort against Eibar took his tally to 400 La Liga strikes, remarkably in just 435 games. Coach Ernesto Valverde summed Messi up that day,

218 Miguel Ángel Lara, 'Barcelona's 6-2 win over Real Madrid, Guardiola's masterpiece', *Marca*, 17 August 2018 https://www.marca.com/en/football/spanish-football/2018/08/17/5b768c7dca4741bb0f8b4635.html

219 Ben Jones and Gareth Thomas, *Football's Fifty Most Important Moments* (Worthing: Pitch Publishing, 2020) p.184

'He is from another galaxy… They are incredible numbers.'[220] With a record six Ballons d'Or to his name (as of the 2019 award), there aren't really the words to do justice to the lasting impact Lionel Messi has left on the beautiful game. He will never, ever be forgotten.

220 *The Telegraph*, 13 January 2019

54

'Hello, hello … here we go' – The Miracle of Istanbul (2005)

THE WORDS of commentator Clive Tyldesley are etched into the memory of every Liverpool supporter. It seemed as if he knew what was to come. The rollercoaster of emotions those at the Ataturk Stadium and the millions watching at home felt following Steven Gerrard's 54th-minute header would be hard to imagine. Upon it hitting Milan's net, the following six minutes set in motion arguably the greatest of all footballing comebacks.

The 2005 Champions League Final saw AC Milan, featuring an XI of world-class talent, face Rafael Benitez's Liverpool side. Although boasting a strong spine, the Reds were lacking real quality. The half-time score was clear evicence of this – Milan 3 Liverpool 0. Carlo Ancelotti's players had torn Liverpool to shreds with a first-minute goal by Paolo Maldini being followed up by a sublime Hernán Crespo brace. With Brazilian midfielder Kaká pulling the strings and Liverpool offering little attacking threat, any hope of a comeback seemed feeble.

Perhaps *The Guardian* summed it up best, 'If the Liverpool team was a dog, you'd shoot it at this stage.'[221] Arguably most sides would indeed have crumbled or looked to hold out and keep the scoreline as low as possible, but Liverpool are different. The

221 *The Guardian*, 25 May 2005

club's remarkable football history is one which best exemplifies the 'never say die' attitude. Stunned, but not totally discouraged, the Liverpool fans tried to will their side on at half-time through a sombre, yet encouraging version of their anthem, 'You'll Never Walk Alone'.

For many, the chorus was a way in which to motivate the Reds into a second-half revival. For others, it was a chance to demonstrate that the support was still there for the side despite the inevitable defeat. Liverpool's home-grown heroes, Steven Gerrard and Jamie Carragher, would both later write that the supporters were key to their team's recovery. Just nine minutes after the restart the comeback began as John Arne Riise's cross flew into the Milan box. Captain and talisman Gerrard rose highest to score a brilliant header past the helpless Dida.

Few could have predicted that the goal would be more than a consolation. For Gerrard, however, he wrote that it was a repayment to the fans, 'Liverpool fans lifted the players and I wanted to lift the supporters. The volume rose.'[222] Milan would have to react, but a sense of complacency had entered their game. Two minutes later, Vladimír Šmicer crashed in a second before Gerrard won the Reds a dramatic penalty. In just six minutes, Liverpool had an opportunity to equalise. Despite Dida initially saving Xabi Alonso's effort, the Spanish midfielder thumped the rebound high into the roof of the net. The miracle was almost complete.

'Istanbul was madness, pure, utter, wonderful madness,' wrote Gerrard.[223]

Those words are right. There had never been a major final like it and the drama involved is yet to be repeated since. The extra-time period following the final whistle was tense and lacked any real opportunities until Jerzy Dudek somehow saved twice from Milan striker Andriy Shevchenko. At that moment, Gerrard knew that the footballing gods were on his side. A

222 Steven Gerrard, *My Autobiography* (London: Bantam: 2006) p.323
223 Ibid

penalty shootout victory would follow and the Reds' skipper euphorically lifted the cup up to the thousands of Liverpool fans inside the Ataturk Stadium.

The Miracle of Istanbul is one of football's greatest ever matches. It helps to prove that there is so much more to the game than just scorelines. Of course, its greatest message is one about not giving up, even in the face of immense adversity. Furthermore, it promotes the importance of supporters in enabling their side to achieve the impossible. For Milan too, it created a powerful message that 'feeling invincible is the first step on the path to the point of no return'.[224]

One quote perhaps sums it up perfectly, 'In just six unpredictable minutes, you can go from forlorn despondency to the centre of the universe.'[225]

224 Andrea Pirlo, *I Think Therefore I Play* (London: BackPage Press, 2014) p.87

225 Ben Jones and Gareth Thomas, *Football's Fifty Most Important Moments* (Worthing: Pitch Publishing, 2020) p.167

55

Hal Robson-Kanu turns into
Johan Cruyff (2016)

ON 9 May 2016, Hal Robson-Kanu was released by Championship side Reading just a month before he would be part of the Wales squad at Euro 2016. After 11 years in Berkshire, the 26-year-old had offered a modest record of 30 goals in over 200 appearances for the club. Wales, attending their first major tournament since 1958, would have been hoping that Robson-Kanu could find form in France. On 1 July he went far beyond expectations as he used a Cruyff Turn to throw off three Belgian defenders in one of the most remarkable matches in his country's history.

Wales's tournament bow against Slovakia started shakily as less than three minutes in, Marek Hamšík forced Ben Davies into a stunning goal-saving block. But after ten minutes the Welsh hero Gareth Bale opened the scoring and sent the travelling spectators wild. Ondrej Duda levelled for the Slovakians but the game was won with nine minutes remaining, Robson-Kanu miscuing a shot toward goal that found its way past keeper Matúš Kozáčik. Wales had three valuable points and Robson-Kanu had opened his Euros account.

Their second group fixture was against bitter rivals England in Lens. The Three Lions had drawn to Russia in their opener after conceding late on. Bale again gave Wales the lead, but a Jamie Vardy equaliser was compounded in second-half stoppage time by a late Daniel Sturridge winner. England were victorious and Cymru now required a win to have any hope of topping Group B. Aaron Ramsey, Neil Taylor and Bale all scored in Toulouse as Russia were dispatched while an England 0-0 bore draw with Slovakia saw them finish as runners-up behind the Welsh.

England went on to face a humiliating exit to Iceland in the last 16 (Minute 4), while Wales snuck past Northern Ireland due to an own goal from defender Gareth McAuley. This set up a quarter-final clash with Belgium, a side who Wales had beaten in qualifying to earn their place at Euro 2016. Belgium, meanwhile, had crushed Hungary 4-0 in the previous round and were tipped as one of the favourites for the tournament.

After 13 minutes Welsh fans would have been excused for thinking the worst when a thunderbolt from Radja Nainggolan made it 1-0 to Belgium. However, captain Ashley Williams came to the rescue on the half-hour mark with a header to level the match at half-time. And in the second half, the history books were written.

In the 55th minute, Ramsey's dinked ball into the box from the right found Robson-Kanu on the penalty spot. With his back to goal and three Belgian defenders blocking his path, the free agent did the unthinkable. Emulating (arguably surpassing) the legendary Johan Cruyff (Minute 23), Robson-Kanu, in one motion, turned and sent all three defenders the other way. The forward then hammered the ball past Thibaut Courtois and a nation erupted. In fan parks up and down Wales, there was delirium. Wales were 35 minutes from the semi-final in their first tournament since 1958.

Things were to get even better for Wales. With tensions high as the players hung on, defender Chris Gunter perfectly delivered a cross in the 85th minute for Sam Vokes to head home and secure the game at 3-1. Robbie Savage, emotional on commentary, uttered the now famous words, 'Go and wake your kids up, something special is happening here tonight!'[226]

226 Robbie Savage, commentating on the match for BBC Sport

The dream would be ended by eventual winners Portugal in the semi-finals, but for clubless Robson-Kanu it was a career renaissance. Former Wales international John Hartson said after the Belgium game, 'What a goal. He sent Thomas Meunier for a cup of tea and a piece of toast with that turn.'[227] The performance caught the eye of Premier League West Bromwich Albion, who snapped the number nine up post-tournament, but this moment is greater than just that a transfer. This was a Cruyff Turn that made a nation proud.

---

227 Dafydd Pritchard, 'Wales 3-1 Belgium, BBC Sport, 1 July 2016 https://www.bbc.co.uk/sport/football/36613679

56

Gini Wijnaldum equalises in the Miracle of Anfield (2019)

LIVERPOOL'S LOVE affair with the European Cup has become legendary among supporters of the Merseyside club. At their home ground of Anfield, there have been many dramatic matches which have left long-lasting memories on the thousands who watched. In May 2019, Liverpool's semi-final against Spanish giants Barcelona had appeared to be all but over following a damaging first-leg defeat at the Camp Nou. Lionel Messi had helped to punish the Reds with two goals, the second of which was surely one of his finest in a Barça shirt.

As Messi's 30-yard free kick sailed around the wall and past keeper Alisson into the net, it seemed that Liverpool's hopes of a second successive Champions League Final were dead and buried. A 3-0 semi-final first leg deficit would be almost impossible to overturn. Indeed, it had never been accomplished in the tournament's history. Furthermore, Barcelona would be extra careful following an embarrassing exit to Roma a season earlier, having led 3-1 after their quarter-final first leg. BBC Sport was sceptical as to Liverpool's hopes, writing, 'Is there anything that offers them the belief they can somehow turn this around?' [228]

228 Phil McNulty, 'Barcelona 3-0 Liverpool: How Lionel Messi Proved a Force Too Powerful for Liverpool', BBC Sport, 1 May 2019 https://www. bbc.co.uk/sport/football/48129168

To further compound Liverpool's misery there were sudden injuries to the influential Roberto Firmino and talismanic forward Mohamed Salah. Salah had landed awkwardly in the Reds' league match against Newcastle just days before the Blaugrana visited Merseyside. Liverpool had completed many famous comebacks in the past, most notably against Milan in 2005 (Minute 54) and Borussia Dortmund in 2016, but this still seemed a test too far. Manager Jürgen Klopp knew all too well what the injuries would mean and appeared resigned to a semi-final exit in his pre-match press conference, 'Two of the world's best strikers are not available tomorrow night and we have to score four goals. It doesn't make life easier, but we will try for 90 minutes to celebrate the Champions League campaign to give it a proper finish.'[229]

Even with this in mind, the Liverpool supporters hadn't given up hope. Too many times they had seen their side rise from the ashes to produce a memorable European night at Anfield. An early goal would be vital and through stand-in striker Divock Origi that was what they acquired after just seven minutes. Anfield was rocking and Barcelona began to fear a repeat of the debacle in Rome. Liverpool went in at half-time a goal to the good, but still needed three more to progress.

Left-back Andy Robertson was the next to succumb to Jürgen Klopp's injury list and was replaced at half-time by Dutch central midfielder Gini Wijnaldum. Wijnaldum had been asked to play in an attacking role and immediately began to cause the Barça back line some problems. After he scored to put the Reds within a goal of extra time, the stadium reached new levels of pandemonium in the 56th minute. A superb cross from Swiss winger Xherdan Shaqiri was powerfully headed, once again by Wijnaldum, past Marc-André Ter Stegen and into the net. The Kop erupted.

Alan Shearer, on BT Sport, later said of the moment, 'That header from the left [for Liverpool's third goal] was a sublime

229 Jürgen Klopp's press conference, 6 May 2019

one, I would have been proud of that one. I've never seen Anfield like this and the fans were driving their players forward from start to finish. It's just been relentless. It was incredible from all the players. Wow.'[230]

Barcelona's confidence was shot and history looked certain to repeat itself. Just 11 minutes before the final whistle a quick corner by Trent Alexander-Arnold caught the Barcelona defence napping and Origi fired into the unguarded net. Anfield once again erupted, but not quite to the levels of Wijnaldum's equaliser. Why? Alongside the Barcelona back line, the corner managed to be missed by half of the stadium too!

At full time, Anfield was in a state of delirium. The players had seemingly achieved what most believed impossible. Mo Salah, wearing a t-shirt with 'Never Give Up' on the front, joined his team-mates on the pitch. The whole squad, together with the staff and supporters, burst into an impromptu rendition of the club's anthem, 'You'll Never Walk Alone'.

It was a remarkable show of togetherness and the divide between players and fans seemed to be narrower than ever. The result, and celebrations that followed, were testament to the hard work and dedication Klopp had given to the club since his arrival in October 2015. The German manager had managed to revitalise the club and the city in which they played. He had created a true footballing family reminiscent of the work of Bill Shankly in the 1960s and 1970s. Liverpool would go on to defeat Tottenham Hotspur in Madrid and claim their sixth Champions League crown.

230 Alan Shearer on BT Sport, 7 May 2019

57

Angelos Charisteas shocks Portugal to win the Euros (2004)

BEFORE THE start of a major international tournament, it often feels like the winner can only be predicted from a select group of nations. In the European Championship, the likes of Germany, Italy, Spain, Netherlands or France are often at the forefront of most pundits' choices for the top prize. Prior to the start of Euro 2004, it was no different. Alongside the usual suspects, the hosts Portugal and their 'golden generation' completed a strong collection of favourites for the title.

It was of little surprise then, that Portugal reached the final in Lisbon. Barring a shock defeat to Greece in the tournament's opening fixture the side, led by the influential Luís Figo, had impressed in their victories over Russia and Iberian rivals Spain in the group stage. Indeed, even their titanic quarter-final battle against England had further fuelled media speculation that they were destined to win the trophy. A semi-final triumph over Holland meant Portugal were a game away from history. 'I could wish for nothing better,' were the words of Figo after defeating the Dutch.[231]

Football, as we have seen so many times before, doesn't always follow the script. Indeed, the final would see a repeat of the competition's opening fixture as Greece surprised the

---

231 Luís Figo in: BBC, 'Portugal 2-1 Netherlands', BBC Sport, 30 June 2004
    http://news.bbc.co.uk/sport1/hi/football/euro_2004/3844465.stm

continent to reach the showpiece event. Coach Otto Rehhagel had deployed a 'solid, practical and defensive approach' in order to fend off defending champions France in the quarters and neutral favourites the Czech Republic (Minute 105) in the last four.[232] Greece weren't to every supporter's liking and their negative style had earned criticism along the way. However, in 2004, the game had already shown its openness to a new brand of defensive 'catenaccio'-inspired tactics. José Mourinho's Champions League winners Porto were no strangers to the style.

Following a goalless first half at the Estádio da Luz, the game's opening goal would arrive in the 57th minute. Greek striker Angelos Charisteas had risen highest to nod Angelos Basinas's corner past Ricardo and into the net. The goal had been perfect for Rehhagel's pragmatic approach and offered the Greeks something to defend. Propped up by the increasingly impressive defensive duo Traianos Dellas and Michalis Kapsis, the side withstood a Portuguese barrage led by youngster Cristiano Ronaldo. Despite the statistics being heavily weighted in Portugal's favour, Greece would hold firm and produce one of football's greatest shocks.

As captain Theodoros Zagorakis held aloft the Henri Delaunay Trophy to a shell-shocked stadium in Lisbon, the footballing world rejoiced at the victory of the underdogs. So often in the competition, the pragmatic Greek approach had been criticised, but with the European Championships in their hands, no one could deny its worth. BBC pundit Alan Hansen described the victory as a 'triumph for defensive organisation'[233] and Portugal manager Luiz Felipe Scolari, through gritted teeth, refused to criticise the tactics of his opposite number: 'I can say only that the Greek defence was magnificent.'[234]

232 Martin Cloake and Aidan Radnedge, et al, *Football The Ultimate Guide: Updated 2010 Edition* (London: DK, 2010) p.54

233 Alan Hansen, 'Hansen: Dellas Made the Difference', BBC Sport, 4 July 2004 http://news.bbc.co.uk/sport1/hi/football/euro_2004/3865371.stm

234 Luis Felipe Scolari in Phil McNulty, 'Scolari Remains Upbeat', BBC Sport, 5 July 2004 http://news.bbc.co.uk/sport1/hi/football/euro_2004/portugal/3865787.stm

Reaction around the world demonstrated that this victory was one of the game's most significant. The BBC wrote that Greece had indeed 'pulled off one of the biggest shocks in football history'. Furthermore, the win has led to a wealth of books and articles highlighting the achievement of the underdog and the folly of football betting. It showed that even with a wealth of statistics and probabilities, you can never truly predict what might happen on a football pitch.[235]

In Greece, the celebrations were wild. With the Olympic Games also being held in the country, a wave of euphoria gripped the country like no other. For the first time in over 2,000 years, Greece was once again at the centre of the world.

235 Liedy Klotz, *Sustainability Through Soccer: An Unexpected Approach to Saving Our World* (California: University of California, 2016) pp.61–64

58

Michel Platini wins the European Cup which should never have been played (1985)

WEDNESDAY, 29 May 1985 should be considered one of the greatest days in Juventus's history. The Old Lady finally lifted their first European Cup title after twice previously finishing as runners-up. Sadly, the game that night should never have been played following the terrible and tragic scenes pre-match. Violence before kick-off saw the death roll reach 39: 32 Italians (the youngest of whom was 11), four Belgians, two French and one fan who was from Northern Ireland. Those injured that dark night, are believed to have amounted to more than 600.[236]

From 1977 to 1984, English clubs had dominated the European Cup. Liverpool had lifted the title four times, Nottingham Forest twice (Minute 45) and Aston Villa once. And 1985 saw Liverpool reach the final again with Italians Juventus the opponent at Heysel Stadium in Brussels, Belgium. Despite English football being at its height, the problem of 'hooliganism' was killing the game off the pitch. *The Times* stated in 1980 that 'if we do not [do something] there is a real danger that football will die for lack of support, because only thugs will go to watch it... Football is sick, it may be terminal'.[237]

236 *Liverpool Echo*, 23 May 2015
237 *The Times*, 19 September 1980

The month of May 1985 saw football reach a breaking point. The Bradford fire (Minute 40) highlighted the lack of quality of some of the stadia, while a fan was killed at Birmingham City due to tribalistic and violent fan behaviour on the same day as the blaze. The *Sunday Times* called football 'a slum sport, played in slum stadiums, increasingly watched by slum people who deter decent folk from turning up'.[238]

Heysel Stadium had been heavily criticised in the lead-up to the fixture, being labelled a 'dump' by previous visiting fans. This meant that when tensions rose between Liverpool and Juventus supporters before kick-off, it was far too easy for hooligans to break through the 'flimsy wire fencing' that separated fans.[239] Parts of the crumbling stadium became missiles thrown, and in the panic that ensued, Juventus supporters were crushed by a falling wall. The tragedy was unthinkable, with no stretchers available meaning that victims were carried out on fences and advertising hoardings.[240]

Staggeringly, the final was not called off. It was delayed but the authorities, fearing an increase in violence, decided that it would be played. Understandably, many of the players did not want the tie to go ahead, but it did. The deadlock was broken in the 58th minute by Frenchman Michel Platini after Liverpool defender Gary Gillespie brought down Zbigniew Boniek. Liverpool argued that Boniek was outside the box, but referee André Daina gave the spot kick and Juventus had their lead. The single goal settled the final.

Historian Matthew Taylor wrote how in the aftermath English football would be 'ostracised and isolated from Europe and the world'.[241] The FA immediately declared, 'It is up to English football to put its house in order, to ensure that this totally unacceptable behaviour of English supporters at home

238 *Sunday Times*, 19 May 1985
239 *The Guardian*, 28 May 2010
240 Bryon Butler, *The Football League: The First 100 Years* (Guildford: Colour Library Books Ltd., 1988) pp. 328-329
241 Matthew Taylor, *The Association Game* (London: Routledge, 2008) p.319

and abroad becomes a thing of the past.'[242] Liverpool withdrew from European competition the following season but UEFA extended the ban more widely. This saw English clubs barred from Europe for five years, Liverpool receiving an extra year.

Heysel was a wake-up call to try and fix the hooliganism problem. However, the violence continued and historian Richard Holt wrote in 1989, that 'fatal risks are being run each week in stadia where large and rowdy confrontations of young spectators take place'.[243] If Heysel was the alarm, then Hillsborough, where hooliganism played no part, in April 1989 (Minute 6) was finally the catalyst for change. Eventually football would be reclaimed for the everyday fan but not before lives were lost in horrendous circumstances.

242 *Aberdeen Evening Express*, 31 May 1985

243 Richard Holt, *Sport and the British: A Modern History* (Oxford: Oxford University, 1989) p.329

59

The Copa del Generalísimo
begins in Barcelona (1939)

THE 1930S arguably offers football's most dramatic and controversial decade. The wider political, social and economic background of the period provides some of the most researched, documented and analysed pieces of history, and yet the football played during this time is relatively forgotten. We've often heard that history is written by the victor and studies of football's past show it to be no different. In an era dominated by off-the-pitch issues, those on it are beginning to be retold and revised by sports historians. In Spain, the brutal regime enforced by fascist General Franco would have an impact on the game many outside of the Iberian peninsula are still unaware of.

The Spanish Civil War (1936–39) had devastated the nation. Split into Republicans and Nationalists, the latter had claimed victory after the deaths of potentially two million soldiers and civilians. In a fractured country, Franco would seek to impose his regime on his citizens and restrict anti-fascist sentiment across Spain. The renaming of the Copa del Rey (King's Cup) to the Copa del Generalísimo was just one minor step, but one which helped reflect the overarching restructuring of Spain in its general's image.

Franco had three leading ideas disseminated through the use of football. Firstly, football was to be used as an opportunity to promote the ideals of fascism. Secondly, through victory, it would help to improve the dictator's global image and finally it was to become a catalyst to spark regionalist oppositions opposed to Francoism.[244] Sports historian Timothy Ashton wrote that the government had seen an opportunity to use football to reflect its ideals.[245]

One of the first examples of this ideology on display came in 1939 as Sevilla faced Racing Club de Ferrol for the Copa in Barcelona. The choice of city was significant. Barcelona had been at the very centre of Republican resistance throughout the Civil War and Franco saw a chance to demonstrate that he was in charge. The two sides would raise their arms in the fascist salute before the game commenced and enthusiastically sang along to the hymn 'Face to the Sun', together with the capacity crowd. The propaganda machine was in full flow.

The game itself saw Sevilla emerge as victors. A 6-2 scoreline demonstrated Sevilla's talent and featured the feared forward line nicknamed 'Delantera Stuka'. This nickname alone is a clear example of the promotion of fascism in Spain. The name is shared with the first Nazi Luftwaffe bomber which assisted the Nationalist forces throughout the civil war.[246] The focal point of the attack was Spanish international Guillermo Campanal. Campanal had scored twice and captained his side to a 5-0 half-time lead. In the second half, the forward completed his hat-trick in the 59th minute. Two consolation goals for Ferrol (ironically Franco's home town) saw the match finish 6-2 to Sevilla.

Football is never too far from politics and the renaming of the Spanish Cup to the Copa del Generalísimo is further proof of this. Furthermore, the use of football as a propaganda tool by Franco helps to identify just how powerful the game can be on an entire nation.

244 Duncan Shaw, *Football and Francoism* (Madrid, Alianza, 1987)

245 Timothy Ashton, *Soccer in Spain: Politics, Literature and Film* (Plymouth: Scarecrow, 2013) p.28

246 Colin Millar, *The Frying Pan of Spain: Sevilla vs Real Betis: Spain's Hottest Football Rivalry* (Worthing: Pitch Publishing, 2019)

But 1939 would by no means be the end of the Spanish dictator's influence on wider sport and culture and the subsequent repression of regional identities and promotion of nationalistic Spanish ideals became paramount to the nation's future. Lasting until the mid-1970s, it would be decades before Spain embraced the intricacy and abundance of distinct cultures once again (Minute 3).

60

Future full time? (2017)

WHO MAKES the rules of football? The Football Association? UEFA? FIFA? The rich clubs? The media? The broadcasters? Actually, the institution that sets out changes to the 'Laws of the Game' is a body known as International Football Association Board (IFAB). Significantly for those who so often enjoy moaning about foreign influences spoiling the game, the British control IFAB. In 2017, IFAB shocked fans when it proposed the idea of the full-time mark being shifted to 60 minutes.

In 1904, Fédération Internationale de Football Association (FIFA) was founded to meet the 'European hunger for the coordination of football'.[247] The English, Scottish, Welsh and Irish FAs were united in their decision to reject FIFA as they sought to protect their game from outside influences. Historian Richard Holt described the attitude as 'proud and insular',[248] but FIFA would not be deterred and accepted the already established 'Laws of the Game' set out by IFAB (which had been founded in 1886 by the home nations for that role).[249]

The English (1905), Welsh and Scottish (both 1910) and Irish (1911) would eventually join FIFA. In 1913, FIFA was

247 Ben Jones and Gareth Thomas, *Football's Fifty Most Important Moments* (Worthing: Pitch Publishing, 2020) p.35

248 Richard Holt, *Sport and The British* (Oxford: Oxford University Press, 1989) p.273

249 Erik Eggers, in John Turnbull, Thom Satterlee and Alon Raab (eds.), *The Global Game: Writers on Soccer* (Lincoln: University of Nebraska, 2008) p.31

finally allowed access to IFAB and the opportunity to influence the rules of the game, but its votes would be strategically limited to prevent the organisation having too much power. When Ireland was 'partitioned' in 1921, the Irish association became the Northern Irish governing body, and the new Republic of Ireland was then also refused access to IFAB. The home nations now fully controlled 'four-fifths' of the rule-making organisation that dictated the laws across the world, FIFA just having one-fifth.[250]

In 1958, FIFA joined IFAB as a full member, but the voting rules were still tipped in the balance of the home nations. England, Scotland, Wales and Northern Ireland continue to have one vote each to this day, while FIFA has four votes for the rest of the world's associations (currently 207). Any new footballing law must pass with six out of eight votes, and so Britain remains having '50 per cent control of the laws of the game' and the power of veto as a group.[251]

Records suggest that as early as 1865[252] and 1866,[253] 90-minute football matches had been played. These were formally codified in 1897,[254] but in 2017 IFAB proposed the radical idea of games becoming just 60 minutes.

The main aim of the proposal was to 'reduce time-wasting and speed up the game'.[255] This would come from adopting much stricter time-keeping by officials. Other sports where the referee would pause the match clock were compared against, for example rugby, where the counting is halted at the referee's command when play stops. In football, this could incorporate penalty decisions, the cautioning of players, treatment of injured

250 Kevin Moore, *What You Think You Know About Football Is Wrong* (London: Bloomsbury, 2019) p.22

251 Ibid, p.23

252 *Morning Post*, 24 November 1865

253 *Nottinghamshire Guardian*, 23 March 1866

254 IFAB, 'Minutes of Annual General Meeting', *International Football Association Board*, 1897, Available at: https://theifab.com/home

255 *The Telegraph*, 17 June 2017

players, substitutions being made, and the celebration of a goal being scored. With the referee stopping the watch, this would see injury time consigned to the history books, as much like rugby, when the clock hits 30 or 60 and the ball leaves the field, the half-time or full-time whistle would be blown.

IFAB's research had found that the typical match has fewer than 60 minutes of 'effective playing time (EPT)', where the ball was in play. The plan for two 30-minutes halves would mean there would be 'less point in players wasting time' and would also mean every competition and every club in the world would play 'exactly the same amount of EPT' consistently.[256]

The controversial plans to radically alter the beautiful game shocked many fans, social media being awash with criticism of the idea. Many others, though, understood the aims of the proposal and while 60-minute matches have not been enacted upon yet, do not expect this idea to totally disappear in the future.

256 Play Fair!, 'The IFAB strategy to develop the Laws of the Game to improve football 2017–2022', *IFAB*, 2017, Available at: https://www.play-fair.com/

61

Alan Shearer sets a seemingly unbreakable record (2006)

THE PREMIER League changed English football forever. Founded in 1992, the reformatted top flight was an answer to the decline of the game in the 1980s and a direct result of hooliganism. With an average attendance of 21,723 in 1991/92, 25 per cent lower than a decade previous, something needed to change. The new Premier League was backed by Sky's £304m broadcasting deal, and the traditional 3pm kick-offs would no longer be protected to accommodate television viewers.[257] Brian Deane would net the first goal of this new league (Minute 5), but when you consider the all-time greats of the division, it is hard to look past striker Alan Shearer's 260 goals.

Shearer began his career at Southampton and following his breakthrough in the late 1980s, he recorded 23 goals in 118 matches in the 'old' First Division. Shearer transferred from Southampton to Blackburn for a British record £3.6m in the summer of 1992, just in time for the debut season of the new Premier League.[258] His time with Blackburn would be incredibly productive, scoring over 30 league goals in each of 1993/94, 1994/95 and 1995/96. This earned him two Golden Boots and the Premier League title in 1994/95 as part of the lethal 'SAS'

257 Ben Jones and Gareth Thomas, *Football's Fifty Most Important Moments* (Worthing: Pitch Publishing, 2020) pp.143–144

258 *The Independent*, 27 July 1992

combination with strike partner Chris Sutton (49 between them that year).

The goals attracted great interest from clubs across the world, most notably Alex Ferguson's Manchester United. Ferguson had first attempted to attract the Geordie to Old Trafford in 1992 and after his deadly form for Blackburn he came calling again. However, for Shearer, the lure of his home-town club would prove too much and in 1996 he made the £15m switch to Newcastle United.[259]

Goals continued to flow on Tyneside, with 25 securing another Golden Boot in 1996/97. While the number nine would not lift another Premier League title at St James' Park, or a domestic cup, Shearer did establish himself as Britain's best goal-getter. Comfortable with 'tap-ins, long-range beauties, headers and penalties', Shearer is considered perhaps the 'most natural goal scorer this country [England] has ever produced'.[260]

With his trademark simple celebration, the right arm raised above his head, Shearer would surpass 200 Premier League goals with ease. On his first senior start at 17 Shearer had scored a remarkable hat-trick against Arsenal for Southampton. His last senior goal came at the age of 35. On 17 April 2006, Newcastle played rivals Sunderland away from home. In the 61st minute of the 4-1 victory, Shearer scored a penalty to take his Premier League total to an imperious 260. Sadly for Shearer, who had already announced his impending retirement, a knee injury picked up in the 71st minute ended his career three games earlier than planned.

Nonetheless, Shearer's goal record is one that many believe will stand for years and years to come. Wayne Rooney is the only man to come close in the interim with 208 goals and no doubt the mark will be surpassed eventually, but one thing is for certain, they don't make strikers like Alan Shearer any more.

259 Jo Tongue, Simon Poole and Paolo Hewitt, *The League Doesn't Lie: The 606 Book of Football Lists* (London: BBC Books, 2012) p.282

260 Ibid, p.111

62

Tommy Gemmell equalises in Lisbon (1967)

THE EARLY years of the European Cup had been dominated by sides from Latin Europe. Real Madrid, Benfica, AC Milan and their city rivals Inter had all conquered the continent in the competition's opening 12 campaigns. In 1967, Inter were aiming for a third European crown following victories in 1964 and 1965. Playing with a rigid tactical style called catenaccio ('the chain'), they had retained defensive solidity in order to see out matches and crush the opposition.

The style wasn't popular in Britain. Indeed, Inter's semi-final victory over Liverpool in 1965 had won them few neutral supporters and upon their final game of the 1966/67 European Cup campaign, most were in favour of Jock Stein's Celtic. Remarkably, the Celtic side had all grown up within 30 miles of the club's home ground, Parkhead.[261] A close bond was felt between supporters and players with many of those playing having been raised in Glasgow's poorest neighbourhoods.

Celtic had reached the final in Lisbon by playing an attractive style. They were in many ways the antithesis of Inter. Their brand of football had promoted the game at its finest and pre-match discussion, particularly in the British press, had

261 David Bolchover and Christopher Brady, *The 90-minute Manager: Lessons from the Sharp End of Management*, 3rd edition (London: Pearson Education Limited, 2006) p. 147

made a point of the all-out attack that 'Celtic's heroes' would display.[262] Despite talk of battles and potential confrontations, Stein was quick to quell the animosity of the media before the game, insisting his side were there to play football and not fight a war.

Sandro Mazzola gave Inter the lead from the penalty spot after just seven minutes. An early goal was usually essential for catenaccio to begin, as it gave the Italians something to defend. Midway through the second half, however, Celtic struck back. In the 62nd minute, Tommy Gemmell rifled in from 20 yards to equalise. An attacking onslaught ensued and eventually Stevie Chalmers was on hand to deflect the ball past Giuliano Sarti and into the net.

A 2-1 victory would see the European Cup head to British soil for the first time. Celtic's brand of positive football had defeated the negativity of catenaccio and paved the way for a new brand of tactical innovation across the continent, particularly in the Netherlands. Even opposition manager Helenio Herrera was quick to express his admiration for the way in which Celtic played. Stein's side would be dubbed the Lisbon Lions after the game for their attacking intent.

For a group of players with many having grown up in 'impoverishment, illness and intolerance', victory meant far more than just a trophy.[263] It was a trophy for Glasgow as much as it was for football. The following year another British side, Manchester United, would win the European Cup and cap a dramatic turnaround for the club since the Munich air disaster (Minute 2). Matt Busby's team had been inspired by Celtic and featured the attacking trio of George Best, Denis Law and Bobby Charlton. Victory for United, and the later introduction of Total Football in Holland, meant the legacy of the Lisbon Lions lived on.

262 *Reading Evening Post*, 25 May 1967
263 *Glasgow 1967: The Lisbon Lions*, BBC documentary, (2017)

63

Khalid Boulahrouz sees red in the Battle of Nuremberg (2006)

THE GROUP stages of the 2006 World Cup had seen football at its finest. With a wealth of goals and arguably one of the finest collections of squads in recent memory, it had been an overwhelming success of host nation Germany. Some 107 goals had flooded the first round and produced some of the tournament's best ever strikes. The superstar talents of Cristiano Ronaldo, Ronaldinho, Wayne Rooney and Alessandro Del Piero were all on display, leading to mouth-watering knockout round ties between the traditional superpowers of world football.

The first knockout round saw the Netherlands face Portugal. In 2004, the sides met in an entertaining semi-final at the European Championships. The Dutch had felt aggrieved by many of the referee's decisions on the night – even culminating in a two-match ban for Ruud van Nistelrooy following 'insulting words'. Before they once again met, this time in Nuremberg, neutrals found it difficult to separate them. With a multitude of attacking talent on display, the only thing safe to predict was goals.

But the game wouldn't be remembered for goals. Instead, it would be the 16 yellow cards and four reds which left referee Valentin Ivanov's pocket like confetti. The first culprit? Who else but Mark van Bommel. The early booking had shown how Ivanov would approach the game. Within minutes of van

Bommel's challenge, Khalid Boulahrouz followed his team-mate into the book. An ugly and forceful tackle on Ronaldo resulted in the then Manchester United man leaving the field. Portugal were no angels either, first-half bookings to Maniche and Costinha meaning both defensive linchpins were treading a fine line. The Portuguese duo were also involved in the first half's biggest moments. Maniche had scored the game's only goal after 19 minutes and Costinha earned the first red card for a deliberate handball just before half-time.

The second half continued where the first left off, with cynical fouls and bookings for Petit and then van Bronckhorst. The latter prompted a fracas between players of both sides. The legendary Luís Figo even headbutted van Bommel, whose reaction was in some ways comical. How Figo stayed on the pitch and escaped with only a yellow is a mystery. In the 63rd minute, Figo would also go down easily after being caught by Boulahrouz's stray elbow. Another melee and another red card, this time for the Dutch right-back.

It was Boulahrouz's red card that saw the tie begin to slip away from the Netherlands. Marco van Basten had built an incredible squad, intent on playing Total Football in the groups, but a mindless flick of the elbow and wider abandonment of Dutch footballing principles would result in the rest of the match being frequently stopped for confrontations between the combustible set of footballers.

Deco was also dismissed before Giovanni van Bronckhorst finally saw red in the 96th minute for a second yellow. After the final whistle, the viewing public were left stunned after watching a petulant, embarrassing and yet gripping 90 minutes of football. Post-match conversation was centred around referee Ivanov's performance. FIFA president Sepp Blatter said, 'I consider that today the referee was not at the same level as the participants, the players. There could have been a yellow card for the referee.'[264]

264 *The Guardian*, 26 June 2006

The 2006 World Cup witnessed more ugly scenes in Berlin when the German and Argentine teams clashed following a tense penalty shootout in the quarter-final. The tournament would, however, create a most memorable final. After Portugal were knocked out by France and Italy defeated Germany in an epic in Dortmund, the Italians lifted the trophy. The 2006 tournament is now remembered for Zinedine Zidane's final headbutt (Minute 110), but the Battle of Nuremberg will live long in the memory as a tragic example of fair play and a sense of déjà vu for the Dutch.

64

Gareth Bale's Champions League overhead brilliance (2018)

REAL MADRID won the inaugural European Cup in 1956 (Minute 14) and the four following it. In 2014 they made it ten titles, La Décima (Minute 118), before adding further Champions League victories in 2016, 2017 and 2018. Each one of those wins were brilliant and significant for one of football's greatest clubs. However, the 2018 final will be remembered for more than just another Real Madrid crown as in the 64th minute, Gareth Bale scored a goal for the ages.

Bale was born in Cardiff in 1989 and began his career as a full-back at Southampton. Tottenham Hotspur purchased the 17-year-old in 2007, but the Welshman failed to make an immediate impact at White Hart Lane. Bale's breakthrough would come on 20 October 2010 in a memorable night against Italian side Inter Milan at the San Siro in the Champions League. Spurs were losing 4-0 inside 35 minutes and down to ten men, but Bale gave a stunning second-half performance as he scored a hat-trick, tearing right-back Maicon to shreds in the process.

Bale's frightening pace and power saw him move upfield to take up the role of a winger. The shift worked and in 2012/13, he scored 21 Premier League goals. Real Madrid legend Zinedine Zidane would describe Bale's season as 'the same level as Ronaldo and Messi',[265] earning him interest from across the world. The

265 *The Independent*, 2 September 2013

form saw Madrid chase Bale, eventually paying a world record fee of over €100m to bring him to the Santiago Bernabéu.

Bale settled into the famous white jersey quickly, the 2014 Copa del Rey Final being a notable highlight. With the scores level at 1-1 against rivals Barcelona and just five minutes left on the clock, Bale showed his blistering pace to win the competition. Beginning inside his own half, he blazed past defender Marc Bartra, even running off the field to beat his man, before poking the ball calmly past keeper José Pinto. This moment would be surpassed in the 2018 Champions League Final, though, by a goal worthy of winning any cup.

Playing Liverpool on 26 May, the match was tied at 1-1. Karim Benzema had given Madrid the lead with Sadio Mané equalising for the Reds. Bale, who had experienced a difficult campaign in Spain, was only a substitute for Los Blancos. He was brought on after 61 minutes and just three minutes later his moment would come. Marcelo's whipped cross flew in to Bale who was on the edge of the box, and with seemingly nothing else to do, he hit a jaw-dropping overhead kick from an unbelievable height that rocketed into the top-right corner of the net past a helpless Loris Karius.

Wales's all-time record international goalscorer had emulated Zidane, by now Madrid's manager, who had himself scored a beauty in the 2002 Champions League Final. Zidane described Bale's hit as 'magnificent', while pundit and former Manchester United defender Gary Neville remarked, 'Not joking. That may be the best goal I've ever seen.'[266] The incredible strike was rightly lauded as one of the best cup final goals ever, but Bale was not done. He added a second to his tally seven minutes from time to firmly sink Liverpool 3-1. Real Madrid had a 13th title and Bale had seized the headlines for himself – something less than straightforward to do with Cristiano Ronaldo also on the pitch.

266 *Daily Express*, 27 May 2018

65

Megan Rapinoe stands tall
for women's football (2019)

THE 2019 Women's World Cup was undoubtedly the biggest women's edition of the competition since it had begun back in 1991 (Minute 20). In the UK, the BBC announced that 6.1 million viewers tuned in for England's opening match with Scotland, a record for women's football.[267] FIFA would confirm that a combined 1.12 billion viewers watched the French World Cup throughout the tournament. The final, where the USA beat the Netherlands, drew an average worldwide audience of 82.18 million, with a total of 'unique' viewership of 263.62 million.[268]

Such figures highlighted the growth of the women's game and the eventual champions were central to its promotion. The USA were victorious in 2019, defending their 2015 title and sealing a fourth global crown. They started their tournament with three successive group wins, scoring 18 and conceding none. Their opener was a record breaker, a 13-0 thumping over Thailand, the biggest in World Cup history. Alex Morgan also set a new best, netting five goals in the match. Chile and Sweden followed with 3-0 and 2-0 wins respectively to set up a last-16

267 Tweeted by BBC Sport, 10 June 2019

268 Alana Glass, 'FIFA Women's World Cup Breaks Viewership Records', *Forbes*, 21 October 2019 https://www.forbes.com/sites/ alanaglass/2019/10/21/fifa-womens-world-cup-breaks-viewership-records/#31c926be1884

clash with Spain. Megan Rapinoe secured USA's passage into the quarter-finals; her brace defeated the Spanish 2-1 and earned a chance to put out the hosts in Paris.

Rapinoe, plying her trade for Seattle-based OL Reign, had already made headlines for an outspoken defence of equality and rights for all people.

In 2016, she 'took a knee' during the American national anthem, supporting NFL quarterback Colin Kaepernick who had started the protest against perceived police brutality and mistreatment towards black Americans.[269] Rapinoe had also openly criticised controversial American president Donald Trump.

The co-captain made it public knowledge that she would refuse an offer from Trump to visit the White House should the USA side be victorious. The rejection was notable due to the joyous scenes of the team visiting Barack Obama after their 2015 success (Minute 16).

On 28 June 2019, the USA lined up against France with the pink-haired Rapinoe fresh from Trump's heavy rebuke of her defiance. The 33-year-old kicked things off in style, a free kick from the left edge of the box finding the back of the net after just five minutes. The goal set the USA on their way, but it was the celebration that stole the headlines. Rapinoe, running to the corner flag, and standing proudly with arms wide and aloft, created a picture that would be captured across the globe.

The image of Rapinoe standing tall would 'go down as one of the moments of this World Cup'.[270] However, the activist was not done, and in the 65th minute she wrapped the game up with her second of the night and her fifth of the competition. She had experienced 'a microscope focused on her' in the lead up to the match, facing 'an onslaught of opinions, praise, criticism, love and hate' but Rapinoe had seized

269 *The Guardian*, 5 September 2016
270 *The Telegraph*, 29 June 2019

the game for herself and her country.[271] The USA would beat England in the semi-final, Christen Press and Morgan scoring in the 2-1 win. Morgan, like Rapinoe, would make headlines with her celebration by pretending to drink a cup of tea – the stereotypical English image.

Into the final on 7 July, Rapinoe again netted from the penalty spot before Rose Lavelle made it 2-0 against the Netherlands. USA's women were World Cup winners once more, but Rapinoe and her team-mates had made more than just an impact on the pitch in France.

271 Alicia DelGallo, 'U.S. star Megan Rapinoe: Love, not hate motivated World Cup win over France', *ProSoccerUSA*, 29 June 2019 https://www. prosoccerusa.com/us-soccer/united-states-womens-national-team/u-s-star-megan-rapinoe-love-not-hate-motivated-world-cup-win-over-france/

66

Welsh hearts broken by 17-year-old Pelé (1958)

THE SUMMER of 1958 is recorded in Welsh football history. The only FIFA World Cup that the national team has ever attended is fondly remembered, perhaps more so because of the lack of appearances that have followed it. However, it is not just a competition that the Welsh remember as it also marked a debut on the international stage for one incredibly significant player in the story of the beautiful game – Pelé.

Wales qualified for their first World Cup in a less than straightforward manner. Coming second in their qualifying group, they were only added to the draw after a play-off against Israel. The teams in Israel's group had refused to play them for political reasons but FIFA decreed that they could not qualify without playing a single game. Belgium were the first team drawn for the play-off but also refused the game, so Wales were the next name out of the hat and the FAW decided to play the two-legged tie.

Pre-match, Wales were heavily favoured with the 'slaughter of the innocents' expected but the Israeli side 'surprised' the Welsh.[272] Despite this, Wales won the first leg 2-0 and sealed their place in Sweden with a 2-0 home win a fortnight later.

272 *Western Mail*, 16 January 1958

Wales's squad contained undoubted talent: Terry Medwin (Tottenham Hotspur), Ivor Allchurch, Len Allchurch, Mel Charles (all Swansea Town) and national superstar John Charles (Juventus). They were missing Trevor Ford though, the PSV forward having been banned from selection for the World Cup by the FAW due to admitting in his 1956 autobiography that he accepted illegal payments while at Sunderland.[273] Charles reminisced that Ford 'frightened lesser men' with his style of play that was 'aggressive and full of energy', so his absence certainly hurt the Welsh team.[274]

In Sweden that summer, Wales began with a draw against Hungary, no mean feat considering they were playing 1954's runners-up (Minute 18). Two more draws followed, 1-1 against Mexico and 0-0 with the hosts. This led to Wales needing a play-off against Hungary to decide who would progress from Group Three. On 17 June, two second-half goals, from Medwin and an Ivor Allchurch volley secured their passage to the quarter-finals.

Their opponents in the last eight would be Brazil, who had advanced from their group with two wins and a draw. The Welsh were dealt a blow, however, with the heroic Charles out injured. Many thought this would firmly tip the balance in favour of the Brazilians, and so a resolute Welsh side keeping the score to 0-0 at half-time was 'a position the most profound British follower could not have anticipated'.[275] Wales continued their good defensive showing after the break, but in the 66th minute, 17-year-old Pelé would finally net for the dominant Brazil.

Pelé's shot was hit straight at keeper Jack Kelsey, yet it was powerful enough to cross the line. The goal was just the beginning for Pelé and his first of 12 career World Cup goals. The youngster had shaken off the weight of expectation, later

273 WalesOnline, 'League legend Ford one of finest Wales players', *WalesOnline*, 1 April 2013 https://www.walesonline.co.uk/sport/football/football-news/league-legend-ford-one-finest-2486582

274 John Charles, *King John* (London: Headline Book Publishing, 2003) p.141

275 *Western Mail*, 20 June 1958

saying, 'I had got rid of that tremendous pressure ... I was crying like a baby, babbling, while the rest of the team pummelled me, almost suffocating me.'[276]

Pelé's strike was enough to win the game 1-0 and send Brazil through while Wales headed home. The *Western Mail* described Wales's display as 'such a courageous performance that only a scrambled goal' would give the 'world wonders of football' a place in the semi-final.[277] France were up next and Brazil, in their 'innovative 4-2-4 formation', had an 'inspired hat-trick' from Pelé and the 'mercurial dribbling genius' of Garrincha to thank for the 5-2 thumping.[278]

The World Cup Final on 29 June 1958 was in front of almost 50,000 spectators at Råsunda Stadium as Brazil and hosts Sweden both aimed to lift their first Jules Rimet Trophy. Nils Liedholm opened the scoring for the Swedes but a Vavá brace was added to by two more from Pelé, taking his tally to six in three knockout matches. Mário Zagallo wrapped up the 5-2 victory as Brazil finally had their world crown. Wales were left wondering 'what if?', while Pelé had announced himself to the beautiful game.

276 Clemente A. Lisi, *A History of the World Cup: 1930–2010* (Plymouth: Scarecrow Press, Inc., 2011) p.88

277 *Western Mail*, 20 June 1958

278 Tom Dunmore, *Encyclopedia of the FIFA World Cup* (Maryland: Rowman and Littlefield, 2015) p.18

67

Redemption for Ronaldo (2002)

BRAZILIAN STRIKER Ronaldo came to define football at the turn of the millennium. A 'fearsome combination of power, pace and skill', the forward would rise to prominence in the mid-1990s before winning the Golden Ball at the 1998 World Cup.[279] The tournament is now arguably synonymous with the mixed and mysterious fortunes of Brazil's number nine. Suffering a seizure in the build-up to the final in Paris, a career at the peak of its powers was under severe threat in the years that followed. Following a series of injuries and misfortune, it would come as sweet relief for 'Il Fenomeno' to feature once more in a World Cup Final in 2002.

In 1998, football was at the mercy of Ronaldo. Making the game look easy, it seemed like no defender on Earth could stop the striker. Arriving in France, he was comfortably the competition's star attraction.[280] Described during the tournament as the 'world's greatest player', Ronaldo fired the Seleção into the final following an impressive four goals. This included a memorable strike against the Netherlands in the semi. Before his side would meet hosts France in the showpiece, the media were firmly of the belief that Ronaldo would be the game's determining factor.

279 Tim Barnett, 'A-Z of Players' in Glenn Moore (ed), *The Concise Encyclopedia of World Football* (Bath: Parragon, 1999) p.54

280 Geoff Hurst, *Geoff Hurst's 50 Greatest Footballers of All-Time* (London: Icon, 2016)

Before kick-off, and to everyone's surprise, Ronaldo was a notable absentee from the Brazilian starting XI. Having suffered a convulsion in his hotel room the night before the match, he had been rushed to hospital.[281] The episode had left a number of the Brazilian squad visibly shocked and distressed before the game – their World Cup dreams had appeared to be over. To add to the confusion of the global sports media, a second teamsheet was handed in half an hour before kick-off. This time, Ronaldo's name was included in the line-up.

A shadow of his usual explosive self, Ronaldo failed to impose himself on the event with the French fired up for what they had initially believed to be 'mind games'.[282] A Zinedine Zidane brace and a last-minute strike from Emmanuel Petit secured French victory on home soil and left Ronaldo reflecting on what might have been. Over the next four years Ronaldo's career was dominated by 'conspiracy theories, inquiries and doubts'. A further cruciate ligament injury in 2000, described by his former physiotherapist as the 'worst injury I have ever seen', looked to push Il Fenomeno's once-booming career towards an anticlimactic end.[283]

Despite having not played in Brazil's qualification campaign, Ronaldo managed to regain his fitness and form in time for the 2002 World Cup in Japan and South Korea. Scoring six goals, the Seleção's number nine appeared to be demonstrating the form which had brought him superstar status in the late 1990s. The ghosts of 1998, however, were never far away with 'everyone … reminding me [Ronaldo] of

281 Lisi, Clemente A., *A History of the World Cup: 1930–2010* (Plymouth: Scarecrow Press, Inc., 2011) pp.288–289

282 Didier Deschamps speaking in FIFATV, 'When France ruled the world', FIFA on YouTube, 13 September 2012, Available at: https://www.youtube.com/watch?v=lFeRvBPdssU

283 Nilton Petrone, 'Ronaldo's knee cap exploded, it was by his thigh', *FourFourTwo* https://www.fourfourtwo.com/performance/training/ronaldos-kneecap-exploded-it-was-his-thigh

1998 but I don't know why'.[284] On sport's greatest stage of all, the final against Germany offered him an incredible chance of redemption.

In the 67th minute the goal that Ronaldo – and everyone who had followed his career – craved, duly arrived. A fierce strike from Rivaldo was spilled by the tournament's leading goalkeeper Oliver Kahn into the path of Ronaldo who duly dispatched the ball into the Yokohama net. Brazil's celebrations were euphoric and perfectly captured the outpouring of relief at the sight of their number nine scoring the game's defining goal. Twelve minutes later, Ronaldo scored again. This time a dummy from Rivaldo led the ball into Il Fenomeno's path. A powerful shot to Kahn's left was enough to put the result beyond doubt. Brazil had won and Ronaldo's redemption was confirmed.

Football's history has been littered with redemption stories. They serve as a vital reminder of the power the sport has in changing opinions, altering the status quo and saving the careers of many of its most faithful servants. Whether it be Brazil's 1958 World Cup triumph eight years after the Maracanazo (Minute 79), Paolo Rossi's goalscoring run in 1982 (Minute 68) after his role in an alleged match-fixing scandal or Ronaldo's winner in 2002 – there is far more to football than just the scorelines.

284 *The Guardian*, 29 June 2017

68

Falcão equalises for Brazil
in Barcelona (1982)

WHENEVER THE question of which World Cup was the best appears, the Spanish tournament in 1982 is usually at the forefront of popular opinion. A competition of undeniable entertainment and intriguing stories, it provokes a wealth of nostalgia for all who recall it. Despite Italy going on to win the final 3-1 against West Germany, the 1982 World Cup is now remembered for the exploits of the side they beat in the second group stage – Brazil. Coached by Telê Santana, the Seleção demonstrated some of football's finest ever team play as positive intent outweighed defensive solidity.

An attacking side which lacked a true goalscorer, the Brazilians would rely on a sweeping midfield which was relentlessly focused on getting forward to support. Zico, Léo Júnior and Sócrates were just three of the household names millions around the world were eager to see. More recent Brazilian World Cup sides have featured more pragmatic approaches to the game with many believing the class of '82 to be the last squad to 'live up to the stereotype'. The team was indeed 'grotesquely and excessively talented' and it would take a monumental effort to beat them.[285]

285 Gabriele Marcotti, 'Best teams never to win a World Cup: Brazil 1982, *ESPN*, 09 May 2014
https://www.espn.com/soccer/blog/name/93/post/1845214/headline

Their opponents in the final match of the second group stage were Italy. With both sides beating Argentina in their opening fixture, this was truly a 'winner takes all' battle. The Italians had been unfancied from the tournament's outset. As has been so often the case with Italian World Cup history, off-the-pitch drama had overshadowed their preparations for the competition in Spain. Star striker Paolo Rossi had been embroiled in a betting scandal and few gave the Azzurri a chance of progressing past Brazil.[286]

Against the odds, it was Rossi who opened the scoring in a sweltering Estadi de Sarrià. Arriving late at the back post, his header flew past Waldir Peres and into the net. The Azzurri's lead lasted for just seven minutes as Sócrates danced through the Italian backline and lashed the ball past Dino Zoff. Just 12 minutes into the game and already it was shaping up to be a classic, showcasing the brilliance of the Seleção's attack but also the fragility of its defence.

The lack of focus of defence began to show once more as Italy scored a second before half-time. Latching on to a loose ball, Rossi exploited the lacklustre pass from Toninho Cerezo and thumped the ball into the net from just outside the area. At 2-1 up, Italy were dreaming of progression to the semi-finals. However, this Brazilian side would keep on attacking and in the 68th minute they got their reward through Falcão. Allowed an incredible amount of space on the edge of the Italian penalty box, his left-footed drive flew past Zoff to spark wild celebrations. Lifting his sweaty arms high into the air, it seemed that Italy's number was up.

If the scoreline remained the same, Brazil would progress on goal difference and meet a strong Polish side in the last four. But a final twist in the tale arrived six minutes later and again Rossi was at the centre of the play. A 'great opportunist', he swivelled on to a knockdown and stroked the ball into the net.[287]

286 John Foot, *Calcio: A History of Italian Football* (London: Harper Perennial, 2008) p.206

287 Ibid, p.505

The euphoric celebrations of the Italian number 20 were met with even greater ones after the final whistle blew. Brazil were a side of 'beautiful flair merged with supreme confidence', but a side which had been beaten. Like so many of football's greatest teams the question of 'what might have been' has helped them to become perhaps even more legendary.[288]

The legacy of this match is remarkably strong. John Foot wrote that 'nobody who saw it can forget it'.[289] Rossi's hat-trick has led to him being known in Brazil as 'The Executioner' and his own autobiography was entitled *I Made Brazil Cry*. The name chosen shows that the Italian striker was being modest, with a more accurate heading perhaps being 'I Made the World Cry'. It is not difficult to find articles or comments of writers and pundits in which they admit to shedding a tear as the beautiful Brazilian side crashed out.

Like Hungary in 1954 (Minute 18), the favourites for the World Cup had come crashing down to Earth and ever since that defeat in Barcelona, you could argue that Brazilian football has distanced itself from the 'joga bonito' and samba skills it had become synonymous with. Telê Santana summed up the 1982 World Cup side best as he spoke to his dejected squad after the match, 'We gave it our best shot… the whole world was enchanted by you. Be aware of that.'[290]

288 *Daily Mirror*, 10 June 2014

289 John Foot, *Calcio: A History of Italian Football* (London: Harper Perennial, 2008) p.206

290 Telê Santana in Tim Lewis, '1982: Why Brazil V Italy Was One Of Football's Greatest Ever Matches', *Esquire*, 11 July 2014, https://www.esquire.com/uk/culture/news/a6396/1982-why-brazil-v-italy-was-one-of-footballs-greatest-ever-matches/

69

Benfica's final European triumph before the Curse of Béla Guttmann (1962)

DO YOU believe in curses? Perhaps not, but if you are a Benfica supporter, the 'Curse of Béla Guttmann' is enough to make you wince. In the 69th minute of the 1962 European Cup Final, Eusébio scored his second and Benfica's fifth in the 5-3 rout of Real Madrid. Benfica would lift a second successive European Cup, but to this day the triumph remains their last continental title, as manager Béla Guttmann walked out of the club and placed them under a 'curse' as a parting gift.

Béla Guttmann is one of football's greatest all-time characters. The Hungarian was born into a poor Jewish family where he lived with 'empty pockets and a hungry stomach'.[291] Football would be his saviour though, experiencing a journeyman playing career across the world as a centre-half and then later as a coach before becoming the most successful manager to come from Hungary.

Guttmann was outspoken and colourful throughout his playing days and the stories about him are endless. Following a humiliating 1924 Olympics defeat to Egypt, Guttmann recalled how he and his team-mates were so unhappy with the accommodation arrangements that they nailed rats to the hotel doors of the leadership in protest. Whether true or not,

291 Jonathan Wilson, *The Names Heard Long Ago* (New York: Bold Type Books, 2019) p.57

Guttman never played for Hungary again after this. He would also stand up to Jewish racial slurs, once punching an opponent who had been anti-Semitic, and while playing in America he would own a prohibited drinking bar, a speakeasy, only to lose it all in the 1929 Wall Street Crash.[292]

Guttmann's Jewish roots never escaped him. During World War Two, Hungarian Jews were persecuted by the Nazis and Guttman lost many family members, friends and team-mates in the Holocaust. Guttmann himself spent time in a slave labour camp in 1944 as part of the persecution, and in 1981 he recalled the horrors experienced, 'Was I a footballer from the national team? Was I a successful coach? Was I even a man? Who cared, you had to forget all about it.'[293]

After the war, Guttmann would flourish as a coach, all the while retaining his colourful nature. One occasion, when 4-0 down as manager of Kispest (later called Honvéd), Guttmann is said to have instructed his full-back not to take the field in the second half, despite this leaving his side with ten men. When the player refused, Guttmann took to the stands to read a 'racing paper', taking the tram home and quitting the club.[294] Another story says that he resigned as Honvéd boss a second time in 1957 to avoid a court case in Milan. This was while the club was on a tour of Brazil, and Guttman became São Paulo manager instead.[295]

Guttmann's motto was 'the third season is fatal',[296] and his varied career path certainly proves he lived by this. In 1959, he

---

292 Ibid. All appearing in Wilson's excellent book: nailing rats to hotel doors (pp.74–78), hitting an anti-semitic opponent (p.96), owning a speakeasy (pp.104–105)

293 From an interview with David Bolchover, author of the biography of Béla Guttmann: *The Greatest Comeback: From Genocide To Football Glory*, in *Daily Mirror*, 27 September 2019

294 Jonathan Wilson, *Inverting the Pyramid: The History of Football Tactics* (London: Orion, 2010) pp.97–98

295 Jonathan Wilson, *The Names Heard Long Ago*, pp.359–360

296 David Bolchover, *The Greatest Comeback: From Genocide to Football Glory* (London: Biteback Publishing Ltd., 2018) p.121

would lift the Portuguese league title with Porto, but the next season he would be tempted to join their fierce rivals, Benfica. At Benfica he would lift two more league titles in a row, but more notable would be the European Cup victories.

In 1961, Benfica became the first side who were not Real Madrid to lift the trophy, their 3-2 win against Barcelona in Bern bringing glory to the Lisbon-based side. That summer, following a chance barber shop meeting with a Brazilian coach, Eusébio would be signed. The Mozambique-born striker was set to sign for city rivals Sporting Lisbon, but Guttmann hijacked the deal.[297] Eusébio's impact was immense.

In 1962, Benfica reached the European Cup Final again, this time with the great Real Madrid as opponents. In a breathless match, Hungarian legend Ferenc Puskás would net a hat-trick for Los Blancos but it was all in vain. Guttmann's free-scoring Benfica scored five of their own in Amsterdam with 20-year-old Eusébio scoring a brace, the last goal in the 69th minute in the 5-3 win.

Guttmann demanded a bonus for the triumph, complaining that he had been paid $4,000 less for winning the European Cup than the Portuguese league title. His request was rejected by the club's board and Guttmann walked.[298] As he did so, he remarked, 'In the next 100 years, no Portuguese team will win two European titles, and Benfica will never be champions of Europe again without me.'[299] While Porto have seen European victories, Benfica to this day remain unable to shake off the 'curse'. Even with Eusébio praying for the curse to be lifted at the Vienna grave of Guttmann,[300] Benfica have now lost in eight European finals since – will the curse continue until 2062?

297 Jonathan Wilson, *Inverting the Pyramid: The History of Football Tactics*, p.99

298 Ibid, p.100

299 Gary Thacker, 'Benfica and the Curse of Béla Guttmann', *These Football Times*, 29 June 2015
https://thesefootballtimes.co/2015/06/29/benfica-and-the-curse-of-bela-guttmann/

300 *The Independent*, 15 May 2014

With two European Cups, six league titles, two domestic cups and a Mitropa Cup, Guttmann was certainly successful. Guttmann's 4-2-4 formation and Hungarian style as São Paulo boss so influenced the Brazilian game, that it 'provided the tactical basis' of the 1958 World Cup victory (Minute 66).[301] His impact on the beautiful game was wider than trophies, though; he brought tactical developments, new ideas about diet and fitness regimes, a firm approach to man management and cleverly used the media to his advantage.[302] Guttmann was everything we see in a modern manager – he was just decades ahead of the rest.

301 Colin Shindler in Rob Steen, Jed Novick and Huw Richards (eds), *The Cambridge Companion to Football* (New York: Cambridge University Press, 2013) p.149

302 *Daily Mirror*, 27 September 2019

70

Sammy Thomson completes English football's first double (1889)

THE FOOTBALL Association was founded in 1863 as the governing body seeking to organise football across the nation. Following this, the first FA Cup was held in 1871/72 as Morton Betts scored the winner for Wanderers (Minute 15). In 1883, Blackburn Olympic won the annual tournament, becoming football's first professional club to do so (Minute 107). By April 1888, it was decided that the Football League would be founded ready for the next season. Twelve teams would compete, with Aston Villa's William McGregor elected chairman.[303] Less than a year later, Sammy Thomson's 70th-minute strike put the icing on the cake of an invincible, double-winning year for Preston North End.

The Football League's debut campaign ran from September 1888 until February 1889, with sides playing each other home and away. On Saturday, 8 September 1888, the first round of fixtures kicked off. Preston North End hosted fellow Lancastrians Burnley in front of 5,000 supporters and saw off the visitors 5-2, courtesy of a goal from Jack Gordon, two from Jimmy Ross and two more from Fred Dewhurst.[304] The next week, they travelled down to Wolverhampton Wanderers and

303 *Blackburn Standard*, 21 April 1888

304 *Sheffield Independent*, 10 September 1888

claimed a comfortable 4-0 win that saw them top the fledgling league, a position they would not give up all season.

Preston would march through the rest of 1888/89 in style. They were described by contemporary media as 'the most perfect, most consistent team in the history of the game'.[305] The combination of 18 league wins with just four draws and significantly no losses guided them to a first official league title. Five goals would be struck five times, while the Lilywhites hit seven against Stoke and Notts County. John Goodall's 21 goals in 21 matches was enough for a first Golden Boot.

Preston had shown their quality in the season before the Football League had begun. In that campaign, they won 59 of their 70 matches, only losing seven.[306] One of those losses was the 1888 FA Cup Final to West Bromwich Albion (2-1). In 1889, they had a chance to right that wrong, as they reached the final to play Wolves. North End had waltzed through the earlier rounds of the competition without conceding a goal.

Bootle were swept aside 3-0 in the first round, with Grimsby Town beaten 2-0 away from home. Birmingham St George's were seen off in the quarter-finals, earning them a semi-final clash to repeat 1888's final – West Bromwich Albion at Sheffield's Bramall Lane. The March rematch was hotly anticipated, the *Preston Herald* reporting how fans were '40 or 50' deep in places, with the 'upper windows and even the roofs of the houses overlooking the ground' packed with onlookers. The crowd was so vast that a 'request for hats off' was called for in one corner of the stadium, presenting a 'curious effect and remarkable contrast' to the usual attire of football supporters at the time.[307]

305 Bryon Butler, *The Football League: The First 100 Years* (Guildford: Colour Library Books Ltd., 1988) p.12

306 Jack Portley, 'Why Preston North End are football's greatest invincibles', *These Football Times*, 23 November 2016 https://thesefootballtimes. co/2016/11/23/why-preston-north-end-are-footballs-greatest-invincibles/

307 *Preston Herald*, 20 March 1889

Preston dominated the game, with Thomson having a goal ruled out for offside, but just a single strike from Dave Russell separated the teams – Preston would return to the final for a second consecutive year. On 30 March 1889, at the Kennington Oval, the double was secured by the Lilywhites. Dewhurst, Ross and finally Thomson in the 70th minute would mark the 3-0 victory and write Preston's Invincibles into the history books.[308] Football's first unbeaten season, in the first Football League campaign.

308 Bryon Butler, *The Illustrated History of the FA Cup* (London: Headline Book Publishing, 1996) pp.53–55

71

Lars Ricken lobs Dortmund to the Champions League (1997)

FOLLOWING THE birth of the Champions League in 1992, the competition underwent a number of different formats in its opening five seasons. Starting with an initial set of knockout rounds and the introduction of a league coming later (Minute 17), the tournament gradually adapted to suit its growing list of competitors. In the 1996/97 season, a 16-team group stage opened the competition before the knockout rounds were introduced to the final eight teams. Among that group was German side Borussia Dortmund.

Today, Dortmund are regulars in arguably football's finest club competition, but in 1996 they were relatively unfancied on the continent. Domestically, they had performed well in the mid-1990s, winning their first Bundesliga for 32 years in 1995. The following season they entered the Champions League again, hoping to fare better than their quarter-final exit in 1995/96. Manager Ottmar Hitzfeld had created a decent side with a strong spine featuring the likes of Paul Lambert, Karl-Heinz Riedle and European Footballer of the Year Matthias Sammer.

A solid European campaign led to Dortmund reaching the Champions League Final in 1997. Despite their strength they were 'widely considered to have little chance' against their opponents, Juventus. Following his side's heavy semi-final defeat at the hands of the Old Lady, Ajax defender Frank de Boer had described the Italian giants as 'a team from another planet' who surely couldn't fail.[309] Dortmund's side, although full of talent, was ageing and would be unlikely to match the speed and guile of the youthful Juventus.

'That Juventus team with Zidane, Deschamps, Bokšić and Co., they were a fantastic team at that time. They were almost unbeatable,' midfielder Lars Ricken later said.[310]

Despite the odds being stacked against them, Dortmund went in at half-time two goals to the good. Riedle had scored a brace to put his side firmly in the driving seat. Young forward Alessandro Del Piero pulled a goal back for the Italians after half-time and the game looked set to be heading to a dramatic climax. Withstanding sustained Juve pressure, in the 70th minute, Hitzfeld sent on 20-year-old Ricken to see out the game. Just 16 seconds after entering the field of play as the minute ticked over into the 71st, a through ball set Ricken clear on goal. Spotting keeper Angelo Peruzzi off his line, Ricken sent a sumptuous lob from 25 yards over the Juventus captain and into the net.

Dortmund had done it. A 3-1 victory was secured, and the Champions League returned to Germany after a 14-year absence. The win had upset the odds and proved that, in football, nothing is ever certain. Even in the face of Juventus's territorial domination and superior creativity, the tactical nous of Hitzfeld and the discipline of the team had provided Ricken with a chance to lob his side into the history books.

Defeat would also secure Juventus's place as the competition's nearly men. Juve would also lose the following season's final to Real Madrid before losing three more in 2003, 2015 and 2017.

309 Alan Tomlinson, *Sport and Leisure Cultures* (London: University of Minnesota, 2005) pp.29–30

310 Lars Ricken from Bundesliga website, 'THAT Lars Ricken chip for Borussia Dortmund in the 1997 UEFA Champions League final 20 years on', *Bundesliga*, 2017 https://www.bundesliga.com/en/news/Bundesliga/ lars-ricken-borussia-dortmund-chip-goal-juventus-champions-league-1997-454861.jsp

72

Luís Figo welcomed back to the Camp Nou with a pig's head (2002)

LUÍS FIGO is one of Portugal and La Liga's all-time greats. With 127 caps for his country, eight league titles, four domestic cups, five domestic super cups, a Champions League, two UEFA Super Cups and a Ballon d'Or, Figo can rightly look back proudly on an incredible career. Although full of remarkable achievements, his playing days cannot be reflected upon without mention of an infamous moment at the Camp Nou. Returning to the club for the second time since his departure to bitter rivals Real Madrid, a pig's head was launched at him from the partisan crowd.

Figo was a product of the Sporting CP academy in his native Portugal. Originally a winger, he would become a vital cog in the Sporting squad in the early 1990s. Showing real talent and promise, Barcelona would part with just £2.2m to bring him to Catalonia in 1995 to replace the departing Michael Laudrup. Figo found a home at the Camp Nou and league titles would be won in 1997/98 and 1998/99 and joined by two Copa del Reys.

Figo was adored by the fans, accepted and loved like he had been born and brought up in Barcelona. He had emulated the legendary Johan Cruyff in winning the city and although he 'may not have been born of Catalonia, he was deemed to be of Catalonia'.[311] Perhaps this is what made his treachery and

311   Steven Scragg, 'Building and destroying a legacy: Luís Figo at Barcelona', *These Football Times*, 14 September 2018 https://thesefootballtimes. co/2018/09/14/building-and-destroying-a-legacy-luis-figo-at-barcelona/

betrayal so great in 2000. Following an impressive Euro 2000 tournament, Figo would accept an offer to switch to Barcelona's greatest rivals – Real Madrid. The £37.4m deal made him the world's most expensive player,[312] but significantly it hurt Barcelona's fans in a seemingly unforgivable manner.

The new and extravagant Real Madrid president, Florentino Pérez, had made it a campaign promise to bring Figo to the Santiago Bernabéu. He had even promised to pay the annual subscription fee for each of Real's 70,000-plus registered members if he failed in his pledge to get his prized target.[313] Figo and Barcelona were always destined to meet again when the El Clásico clubs played each other.

His first opportunity to return was in October 2000, when Los Blancos' team coach was pounded with glass bottles, stones and other projectiles. Figo reminisced that he felt 'as if in the skin of a murderer' for the reaction he received. Barça would win 2-0 with Figo 'humbled' and removed from corner duty to prevent angry exchanges with supporters.[314] Real wrapped up the title that season and Figo was presented with the 2000 Ballon d'Or, a personal accolade that proved the importance of the midfielder.

Figo was absent for Real's Camp Nou fixture the next season but in November 2002 the infamous match would come. The Galácticos were missing stars Zinedine Zidane and Ronaldo, hurting the Madrid side in a game that would end 0-0. Despite this, the 72nd minute was the one that would go down in El Clásico history. Figo had decided he would take corners in this game, but each time he did so missiles would rain down upon him. In the 72nd minute, among the rubble, a suckling pig's head – a cochinillo – was one of the objects thrown.

The disturbance was so profound that referee Luis Medina Cantalejo had to delay the game for 12 minutes to try and

---

312 *The Telegraph*, 25 July 2000
313 *The Independent*, 25 July 2000
314 Patrick Surlis, 'El Clásico moments: Luis Figo's return to the Nou Camp and the pig's head', *Sky Sports*, 21 November 2015 https://www.skysports.com/football/news/11828/10070994/el-clasico-moments-figos-pig-head

regain calm. Barcelona boss Louis van Gaal would blame Figo for 'provoking the fans', while Spanish newspapers *Marca* and *AS* would label it the 'derby of shame' and 'Bronx Nou' respectively.[315] Barcelona were initially told to play two games behind closed doors, but this was reduced to a €4,000 fine. The cochinillo would be a lasting image that was beamed across the globe from this memorable El Clásico.

315 Ibid

73

Bert Trautmann breaks his neck (1956)

ONLY 11 years after the dramatic climax to World War Two, football and the United Kingdom were returning to prosperity. Social reforms and changes in the game's infrastructure meant eyes were beginning to open to a new world. However, for Manchester City goalkeeper Bert Trautmann, post-war reconstruction provided something far more personal.

A German paratrooper on both the Eastern and Western fronts during the war, Trautmann had been captured by the British and sent to a POW camp in Lancashire.

Upon his release in 1948, Trautmann refused repatriation and instead stayed in England, working on a farm and playing in goals for local side St Helens. In a decision met with anger and animosity from a large number of supporters, his impressive performances earned him a move to First Division Manchester City in 1949. World War Two had left a gaping wound in society and hostility towards Germans was rife. Cries of 'war criminal' and 'Nazi' were heard among supporters upon Trautmann's transfer to the club.[316] The decision to sign him was met with a widespread boycott from Jewish supporters, with German war crimes still fresh in their memory.[317]

By 1956, opinions had generally changed. Trautmann's service to the club demonstrated commitment and consistency

---

316 Catrine Clay, *Trautmann's Journey: From Hitler Youth to FA Cup Legend* (London: Yellow Jersey, 2011) p.274

317 *Yorkshire Post and Leeds Intelligencer*, 8 October 1949

before all else and his dedication to supporters was warmly received by his earlier critics. The change in general perceptions towards the City goalkeeper was seen no clearer than by his receipt of the Football Writers' Player of the Year prize days before the 1956 FA Cup Final. Meeting Manchester City in the final were Midlands club Birmingham City. Such was his acclaim, for the *Birmingham Daily Gazette*, Trautmann was 'the only real barrier between the Blues and victory'.[318]

Manchester City scored early through Joe Hayes before a 15th-minute equaliser from Welsh international Noel Kinsey. Despite the setback, the Citizens struck twice after the break to lead 3-1. Even though there were four excellent goals, the game's defining moment came in the 73rd minute after Trautmann collided with Birmingham's Peter Murphy. The impact left the goalkeeper in need of urgent medical attention. Despite the trainer's best intentions, Trautmann insisted on playing on and made two further saves as the Citizens won the FA Cup for the third time. As the final whistle blew, the Manchester City number one's bravery was noted by all four sides of Wembley, earning him the respect of the nation.

Under the subheading 'Hefty Clout', the *Daily Herald* reported how Trautmann was holding his 'stiff neck' when receiving his medal.[319] Trautmann's performance and bravery was widely covered by the British media. It was reported that the City keeper 'staggered around his goalmouth in obvious pain'.[320] It was later discovered that Trautmann had in fact broken his neck following the clash with Murphy.

Unfortunately, the injury sustained would lead to a lengthy time out of the game until his return on Christmas Day 1956. For some, his performances would never truly recover, but his legacy as a true Manchester City great was secure. His will to win and undoubted dedication brought previous post-war

318 *Birmingham Daily Gazette*, 5 May 1956
319 *Daily Herald*, 7 May 1956
320 *Birmingham Daily Gazette*, 7 May 1956

perceptions of Germans into question and helped create a more tolerant society. Furthermore, his injury helped to alter the impression of goalkeeper safety. The protection of goalkeepers would become one of the game's next major initiatives.[321]

321 Jonathan Wilson, *The Outsider: A History of the Goalkeeper* (London: Orion, 2012)

74

Hughie Ferguson wins the FA Cup for Cardiff City (1927)

DESPITE BEING founded in 1871 (Minute 15), the FA Cup has only seen one club from outside of England win the trophy. In 1927, Cardiff City made history at Wembley as the Welsh team beat Arsenal 1-0 with Hughie Ferguson scoring the winner in the 74th minute. There is more to this story though, involving the birth of the cup final radio broadcast, a war veteran, a lucky cat and Arsenal's Welshman who blamed his slippery shirt.

The 1920s was arguably Cardiff City's greatest decade. Promoted to the First Division in 1921, they would come second in the league in 1924, narrowly missing out to Herbert Chapman's Huddersfield Town on goal average. Meanwhile, their cup form was also impressive, and two quarter-finals and a semi-final was added to by a 1925 Wembley appearance to face Sheffield United in the final. United were successful, a 1-0 win denying Cardiff's proudest day.

On 23 April 1927, the Bluebirds earned another attempt to lift a maiden FA Cup crown as they faced a well-fancied Arsenal outfit. Cardiff would this time be victorious as Ferguson's shot inexplicably found the back of the net. The forward's attempt should've been 'comfortably' saved by Welsh international goalkeeper Dan Lewis, but it instead slipped through his arms, below his chest and rolled towards the line.[322] Lewis's last-ditch

---

322 Bryon Butler, *The Illustrated History of the FA Cup* (London: Headline Book Publishing, 1996) pp.122–125

scramble was in vain as his elbow knocked it over the line and the game was Cardiff's.

Cardiff's 'chain-smoking', 'hard-tackling' captain Fred Keenor would lift the cup,[323] a moment immortalised by a statue outside the Bluebirds' current home, Cardiff City Stadium. The First World War veteran had fought at the brutal Battle of the Somme and was a local fan favourite, seen as 'an old-fashioned working man' who was 'committed to the community',[324] so it was right he would raise the trophy.

On the losing side, the inquest would begin and end with Lewis. Some speculated he had 'thrown' the fixture, but the disgust with himself was clear; he had reportedly flung his loser's medal into the crowd after receiving it from King George V. Lewis blamed the 'sheen' on his new jersey for allowing the ball to slip from his grip, and this started an Arsenal tradition of never letting a goalkeeper play in a final with a new kit.[325] Slippery shirt or not, in south Wales they would 'proudly treasure' winning 'the greatest event in the soccer world'.[326]

Perhaps it was meant to be that in 1927, media-savvy Arsenal manager Herbert Chapman was involved in the first live radio broadcast of an FA Cup Final. He saw football as a 'media event' and agreed with BBC director-general Lord Reith about the importance of broadcasting matches of national significance. The hymn 'Abide with Me' would be sung for the first time at Wembley to further promote the 'Christian' values of the day, a tradition that remains in cup finals today. The radio transmission was a hit, and the number of UK radio licences rose from two million in 1926, to eight million by 1939.[327] This

---

323 Ibid

324 Martin Johnes, 'Fred Keenor: A Welsh Soccer Hero', *The Sports Historian,* Vol. 17, Issue 1 (May 1998), pp.105–119

325 *The Telegraph*, 11 May 2008

326 *Western Mail*, 25 April 1927

327 Richard Holt, *Sport and the British: A Modern History* (Oxford: Oxford University, 1989) pp.310–312

game was a vital step to the all-encompassing modern sports broadcasting we currently enjoy.

A final tale from April 1927 was match-winner Ferguson crediting an unusual source for his goal – an adopted black cat named Trixie. Cardiff were the clear underdogs (or undercats) in 1927, but manager Fred Stewart took a relaxed approach to the build-up. Taking the team to Royal Birkdale golf course as a pre-game social, they befriended a small black cat while playing. Ferguson took a liking to the moggie, taking it home to south Wales with him. The cat became an unofficial squad mascot and even travelled to Wembley for the game, Ferguson describing Trixie as a 'lucky charm'.[328] So a lucky cat, a slippery shirt and a historic radio broadcast – 1927 is more than just Cardiff's finest hour.

328 Scott Murray and Rowan Walker, *Day of the Match: A History of Football in 365 Days* (London: Boxtree, 2008) p.118

75

José Mourinho self-proclaimed Special One after Champions League victory (2004)

JOSÉ MOURINHO is a manager who has not left the headlines since breaking on to the global scene in 2004. Some 17 years after Portugal's FC Porto had first lifted the European Cup in 1987, they had a chance to add a second crown as they faced AS Monaco on 26 May 2004. In the 75th minute, Russian midfielder Dmitri Alenichev scored his side's third and final goal to wrap up the Champion League victory and give Mourinho his prize.

Mourinho had a fairly insignificant career as a footballer, but as is often the case with many of sport's greatest bosses, the best coaches were not the most talented players. Mourinho took up the role of Bobby Robson's translator at Barcelona after his playing days finished, but his eyes were always on the top job. Following an assistant manager spot at Benfica he would then take over as 'Mister' before moving to União de Leiria, also in Portugal. In 2002, Porto would come calling and success would follow – back-to-back Primeira Liga titles and a 2003 UEFA Cup.

May 2004 would be a major rung on Mourinho's fledgling managerial ladder – a Champions League title. Beating Manchester United, Lyon and Deportivo La Coruña in knockout games en route to the final in Germany, Porto fancied themselves to take victory. In the first half, Carlos Alberto gave the Dragões the lead, Alenichev assisting Deco for the second goal after the break. In the 75th minute, Alenichev would finish the game by making it 3-0, wrapping up an impressive showing. In the aftermath, however, Mourinho, never one to mince words, declared, 'I would like to leave Porto,' as Chelsea circled.[329]

Chelsea appointed Mourinho on 2 June 2004, barely a week after the Champions League Final. In his opening press conference, Mourinho would confidently proclaim the now famous words, 'I think I am a special one.'[330] Ambitious new Chelsea owner Roman Abramovich approved of the bravado as José continued, 'We have top players and, sorry if I'm arrogant, but we now have a top manager.'[331] Mourinho had instantly made himself something of a hero to Chelsea fans but a foe to the rest of the Premier League.

Mourinho's impact was instantaneous. Backed by the wealth of Abramovich, Chelsea secured the Premier League and League Cup in his debut campaign in English football. Sir Alex Ferguson recalls his frustration at the Mourinho effect, 'I didn't win a game at Stamford Bridge after Mourinho arrived.'[332] Yet, despite Chelsea going unbeaten at home for 60 consecutive Premier League games under his management,, Mourinho and Abramovich fell out in September 2007. Mourinho would 'astonishingly'[333] depart the club and join Inter Milan for the beginning of the next season.

José Mourinho's trophy-laden career has spanned four countries, managing some of the biggest clubs in the history of the beautiful game. When he eventually chooses to retire, the Special One will have left much more of an imprint on the sport than just a famous quote.

329 *The Guardian*, 27 May 2004

330 BBC, 'Chelsea appoint Mourinho', *BBC Sport*, 2 June 2004 http://news.bbc.co.uk/sport1/hi/football/teams/c/chelsea/3765263.stm

331 Ibid

332 Alex Ferguson, *My Autobiography* (London: Hodder and Stoughton, 2013) p.164

333 *The Guardian*, 20 September 2007

76

Wolves equalise before becoming 'champions of the world' (1954)

THE INTRODUCTION of floodlights in football surprisingly dates back to the late 19th century. Their use, however, was incredibly infrequent with the Football League apprehensive to utilise them and even banning them in the 1930s. It can be argued that the reasons were primarily based on financial ramifications and even class repression. By extending the sporting day into the evening, an increase in leisure time would have to be granted and players' pay would once more be brought into conversation.[334]

In spite of a two-decade ban on floodlit league fixtures, 1953/54 First Division champions Wolverhampton Wanderers would host a series of floodlit friendlies against the best sides world football had to offer. Under the lights at Molineux, Tel Aviv were humbled 10-0, Spartak Moscow were 'hammered and sickled' 4-0 and a host of other clubs were beaten by the team captained by Billy Wright.[335] All of these were of course impressive victories, but Wolves were yet to be truly tested. Step forward Hungarian giants Budapest Honvéd.

Honvéd were revered throughout Europe and featured a number of the Hungarian national team, the Magical Magyars.

334 Rob Steen, *Floodlights and Touchlines: A History of Spectator Sport* (London: Bloomsbury, 2014)
335 Nick Miller, *The Guardian*, 13 December 2014

In the past year, the national side had twice battered England, including the famous 6-3 Match of the Century at Wembley (Minute 1). Before the match, national newspapers had predicted a close game between the finest side in Europe and the best team in England. Upon their arrival, the Honvéd team were treated like celebrities. Key players Ferenc Puskás, Sándor Kocsis and Zoltán Czibor were by now household names and the presence of young autograph hunters signified Honvéd's popularity.[336]

Despite being from the other side of the Iron Curtain, media reports highlight a sense of awe and admiration for the Hungarians. Words of encouragement and support were given at a banquet dinner from Wolves chairman J.S. Baker. Baker remarked that if Honvéd were to win, then he would be the first to congratulate them.[337] Within 14 minutes, Wolves found themselves 2-0 down as Kocsis and Ferenc Machos had scored to put Honvéd firmly in the driving seat. In spite of the 'heavy pitch', they had managed to control the game.

The pitch would begin to disrupt Honvéd in the second half. The *Yorkshire Post and Leeds Intelligencer* reported that the intricate passing game of Puskás and co. was hampered by the ball being 'stuck in the mud'.[338] Johnny Hancocks pulled a goal back for Wolves four minutes into the second half before Roy Swinbourne equalised with a fine header in the 76th minute. The goal had sent the Wolverhampton fans wild. Not only had they drawn level, they were pushing for a winner. Two minutes later, Swinbourne scored again with a 'perfectly placed shot'.[339]

'WOLVES. CLUB CHAMPIONS OF THE WORLD' was the headline found in the *Birmingham Gazette* the next day. For the English media, winning in the quagmire of Molineux did nothing but confirm Wolves as the world's greatest club. Winning in all weathers was ample proof that *this* was the best

336 *Birmingham Daily Post*, 13 December 1954
337 *Birmingham Daily Gazette*, 13 December 1954
338 *Yorkshire Post and Leeds Intelligencer*, 14 December 1954
339 Ibid

team the globe had to offer and Budapest Honvéd was merely a 'fair-weather' side. The embarrassment of Wembley a year earlier was beginning to be expunged and Wolves were regarded as 'heroes, everyone'.[340]

Such British arrogance would lead to European media calling for a continental trophy to decide who really was the best. Just half a year later, at the start of the 1955/56 season, the first edition of the European Cup began (Minute 14). The success of the friendlies and the promotion of the English game to the wider continent had proven floodlights to be worth their weight in gold. By 1956, the Football League had ratified their use, eventually leading to some of the game's finest future moments.

340 *Birmingham Daily Gazette*, 14 December 1954

77

Jürgen Sparwasser's winner as East meets West (1974)

THE 1974 FIFA World Cup is one fondly remembered by all Germans. West Germany would host the competition and lift a second world title, while East Germany, drawn in the same group as their Cold War neighbours, would pull off an historic, unique victory as in the 77th minute of the two sides' meeting, East Germany's Jürgen Sparwasser netted an unexpected winner at Hamburg's Volksparkstadion.

Following the end of World War Two in 1945, Germany was split into four areas by the Allied powers: Britain, USA, France and the Soviet Union. By June 1948, relations between the countries had 'broken down irretrievably', and eventually the Soviet zone became the German Democratic Republic (GDR), while the other three founded the Federal Republic of Germany (FRG).[341] The divide became greater and more strained until a solid concrete wall was built to separate the former capital, Berlin. The Berlin Wall represented far more than a physical barrier; it represented communism versus capitalism, East (GDR) versus West (FRG).

The West Germans were one of the pre-tournament favourites in 1974. Their squad contained the likes of Paul Breitner, Gerd Müller and their captain, 'Der Kaiser', Franz

---

341 Hester Vaizey, *Born in the GDR: Living in the Shadow of the Wall* (Oxford: Oxford University Press, 2014) pp.1–5

Beckenbauer. They would be led by a man named Helmut Schön, the East German-born manager who had played in the East before escaping in 1950 to further his coaching career and find a better life.[342] East Germany, meanwhile, were appearing in their first (and only) World Cup tournament.

FRG won both their opening matches, 1-0 over Chile and 3-0 against Australia, with GDR winning 2-0 against Australia and drawing 1-1 with Chile. By the time they met on 22 June 1974, both teams had already qualified for the next round, but the battle was worth far more than a dead rubber. The build-up was intense as 3,000 East Germans were allowed to cross the Berlin Wall under guard to watch the fixture, and players were banned from swapping shirts on the pitch.[343]

For GDR this was finally a chance to test themselves against the West, something they had previously been denied. Striker Hans-Jürgen Kreische remembered how the team were relishing the opportunity to compare their abilities against their rivals, saying, 'It was something we repeatedly strived for, but the authorities always prevented.'[344] The first half of the big match was a 0-0 deadlock, but in the 77th minute, history was made by Sparwasser, who connected with a bouncing ball to score the only goal in the 1-0 victory.

The defeat undoubtedly had a big impact on the morale of the West German squad, notably manager Schön. Schön, who had fled East Germany, was 'never the same coach again', nearly 'cracking up' at the stunning result.[345] Beckenbauer also launched a 'scathing attack' on his team-mates post-match.[346] Despite this, West Germany would recover from the shock and

342 *The Independent*, 24 February 1996

343 Clemente A. Lisi, *A History of the World Cup* (Plymouth: Scarecrow Press Inc., 2011) p.132

344 Mani Djazmi, 'World Cup whisky and the Cold War: When East and West Germany met', BBC, 7 March 2019 https://www.bbc.co.uk/sport/football/47456049

345 Ulrich Hesse, *Tor!: The Story of German Football* (London: WSC Books Ltd., 2003) p.193

346 *Reading Evening Post*, 26 June 1974

go on to lift the World Cup by beating the Netherlands in the final (Minute 43).

East Germany refused to play West Germany after this, and they never met again in competitive action. This meant that when the country was reunified in 1990, the only time the fixture took place was a GDR win. East Germany were nicknamed 'Freundschaftsspielweltmeister' ('world champions of friendlies'), due to the tendency of communist nations to play 'friendly' matches against like-minded states, and their proficiency in these games.[347] West Germany may have had the better record on the international stage, but East Germany had the noteworthy one-off victory that mattered.

347 Markus Hesselmann and Robert Ide, in Alan Tomlinson and
     Christopher Young (eds.), *German Football: History, Culture, Society*
     (Abingdon: Routledge, 2006) p.44

78

Handball! But was it a Welsh or a Scottish hand? (1977)

ON 12 October 1977, Wales hosted Scotland at Anfield with the Scottish requiring a win to qualify for the 1978 World Cup in Argentina. Wales, meanwhile, needed a victory to keep their hopes of qualifying alive, but in the 78th minute a contentious handball decision would lead to a penalty that put the Scots ahead in the vital match.

Scotland had already enjoyed a successful 1977, winning the annual British Home Championship with a huge win over the English at Wembley. A 0-0 draw with Wales was followed by a 3-0 thumping of Northern Ireland, meaning a win for England or Scotland on 4 June would see them lift the crown as the best home nation. Goals from Gordon McQueen and Kenny Dalglish were enough to secure the title with a 2-1 victory, beating the Auld Enemy at Wembley making it even sweeter.

The day was marred by violence, however, as 289 fans were arrested in a tie that would be seen as a 'tribal occasion rather than a sporting fixture'.[348] After the final whistle, a mass pitch invasion saw 'louts' dig up the Wembley field and destroy the goalposts in now-famous images. FA secretary Ted Croker described the scenes as 'the worst I have ever seen', with damage amounting to an estimated £15,000. Scotland Yard would

348 *Newcastle Journal*, 6 June 1977

acknowledge that the majority of the fans were 'boisterous but peaceable', but fears of further violence would hang over the key World Cup qualifier.[349]

Wales were unable to host the clash at Cardiff's Ninian Park due to their own crowd disorder at a game versus Yugoslavia the previous year. With Wrexham's Racecourse Ground limited to just 11,000 spectators, the Welsh FA made the decision to switch the match to Liverpool's Anfield. The controversial call saw many believe the FAW were pursuing a cash earner at a risk, a view shared by goalkeeper Dai Davies, who recalled that the squad felt they'd 'lost home advantage'.[350]

Over 50,000 tickets were sold, the majority to Scottish supporters. Scotland's forward Joe Jordan would remember Anfield being like a 'mini Hampden that night' with a raucous Tartan Army dreaming of a 1978 World Cup spot.[351] The game was an open affair, with both Scotland and Wales having opportunities to take the lead. In the 78th minute though, this game would hit the headlines.

Scotland's Asa Hartford delivered a long throw into the Welsh box, with Jordan and Wales's David Jones challenging for the header. The ball appeared to clearly strike a hand, but which player? French referee Robert Wurtz seemed certain it was Jones's and pointed to the penalty spot. The Welsh were immediately incensed and claimed it was in fact Jordan who had handled the ball.

Don Masson stepped up to coolly slot home the spot kick and make it 1-0, a goal that was added to by Dalglish in the 85th minute.

Post-match, the controversy was far from over, the *Daily Mirror* labelling it a 'mystery' as Jordan denied he had made any illegal contact with the ball. Wales manager Mike Smith was

349 *Daily Mirror*, 6 June 1977

350 *Daily Record*, 11 October 2012

351 *The Telegraph*, 11 October 2012

likewise firm that 'none of my players handled it'.[352] Television replays confirmed that it was Jordan who had used his arm and Wales had been wronged.

Scottish forward Andy Gray, who missed the game, highlighted the importance of the decision in the coming days, 'If we had not got that penalty then I don't think we would have scored at all. It was that sort of game.'[353] The Welsh squad would rue the call for years to come. 'Two years of hard work had been wasted because of one mistake by a referee,'[354] remarked Davies in 2002.

Scotland's 1978 World Cup would not go as hoped, a 3-1 loss to Peru and a 1-1 draw with Iran meaning their final 3-2 victory over the Netherlands counted for little. They would be sent home after just three matches. For Wales, the day would add to their long wait for another World Cup opportunity, a run that extended back to 1958 (Minute 66).

352 *Daily Mirror*, 13 October 1977

353 *Sports Argus*, 15 October 1977

354 'Jordan's handiwork 25 years on', BBC Sport, 12 October 2002 http:// news.bbc.co.uk/sport1/hi/wales/2322845.stm

79

Alcides Ghiggia scores the winner
in Maracanazo (1950)

GREAT NATIONS are not just remembered for their finest victories, they are also shaped by their most harrowing defeats. Maracanazo (Agony of Maracanã), on 16 July 1950, is a day that is etched throughout Brazilian footballing history and continues to haunt the country to this day.

As nations sought to get back on their feet after the horrors of World War Two, Brazil was chosen to host the 1950 World Cup. Sport was to play an important role in post-war reconstruction and the Jules Rimet Trophy was uncovered from its wartime hiding place, a shoebox under the bed of FIFA vice-president Ottorino Barassi, ready to be awarded to the successful country.[355] Alongside the hosts, although just 12 of the other 15 qualified teams would arrive in South America in 1950, the opportunity to compete on a global scale once more was warmly anticipated.

This tournament was uniquely split into two separate group stages with no knockout ties, meaning the country topping the second group would lift the trophy. Brazil marched through their initial group 4-0 v Mexico, 2-2 v Switzerland and 2-0 v Yugoslavia, qualifying for the second stage along with Uruguay, Sweden and Spain. England, meanwhile, had been humiliatingly

---

355 Clemente A. Lisi, *A History of the World Cup,* (Plymouth: Scarecrow Press, Inc., 2011) p.44

dumped out of their debut World Cup after a loss to the USA in the Miracle on Grass (Minute 38), followed by a defeat to Spain.

In the second group stage, Brazil decimated Sweden 7-1, before destroying the Spanish 6-1 just four days later. With Uruguay having drawn against Spain and narrowly beating Sweden, the World Cup would be decided in the final match of the competition, Brazil v Uruguay on 16 July. A draw would hand the cup to the hosts, while Uruguay needed an unlikely win to seize the glory.

Brazil had netted 23 goals in five games, 13 in their previous two and in their 1949 Copa América victory, they had scored a staggering 46 in eight matches. Perhaps understandably Brazilian confidence was so high that the day before the game *Gazeta Esportiva* declared, 'Tomorrow we will beat Uruguay.'[356] Another newspaper, *O Mundo*, even published the headline 'Here Are The World Champions' with a picture of the Brazil squad filling the page.[357]

The bravado infuriated the Uruguayan team and inspired a famous moment. Captain Obdulio Varela took 20 copies of *O Mundo*, scattered them across the toilet floor of the Paysandú Hotel, and instructed his team-mates to 'trample and urinate' upon them.[358] Uruguay were not about to roll over and let Brazil waltz to the title. They were unbeaten in their own World Cup history having won the 1930 competition (Minute 19) and been absent in 1934 and 1938, so they planned to stay undefeated.

The match would be watched by an official 'paid' attendance of 173,850, but upper estimates suggest that almost 200,000 fans packed the Maracanã.[359] After a goalless first half, Brazil took the lead in the 47th minute before Juan Alberto Schiaffino

356 Alex Bellos, *Futebol: The Brazilian Way of Life,* (London: Bloomsbury, 2002), p.49

357 FIFA website, 'The Maracanazo marvels in numbers', *FIFA*, 26 September 2017 https://www.fifa.com/worldcup/news/the-maracanazo-marvels-in-numbers-2909382

358 Ibid

359 Alex Bellos, *Futebol: The Brazilian Way of Life*, p.49

equalised in the 66th. Then, with 79 minutes on the clock, Peñarol wide player Alcides Ghiggia would shoot from a tight angle at close range and score the decisive strike.

The *Northern Whig* reported how 'few had given Uruguay a chance',[360] but against the odds the crown was theirs. After the game, mass mourning broke out across Brazil as 'stadium doctors treated 169 people for fits of hysteria', with 'six taken to hospital seriously ill'.[361]

Maracanazo had occurred and Brazil sought change. Even their white kit, played in since 1919, was dropped in favour of a more 'patriotic' blue and yellow.[362] The humbling could never happen again and so the 2014 Brazilian World Cup was a moment for the Seleção to finally banish the ghosts of Maracanazo. Instead, Mineirazo would later leave an even worse taste in the mouths of the nation (Minute 29).

360 *Northern Whig*, 17 July 1950
361 *The Guardian*, 15 March 2018
362 *Daily Mail*, 05 March 2019

1' – After Nándor Hidegkuti's early opener, Ferenc Puskas celebrates Hungary's third goal in the 3-6 demolition of England at Wembley on 25 November 1953.

5' – Brian Deane thumps an early header past Manchester United goalkeeper Peter Schmeichel in August 1992. The goal would be the first in the Premier League and introduce a new era of football.

22' – *Mario Balotelli celebrates scoring the opening goal for Manchester City at Old Trafford in 2011, by asking the media 'Why Always Me?' The 1-6 thumping of their rivals followed another week of Balotelli headlines in the press.*

28' – Spain's Xabi Alonso is on the receiving end of Nigel De Jong's infamous 'kung-fu kick' during a brutal 2010 World Cup Final. Incredibly, the Dutchman was only shown a yellow card.

34' – Ivan Perišić's handball in the 2018 World Cup Final becomes a historic moment, as VAR gives a penalty to France.

37' –
Wimbledon manager Bobby Gould is crowned with the FA Cup, after his 'Crazy Gang' seized an unlikely 1-0 victory over Liverpool in 1988, thanks to goalscoring hero Lawrie Sanchez (second from left).

64' – Liverpool's defence can only watch in wonder as Gareth Bale scores a ridiculous bicycle kick in the 2018 Champions League Final.

66' – Pelé slots the ball past goalkeeper Jack Kelsey during Brazil's closely-fought 1958 World Cup quarter-final against Wales.

74' – Hughie Ferguson's shot squirms through Arsenal goalkeeper Dan Lewis's 'slippery shirt' as Cardiff City become the first and only Welsh side to lift the FA Cup in 1927.

85' – The Bundesliga was the first professional league to return after the coronavirus (COVID-19) pandemic. Erling Haaland of Borussia Dortmund celebrates 'socially distanced' from his team-mates in an empty Westfalenstadion in May 2020.

90' – Following an exquisite first touch and a wonderful turn past Roberto Ayala, Dennis Bergkamp thumps the ball past Carlos Ángel Roa to send the Netherlands into the 1998 World Cup semi-finals.

106' – Roger Milla's celebration has become an iconic image, as the forward scored both of Cameroon's goals during the 2-1 a.e.t World Cup last-16 victory over Colombia at Italia 90.

119' – Time appears to stop as Italian and German players watch Fabio Grosso's late strike seal the Azzurri's place in the 2006 World Cup Final.

Brandi Chastain drops to her knees after scoring the winning penalty in the 1999 Women's World Cup Final. Over 90,000 fans were there to witness history being made.

80

Number eight Jimmy Dunn scores Everton's third in the FA Cup Final (1933)

KIT NUMBERS are a fully accepted part of modern football. Players will choose a number with meaning to them, or clubs may allocate numbers to their best players to maximise commercial value. Despite this, there has long been an accepted view that a player's shirt number was the 'equivalent of wearing a job title' on their back. It was like they had been 'branded' by a poker into the role the number gave them.[363] The 1933 FA Cup Final made history as the first in which players wore a kit number on their back. The game was secured in the 80th minute by Jimmy Dunn, clearly wearing the number eight.

The legendary Herbert Chapman was an innovator. He constantly sought to improve his teams and after success at Huddersfield Town, he joined Arsenal in 1925, planning to take the club to great heights. He introduced the white sleeves to Arsenal kits, believing players saw white in their peripheral vision more than any other colour, and he introduced tactical meetings before matches too. His support of kit numbers, however, was blocked by the 'instinctively conservative' FA.[364] Chapman's side

363 Daniel Gray, *Black Boots & Football Pinks: 50 Lost Wonders of the Beautiful Game* (London: Bloomsbury, 2018) pp.44–45

364 Jonathan Wilson, *Inverting the Pyramid: The History of Football Tactics* (London: Orion, 2010) pp.50–51

became one of the first in Britain to trial numbers, in August 1928, playing away at Sheffield Wednesday, where the home side wore 1-11 and Arsenal 12-22.[365] The same day, Chelsea wore numbers 2-11 at home to Swansea Town in the Second Division, the goalkeeper remaining blank.

Following further trials, it was decided that for the 1933 FA Cup Final, shirt numbers would be exhibited again. The *Derby Daily Telegraph*'s build-up to the game warned readers of the approach of the 'most novel cup final in the history of football'. With neither team wearing their usual jerseys because of a kit clash, Everton (white) and Manchester City (scarlet) would wear unfamiliar colours. Stranger than that though, each player would have a 'huge distinguishing number on his back'.[366] Again the numbers would be separated by team, Everton donning 1-11 with City wearing 12-22.

Everton put City to the sword on 29 April. Jimmy Stein opened the scoring and Dixie Dean made it two before Dunn wrapped up the 3-0 victory in the 80th minute. Everton would lift a second FA Cup, but the significance of seeing kit numbers was not lost on journalists. The *Liverpool Echo*, in favour of the development, wanted the 'simplicity' of both sides wearing 1-11, beginning with the goalkeeper and finishing with the left-winger. The newspaper noted how it would be 'much easier to spot your man and his position from a glance at your programme'.[367] Another meeting of the Football League and the FA would reject the idea once more and kit numbers were not formally implemented.

It would be the growth of television and the commercialisation of the sport that finally saw kit numbers accepted. The first BBC television broadcast of football was in 1937, and the 1938 FA Cup Final between Preston North End and Huddersfield

365 Arsenal club website, '27. Gunners wear numbered shirts', *Arsenal*, 1 June 2017 https://www.arsenal.com/news/news-archive/gunners-wear-numbered-shirts

366 *Derby Daily Telegraph*, 22 April 1933

367 *Liverpool Echo*, 29 April 1933

followed it. This saw the need for methods for distinguishing players on grainy TV sets. In June 1939, the Football League voted by 24 to 20 to include kit numbers for the 1939/40 season (cut short by World War Two). The FA 'insisted' that these would be 1-11 for both sides with the goalkeeper allocated the first jersey, the full-backs taking two and three, up to the left-winger at number 11.[368]

The move was labelled as a 'progressive step' by the *Grimsby Daily Telegraph*,[369] although it would never foresee the future crimes of centre-back William Gallas wearing ten for Arsenal, striker Milan Baroš donning five for Liverpool or midfielder Edgar Davids turning out with number one on his back for Barnet.

368 Gavin Mortimer, *A History of Football in 100 Objects* (London: Serpent's Tail, 2012) pp.92–94

369 *Grimsby Daily Telegraph*, 5 June 1939

81

Alejandro Villanueva scores for Peru at the 1936 Olympics (1936)

A TURBULENT decade, the 1930s would see the very fabric of society torn apart by the emergence of ruthless dictatorships and repressive ideologies. It perhaps comes as a shock, therefore, that Germany, under the brutal fascist regime of Nazi leader Adolf Hitler, was chosen to host the 1936 Olympic Games. Centred in the eastern capital of Berlin, the Summer Games proved an opportunity to demonstrate Germany's rebirth to the watching world.

The 1930s had seen football become increasingly less popular at the Olympics. The development of the World Cup at the start of the decade meant the Olympics were only open to amateur players. Even though there was a lack of recognisable faces, the absence of the game's professionals would help the final tournament to be incredibly competitive, with the forthcoming World War Two's key nations all taking part in Berlin. Sport in Nazi Germany had become heavily politicised in order to promote its leader's ideology on the watching masses.[370] The appearance of Nazi salutes seen before matches leaves a bitter taste today.

Despite the success of black athlete Jesse Owens in the Olympic Stadium humiliating the Aryan 'master race', including

---

370 Matthew Taylor, *The Association Game* (London: Routledge, 2008) p.165

football in the Games had proven relatively worthwhile for Germany and her international allies. Italy, the 1934 World Cup winners, had raced through to the final, even in light of making a wealth of changes to their squad, with Japan surprising the watching spectators by reaching the quarter-finals. Germany's neighbours to the south, Austria, had also enjoyed a run of success to make the last eight, where their opponents, perhaps surprisingly, would be the South Americans of Peru.

Peru was by no means known for its footballing prowess and in the shape of Austria found one of the world's most renowned international sides. It came as little surprise then that by half-time, the Europeans, who had resorted to 'rough play', were two goals to the good.[371] An Austrian victory would be pivotal to Hitler's foreign policy, with the 1938 'Anschluss' very much at the forefront of future Nazi plans. Remarkably, with the odds stacked against them, Peru hit back in the second half, scoring through Jorge Alcalde before Alejandro Villanueva equalised in the 81st minute to send the game into extra time.

Incredible drama was about to unfold in the additional half-hour. Minutes before the end of time, Peruvian supporters, some apparently wielding revolvers, stormed the pitch and attacked the Austrian XI. Shaken by the assault, which had reportedly left a player 'covered in blood', Austria would concede twice in the final three minutes to lose the game 4-2.[372] Peru's national celebrations would be cut short after the game's dramatic climax as a complaint was lodged and upheld, leading to an arranged rematch. Peru refused to play, arguing that the denial of their legitimate victory had been merely an example of 'latter-day colonialism' against South American nations.[373]

In Peru, anti-German sentiment was rife. Political leaders would do little but intensify the feeling of robbery throughout the country, eventually withdrawing their entire delegation from

371 David Clay Large, *Nazi Games: The Olympics of 1936* (London: W.W. Norton, 2007) pp.275–277

372 *Yorkshire Post and Leeds Intelligencer*, 11 August 1936

373 David Clay Large, *Nazi Games: The Olympics of 1936*, pp.275–277

the 1936 Olympics. It has been argued that the outrage may well have been exaggerated by those at the top, with national elections around the corner.[374] This has also done little to quell conspiracies regarding possible Nazi involvement in the farce. Some historians have suggested that propaganda minister Joseph Goebbels, fearing an Austrian exit, had prompted the invasion and that the 'Peruvian supporters' may not have been native to South America after all.

Austria would go on to win a silver medal at the Games in a final acceptable to the Nazi regime. Gold medallists Italy would promote their triumph as one of national victory and further proof for Mussolini's government that theirs was a country to be regarded above all else. Two years after the Olympics, Austria would be annexed into Germany and the wheels of war were to be set in motion once more. This minute of football offers a clear example of its entanglement within the confines of global politics.

374 Ibid

82

Robert Ullathorne's injury ends the Battle of Bramall Lane (2002)

THE THIRD law of football is centred around the players. It states that a team is allowed no more than 11 players, but 'a match may not start or continue if either team has fewer than seven players'.[375] It is extremely rare for any game to reach this point and other than a 'snapping match' on the *FIFA* video game, it is unlikely to happen anytime soon. However, in 2002, a First Division (Championship) fixture between Sheffield United and West Bromwich Albion saw the antics of the home team lead to what can only be described as a farce.

The Blades started terribly and in the ninth minute, goalkeeper Simon Tracey handled outside of his area and was promptly sent off by referee Eddie Wolstenholme, reducing Neil Warnock's side to ten men. West Brom made use of their man advantage with a goal through Scottish striker Scott Dobie and led going into the break. The Baggies had been enjoying a successful season in their push for automatic promotion to the Premier League and in the second half, captain Derek McInnes put them two goals to the good.

In the 64th minute, and chasing the game, Warnock introduced forward Patrick Suffo and combative midfielder Georges Santos into the mix. A season earlier, Santos had

---

375 Law 3: The Players, in IFAB, 'Laws of the Game', *International Football Association Board*, available at https://www.theifab.com/laws/chapter/4

fractured his cheekbone following an elbow from Nottingham Forest's Andy Johnson. Johnson had signed for West Brom soon afterwards and found himself playing against Santos for the first time since the incident. Seconds after entering the field, a loose ball was heading towards Johnson. Without a moment's hesitation, Santos lunged in two-footed and wiped out his rival. Rewatching the footage shows that it is perhaps one of the worst tackles in football history.

Chaos erupted in the aftermath as players from both sides piled into the ensuing melee. Blades midfielder Michael Brown recalled in an interview with Sky Sports that the introduction of Santos had led to the game becoming a bizarre farce.[376] It came as no surprise when Santos was shown a straight red card for his challenge, with fellow substitute Suffo following him down the tunnel for a headbutt in the resulting fracas. With United reduced to eight players, the game would become a mere training exercise for West Brom.

Dobie added to his tally with 13 minutes to play to put the result beyond doubt as the Baggies strolled towards another valuable three points. Two minutes later, Michael Brown limped off with an injury before left-back Robert Ullathorne was also deemed unfit to continue in the 82nd minute. With only six players left on the pitch, Wolstenholme had no other choice but to abandon the match. Upon the referee's signal to cancel the fixture, a media frenzy began with the tie being dubbed the 'Battle of Bramall Lane'.

West Brom manager Gary Megson claimed he had never seen anything like it on the football pitch and brandished Sheffield United a 'disgrace' for their antics. Megson would suggest in the aftermath that Warnock had instructed both Brown and Ullathorne to go down, thus leading to the game's abandonment. Such suggestions disappointed the two players in

376 Adam Bate, 'Battle of Bramall Lane: Sheffield United and West Brom have history', *Sky Sports*, 14 December 2018 https://www.skysports.com/football/news/11688/11579928/battle-of-bramall-lane-sheffield-united-and-west-brom-have-history

question, as both would miss a significant number of Sheffield United's resulting league matches. West Brom would use the victory to reignite their promotion challenge and pip West Midlands rivals Wolves to the Premier League on the season's last day …

83

Dixie Dean scores 60 in a season (1928)

'He belongs to the company of the supremely great, like Beethoven, Shakespeare and Rembrandt.' [377]

WILLIAM 'DIXIE' Dean was a goalscorer. Beginning his career at Tranmere Rovers in 1923, it would be with Everton (1925–37) that he made his name. Throughout his career, he scored 473 goals in just 502 appearances for club and country, with 18 in 16 for England. The 1927/28 campaign was Dean's most prolific, scoring 60 First Division goals. During the 1928 calendar year, he recorded a remarkable 85 goals in all competitions. [378]

Dean tormented defences, so much so that in February 1924 he was hacked by an opposition player between his legs. The kick to Dean was so significant that he would lose one of his testicles. Seventeen years later at a Chester bar, Dean is reported to have spotted the man he believed responsible, knocking the

---

377 The legendary manager Bill Shankly, quoted in Stuart Maconie, *The People's Songs: The Story of Modern Britain in 50 Records* (London: Ebury Press, 2014) p.306

378 National Football Museum website, 'Dixie Dean Hall Of Fame Profile', *National Football Museum*, https://www.nationalfootballmuseum.com/halloffame/dixie-dean/

perpetrator out with 'one punch'.[379] While it later turned out Dean had punched the wrong person, he proved he was not a man to be messed with.

In March 1925, 18-year-old Dean was offered the opportunity to join his boyhood club, Everton. The move to Goodison Park paid dividends and in his first full season (1925/26), he scored 32 times. However, a motorcycle accident in the summer of 1926 in north Wales threatened his career, Dean sustaining a fractured skull and a badly broken jaw.[380] Recovering from his injuries, Dean scored on his return to the blue jersey and kept winning admirers.

The 1927/28 season was Dean's greatest. Scoring in Everton's opening day 4-0 win over Sheffield Wednesday, the tone was set, and he would net in the next eight too. On 8 October 1927, Dean scored five against Manchester United in the 5-2 victory, taking his tally to 17 in just nine matches. United's keeper Lancelot Richardson described Dean as 'the best forward I have met'.[381] By May 1928, Dean had 57 goals and Everton sat at the top of the First Division.

Everton's third league title was secured days before the final game of the season as Huddersfield Town were defeated at Aston Villa. Newspapers paid tribute to the 'wonderful marksmanship of Dean',[382] who needed a hat-trick in the last game of the campaign at home to Arsenal to set a new record of 60. The fixture, on 5 May 1928, would be all about whether Dean could write his name into the history books.

Dean started the game rapidly, scoring twice within ten minutes (a header and a penalty) to match the previous record of George Camsell (Middlesbrough) and needing one more to take it for himself. Two from Arsenal would see the scores level

---

379 Paul McParlan, 'The Unbreakable Goalscoring Records of Dixie Dean', *These Football Times*, 11 February 2019 https://thesefootballtimes. co/2019/02/11/the-unbreakable-goalscoring-records-of-dixie-dean/

380 *Athletic News*, 28 June 1926

381 *Liverpool Echo*, 5 May 2018

382 *Hartlepool Northern Daily Mail*, 3 May 1928

at the break, and it stayed that way until the final ten minutes. There is some debate over the exact time of Dean's hat-trick goal, reports varying and timings less well recorded, but with seemingly around eight minutes remaining, Everton earned a corner. The delivery then found Dean who, with 'unerring accuracy', headed the ball past the Arsenal keeper for his 60th of the season.[383] The delight was evident, with some fans invading the pitch to celebrate with Dean. Despite conceding a last-minute equaliser, the crowd witnessed Everton lift the title and Dean make history.

Everton were shockingly relegated in 1930 but in 1930/31, Dean notched 39 in the Second Division as they won promotion back to the top flight. The following season, Dean netted 44 league strikes as Everton went on to win the First Division title and added to it with an FA Cup in 1933 (Minute 80). In English football, no player has ever come close to taking that 60-goal record from Dean, and nor does it look likely it will ever be broken.

383 *Liverpool Echo*, 5 May 1928

84

Super-sub David Fairclough makes the Kop go wild (1977)

AS THE 56th minute of this book suggests, Liverpool's home ground of Anfield is no stranger to incredible European nights. In March 1977, the side managed by Bob Paisley were yet to record the first of their six European Cup titles and were craving the final piece to their ever-expanding trophy cabinet. Despite winning the previous season's UEFA Cup, the European Cup was by no means a foregone conclusion. Meeting the Reds in the last eight were French champions Saint-Étienne.

Saint-Étienne had been beaten in the 1976 final by Bayern Munich and had serious European pedigree. Winning the first leg against Liverpool 1-0, the French side entered Anfield as favourites to progress. Anfield, however, was ready. Since Paisley's promotion to manager in 1974, Liverpool had built on predecessor Bill Shankly's foundations and created a strong winning mentality. Chasing an unprecedented treble, a potential passage into the semi-finals ignited the Kop into life.

The atmosphere in France a fortnight earlier had been incredible, but Anfield, according to commentator Gerald Sinstadt, had matched it. Kevin Keegan would put the Reds into the lead on the night with a cross-cum-shot which looped over the Saint-Étienne keeper and into the net. Étienne would push for an equaliser and at the start of the second half they scored through a 30-yard Dominique Bathenay screamer. For many of the Liverpool side, along with substitute David Fairclough, such a fantastic strike meant they believed Étienne had too much for them.[384]

Liverpool now needed two goals to progress and a quick response was essential in order to drown out the vociferous singing of the 5,000 travelling French fans. Through Ray Kennedy's low drive in the 59th minute, they found it. Anfield once again erupted into a frenzy and began chanting 'Allez Les Rouges' in response to Étienne's earlier singing.[385] In need of another goal to reach the semi-finals, Paisley sent on 20-year-old David Fairclough with less than 20 minutes to play.

Fairclough had spent most of his early career on the bench as the dream partnership of Keegan and John Toshack became almost impossible to replace. In the 84th minute, a hopeful ball over the top of the Saint-Étienne defence was taken under control by Fairclough who raced into the box. 'This now could be interesting' were the words of Sinstadt as the Kop held its collective breath. Calmly rolling the ball under the goalkeeper and into the net, the super-sub had struck again.

The noise which greeted the final whistle has been described as louder than even that which met Fairclough's goal.[386] Liverpool had seen off arguably Europe's best side and progressed to the European Cup semi-finals for the first time since 1965. Later victory over Borussia Mönchengladbach in the final would see Emlyn Hughes lift the trophy for the first time in Reds history. Without Fairclough's 84th-minute intervention, it is difficult to see the subsequent emergence of Liverpool into the realms of European royalty. The Kop's presence became legendary as a result of the match and helped to play a significant role in future triumphs. Chelsea '05, Dortmund '16 and Barcelona '19 all owe a lot to a ginger-haired Scouse super-sub called Fairclough.

384 David Fairclough in Mark Platt, *Cup Kings: Liverpool 1977* (Bluecoat Press, 2003)

385 Stephen F. Kelly, *The Kop: Liverpool's Twelfth Man* (London: Virgin Books, 2008) p.157

386 Steve Wilson, *Glad All Over* (London: Lulu, 2014) p.42

The final Premier League goal before COVID-19 suspends play (2020)

AS HARVEY Barnes scored the final goal in the 85th minute of Leicester City's 4-0 victory over Aston Villa on 9 March 2020, fans would not realise quite the significance of that moment. It was not a goal to win the title, like their shock 5,000/1 Premier League victory in 2015/16, but it was the last goal that would be scored in the English top flight for three months. Just days later, British football joined large parts of the world in suspending all sport as the rapidly spreading coronavirus, COVID-19, saw countries across the globe grind to a halt.

The 2019/20 season had seen Liverpool continue their fine 2018/19 campaign with Premier League domination. In 2018/19, the club had missed out on the title by a single point, despite accumulating 97 points and losing just one league fixture. Manchester City's total of 98 had been enough to pip Jürgen Klopp's Reds to the crown but the Champions League trophy, the club's sixth European Cup (Minute 56), had sweetened the blow. The following year, many expected a close title race but this time around, City could not keep up with the pace set by the Anfield men.

By March 2020, Liverpool had played 29 league matches, accumulating 82 points with just one draw and a single loss – City, chasing behind, were 25 points worse off. The Reds looked set to lift a maiden Premier League crown and their first top-flight title since 1989/90. Liverpool supporters hotly anticipated their triumph, expecting the competition to be wrapped up in the coming weeks. Then the coronavirus struck.

COVID-19 originated in the city of Wuhan, in the Hubei province of China, at the end of 2019. The contagious virus could cause a fever, cough, chest tightness, loss of taste and smell and lead to death in some patients. After the virus was reported in Europe, it began spreading rapidly, causing the abandonment of all mass gatherings with sport of course impacted. Italian football was formally halted on 9 March,[387] but when Harvey Barnes scored the same day, many British fans did not expect the domestic game to be next.

In fact, with cases numbers growing, it was controversially decided that Liverpool's Champions League home tie to Atlético Madrid on 11 March would go ahead. Amid criticism, many thousands of fans from the Spanish capital would fly to Merseyside for the last-16 second leg. Finally, on 13 March, after Arsenal manager Mikel Arteta was the highest profile professional to test positive for the virus, English football was suspended. A statement cited 'increasing numbers of clubs taking steps to isolate their players and staff' as the reason, with 3 April 2020 being the point at which football would hopefully restart.[388]

Tragically, with the number of deaths increasing throughout Europe and notably in the UK, the suspension was extended indefinitely. The lack of sport was something of an unprecedented shock to fans, Euro 2020 being postponed until 2021 and the Tokyo Olympics also being pushed back a year. Scottish, Belgian, Dutch and French football would be cancelled, authorities deciding it was not safe to restart with 'social distancing' (people keeping at least two metres apart)

387 *The Guardian*, 9 March 2020

388 'Professional Football Suspended in England until Friday 3 April at the earliest', The Football Association, 13 March 2020 http://www.thefa.com/news/2020/mar/13/fa-premier-league-efl-statement-football-suspended-130320

meaning games would have to be played behind closed doors, hurting clubs financially.

English Leagues 1 and 2, as well as non-league football, would all decide against completing the current campaign, leaving many unanswered questions. What would they do with the previous results? Would they void the campaign as unfinished and invalid? How would they decide the final league table? Would football clubs survive the financial consequences?

On 17 June the Premier League returned. With no fans allowed inside stadiums, Sky, BT, Amazon and even the BBC shared the broadcasting of matches for fans. The odd scenario was replicated in the Championship too with 'fake fan noise' piped into television games to give the illusion of full grounds. The completed fixtures allowed Liverpool to lift that elusive Premier League title, while Leeds United lifted the Championship trophy to return to the top flight after a 16-year absence.

Likewise, UEFA took the decision to host an unprecedented men's and women's Champions League and a Europa League summer tournament to complete these competitions. Bayern Munich won their sixth top-tier European Cup in August 2020 after one-legged fixtures hosted in Portugal, Sevilla similarly winning a sixth Europa League in Germany and Lyon's women lifting a seventh crown in Spain.

Sadly, the COVID-19 pandemic had not sufficiently passed to allow fans to return to stadia in the UK in time for the new 2020/21 campaign, after a shortened summer break. This meant for many clubs the financial hurt would continue. Lower-league football and the women's game are sure to feel the devastating impact for years to come, meaning the 2019/20 season is one that will never be forgotten.

86

Carlos Alberto scores *that* goal for Brazil (1970)

WHEN THE conversation about the greatest sides of all time arises, you can be sure that a wealth of responses will return with Brazil 1970 as the winner. The South American nation swept all before them at the 1970 World Cup and their brilliance was gloriously symbolised by their final goal of the tournament. In the final against Italy, a sweeping move starting with skilful midfielder Clodoaldo was finished emphatically by right-back Carlos Alberto and with it came the Seleção's third World Cup in 12 years.

Despite a decade of success, the side had been caught out at the 1966 World Cup by so-called 'power football'.[389] Defeats to Hungary and Portugal saw them surprisingly crash out in the group stage and fail to defend their title. Three months of intense training would see them prepare for the tournament in Mexico with teamwork and strong partnerships becoming essential to their success.

Reaching the final had been relatively comfortable for Pelé's men. Scoring an impressive 15 goals in just five games demonstrated that attacking flair was key to their victories. Meeting them at the Estadio Azteca were two-time winners Italy, whose progression to the final had seen them dramatically

---

389 Carlos Alberto on FIFATV, 'Brazil in 1970: Football's most beautiful team', FIFA on YouTube, 15 May 2014, Available at: https://www. youtube.com/watch?v=rbSgpuwVEok

win their semi-final after extra time against West Germany 4-3 (Minute 111). Perhaps tired from playing in the 'game of the century', the Italians could still boast a squad full of European champions and world class individuals.

The final itself followed the script of the tournament as attacking flair triumphed over negative tactics. Despite going in at the break level at 1-1, second-half goals from Gérson and Jairzinho had put the Brazilians on course for victory. Pelé wrote that the 1970 World Cup had indeed seen football as the real winner and his side were indeed happy to play in the 'best spirit of the game'.[390] With these thoughts in mind, the last goal of the final would see the game at its purest.

In the 86th minute, some neat passing triangles led to the ball landing at the feet of Clodoaldo. With a few drops of the shoulder four Italian players had been effortlessly dribbled past before he laid the ball off to Rivelino on the left wing. A looped pass found Brazil's top scorer at the tournament, Jairzinho, who darted across the pitch before playing the ball infield to Pelé. To his right, full-back Carlos Alberto was steaming around him, unmarked. Colleagues at Santos, their relationship was almost telepathic. Alberto claimed that Pelé didn't even need a shout to know that he was overlapping him and bursting into the box.[391]

As the ball landed at his feet, Alberto crashed the ball to the goalkeeper's right and into the net. The goal had beautifully rounded off the finest performance by an international side at any World Cup. Pelé credited the triumph to the synchronicity of the squad, with the months of preparation clearly paying off.[392] Attacking football was alive and a further nail was put into the coffin of the rigid tactical style – catenaccio. Such flair would pave the way for the Total Football of the Dutch, which would follow four years later. Rounding off an incredible move, Alberto had earned his place in football's remarkable history.

390 Pelé, *Pelé: The Autobiography* (London: Simon and Schuster, 2006) p.186
391 *The Guardian*, 30 October 2016
392 Pelé: *Pelé, The Autobiography*, p.188

87

Lionel Messi makes fools of Real Madrid in El Clásico (2011)

PEP GUARDIOLA'S Barcelona side of 2008 to 2012 are rightly considered as one of the greatest to ever grace the beautiful game, and they recorded some spectacular performances against rivals Real Madrid. In November 2010, the 5-0, La Liga dismantling (Minute 10) was a masterclass, but on 27 April 2011, a major Champions League El Clásico victory was witnessed across the globe. Lionel Messi was the architect that day, providing a spellbinding 90 minutes.

Messi had firmly established himself as Barcelona's talisman by the 2010/11 campaign, scoring 34 goals in La Liga the previous season. Messi had also lifted his first Ballon d'Or in 2009, retaining the honour in 2010. In the 2009 Champions League Final in Rome, Messi had scored Barcelona's second in the 2-0 win over Manchester United, the 5ft 7in magician jumping in between United's centre-backs at a seemingly ridiculous height.

In 2011, Guardiola's men were attempting another assault on the Champions League and had drawn fierce rivals Real Madrid in the semi-finals. Having lost 1-0 in the Copa del Rey Final to José Mourinho's Real a week earlier, Barça wanted revenge on Los Blancos. The clash at Real's Santiago Bernabéu was the first leg of a gargantuan battle. German team Schalke or England's Manchester United would be awaiting the winners for the final at Wembley.

Barcelona would dominate proceedings with 76.8 per cent of the ball, but the affair would be described as 'bad-tempered' and 'ugly', as Mourinho instructed his side to employ their finest dark arts to break up the game.[393] The feisty occasion would see Barcelona's substitute keeper José Pinto sent off for a scuffle in the tunnel at half-time. The second 45 saw the bitterness continue, and in the 61st minute, Madrid defender Pepe was given his marching orders for a challenge on Dani Alves. The red card was the fourth received by Madrid in four El Clásico fixtures in 2010/11, and Mourinho's anger exploded on the sidelines leading to him also being dismissed.[394]

In the 76th minute, Barcelona finally broke through the resolute Los Blancos defence. Messi had his 51st goal of the season as he latched on to Ibrahim Afellay's low cross inside the six-yard box. The valuable away goal had been secured but it would be in the 87th minute that Messi provided his headline-stealing moment.

Following a quick piece of thinking, Messi played a one-two with Sergio Busquets just inside the Madrid half. He then set out on a mazy run beating Lassana Diarra, Raúl Albiol and Marcelo before evading Sergio Ramos's last-ditch attempt to block him. Messi passed the ball beyond keeper Iker Casillas to win the game 2-0 and give Barça an unassailable semi-final lead.

The Guardian reflected upon 'one of the finest goals this competition [the Champions League/European Cup] has ever witnessed',[395] while the *Daily Mail* called it a 'beautiful goal from a beautiful player'.[396] Messi had left his mark once again and the 1-1 draw a week later set up a 2009 rematch versus Manchester United at Wembley.

393 Rob Parrish, 'Messi magic inspires Barca', *Sky Sports*, 27 April 2011 https://www.skysports.com/football/r-madrid-vs-barcelona/report/234365

394 Ibid

395 *The Guardian*, 27 April 2011

396 *Daily Mail*, 28 April 2011

The La Liga champions would party once more in the final on 28 May 2011. Pedro, David Villa and Messi again (netting his 12th Champions League goal of the campaign) made the score 3-1, as Guardiola's men secured a second European crown under his tutelage. Messi, of course, would go on to break many more personal records, with his 400th La Liga goal (Minute 53) coming in 2019, but his impact on the sport will last much longer than just the memories of stunning goals.

88

Hosts South Korea equalise in one of the game's most controversial matches (2002)

CONTROVERSY IS never far away in football. From the game's modest infancy to its gargantuan present day, certain decisions (on and off the pitch) have led to the most heated and passionate debates. The World Cup is perhaps where the most infamous of these contentious moments have taken place. For all its futuristic splendour and attacking football, the 2002 tournament in Japan and South Korea was open to many peculiar and disputable calls from the officials. This was perhaps seen no more clearly than in the first knockout round tie between co-hosts South Korea and three-time champions Italy in Daejeon.

The Italians were no strangers to remarkable matches at the World Cup. The entirety of their 1938 campaign (Minute 35), the Battle of Santiago (Minute 41) and their shock defeat to North Korea in 1966 (Minute 42) all hold a certain resonance to this day. Upon Italy's meeting with South Korea for a place in the last eight, talk before the game reflected back to 1966. Despite victory then being won by the North, the Korean peninsula revelled in a shared sense of patriotism before the match, using the history of the fixture to ignite the vociferous southern support.[397] 'AGAIN 1966' was spelled out in capitals for Italian supporters to see.

In a shock to the watching world, Korea earned a penalty just five minutes into the game. Gianluigi Buffon would deny Ahn Jung-Hwan from the sport before Italy, then ranked sixth in the world, took control of the tie in the 18th minute through Christian Vieri. For all of Italy's domination and abundance of goalscoring opportunities, they couldn't get the killer goal to see off the challenge of a side ranked 34 places below them.

As the tension inside the stadium rose, the South Koreans resorted to robust challenges. Italian frustration at a lack of protection from referee Byron Moreno was evident on the pitch. Giovanni Trapattoni's makeshift defence was later undone in the 88th minute when a hopeful ball into the box was controlled and finished by Seol Ki-Hyeon. The match finished 1-1 and a period of golden goal extra time would be needed to settle the score. The noise in Daejeon grew once more with the South Korean players growing in confidence and the tempo with which they played. 'Chubby' Moreno was struggling to keep up with play.[398]

The fitness of the referee may go some way to explaining the game's next controversial decision. Roma forward Francesco Totti burst into the box and was brought down by a poor Korean challenge. Fully 30 yards from the action, Moreno judged Totti to have dived and promptly issued a second yellow card. With Italy reduced to ten men, the odds were swinging in favour of South Korea. The second period of extra time saw Damiano Tommasi appear to win the match for the Azzurri, before Moreno brought the play back for offside. Replays suggested that the Italian midfielder had timed his run perfectly.

Just two minutes before the end of extra time, a cross from the left was met by the head of Ahn Jung-Hwan and flew past the outstretched dive of Buffon. The Daejeon World Cup

---

397 *The Guardian*, 21 May 2018

398 Clemente Lisi, *A History of the World Cup: 1930–2010* (Plymouth: Scarecrow Press, Inc., 2011) p.311

Stadium erupted into a cacophony of noise with supporters and players going wild. The Italian side slumped to their knees as another World Cup ended in disappointment. Ahn had written the 'most glorious chapter in Korean football history' and made sure that one of the two host nations would progress to the quarter-finals.[399]

Italy were left bitter and full of resentment for Moreno's performance, claiming a conspiracy had led to their side's early exit. Although their complaints were vehemently denied by FIFA, the performance of Moreno was still criticised by then president Sepp Blatter. Incredibly, Ahn was subsequently sacked from Italian side Perugia for his 'part' in the tragedy. According to club owner Luciano Gaucci, Ahn was the man 'who was the ruin of Italian football'.[400] Who says football isn't emotional?

399 'Korea's golden moment', BBC Sport, 18 June 2002 http://news.bbc. co.uk/sport3/worldcup2002/hi/matches_wallchart/south_korea_v_italy/ default.stm

400 *The Guardian*, 21 May 2018

89

An epic comeback for Turkey
at Euro 2008 (2008)

IT GOES without saying that the later a goal is scored, the more dramatic it is. What takes the sense of drama to new levels is if the goal scored wins a trophy or completes a remarkable comeback. Hosted in Switzerland and Austria, Euro 2008 would be the first major tournament not to feature the home nations or Ireland since 1984. But their absence did little to limit the competition's drama, with Fatih Terim's Turkey offering perhaps the tournament's most memorable moments.

Prior to the competition's start, Turkey had been outsiders to progress from a difficult group. Featuring Cristiano Ronaldo's Portugal, the Czech Republic and co-hosts Switzerland, it was always going to go down to the wire. Before the opening match, Turkey were not even considered tournament dark horses and a swift return home was predicted by most. An opening defeat to Portugal did little to change opinions and further failure to win would see them knocked out. It appeared that BBC Sport's prediction was coming true, 'Struggled a bit in qualifying and will probably not set Euro 2008 on fire this summer. They [Turkey] would settle for a quarter-final berth but are unlikely to get one.'[401]

401 BBC, 'Turkey Team Guide', *BBC Sport*, 15 May 2008 http://news.bbc.co.uk/sport1/hi/football/euro_2008/turkey/7363764.stm

Victory over Switzerland in a rain-soaked St Jakob-Park stadium led to a showdown with 2004 semi-finalists Czech Republic. Both nations entered the match boasting identical group records and a draw would see progress to the next stage decided with a penalty shootout. It was an unprecedented situation but that one many believed to be a real possibility. Such a new rule struck fear into the Czechs who had been victims of law changes in 1996 and 2004.[402] An Oliver Bierhoff golden goal (Minute 98) and a Traianos Dellas silver goal (Minute 105) respectively had seen the side underachieve in recent years.

With that in mind, it was no shock to see Karel Brückner's side race to a two-goal lead after 62 minutes. Jan Koller and Jaroslav Plašil had put the Czechs on the brink of progression and dampened the hopes of the neutral. 'Doesn't look like penalties then,' wrote the BBC's live action reporter.[403] Just 15 minutes from the end, the match began to swing back towards Turkey and a possible shootout was suddenly on the cards. Arda Turan's finish past Petr Čech would bring an onslaught of Turkish attacking pressure.

The match was pulsating and the tension in Geneva was palpable. When the usually unflappable Čech dropped Hamit Altintop's cross at the feet of striker Nihat Kahveci, the resulting goal would mean penalties were on the horizon. Still Turkey pushed for a winner and in the 89th minute, they got it. Altintop's through ball was once more collected by Nihat 18 yards from goal. A glorious right-footed strike was lifted over and around Čech, crashing into the net off the crossbar to send the Turkish side into euphoric celebrations.

'Seeing the ball in the net and knowing that the goal was bringing a win and the quarter-finals, it was an unbelievable feeling,' said Nihat.[404]

---

402 *The Guardian*, 14 June 2008

403 Jonathan Stevenson, 'Turkey 3-2 Czech Republic as it happened', *BBC Sport*, 15 June 2008 http://news.bbc.co.uk/sport1/hi/football/euro_2008/7363029.stm

404 Nihat after the game

Terim hailed the character of his team as they saw out the victory to progress to the quarter-finals. More drama was to follow in the last eight after extra time and a penalty shootout victory saw them move past tournament dark horses Croatia. Turkey's journey through Euro 2008 had been testament to the old cliché, 'it's not over until it's over'. Ironically, it would be a dramatic last-minute defeat to Germany in the semi-finals which ended Turkey's incredible Euro 2008 run but won them the hearts of neutrals around the continent.

90

'Dennis Bergkamp! Dennis Bergkamp! Dennis Bergkamp!' (1998)

THREE WEEKS into the tournament, France 98 had proven to be an overwhelming success. Despite fears that a 32-team format would hinder its overall quality, the emergence of certain players and teams had created a 'festival of football' which had seen a remarkable amount of goals in the group stage.[405]

Entering into the knockout rounds, the drama didn't cease and arguably it improved as the numerous favourites for the tournament met in pulsating and captivating ties. Perhaps none offered finer examples of footballing theatre than the meeting between Argentina and the Netherlands in Marseille.

Both nations had enjoyed dramatic runs to the quarter-finals. The Netherlands needed a stoppage-time winner from Edgar Davids to progress past Yugoslavia before Argentina saw off the English challenge on penalties in Saint-Étienne. Both sides were regarded as favourites for the title with the Dutch squad in particular receiving praise for the attacking manner in which they played.

The side featured the likes of Patrick Kluivert, the de Boer brothers and of course, Dennis Bergkamp. Their style

---

405 Hugh Dauncey and Geoff O'Dare, *France and the 1998 World Cup: The National Impact of a World Sporting Event* (London: Routledge, 2014) p.185

and multicultural squad represented a new, progressive image of Europe.[406]

The match would be regarded as one of the World Cup's finest-ever 90-minute contests. Kluivert opened the scoring early in the first half before Claudio López equalised five minutes later. An end-to-end battle ensued with both sides going close on multiple occasions. Mexican referee Arturo Brizio Carter would be kept busy throughout by full-blooded challenges from both sides as they searched for any weakness to exploit. A late Arthur Numan challenge on Diego Simeone saw him given a second yellow card before Argentina's number ten, Ariel Ortega, followed. Reacting poorly to some choice words from Dutch goalkeeper Edwin van der Sar, his headbutt floored the Netherlands number one and earned him an early bath.

As the clock ticked over into the 90th minute, a hopeful long ball from Frank de Boer found Bergkamp sprinting into the box. With arguably one of the greatest first touches in history, Bergkamp brought the ball under control. Many players would have attempted a first-time strike, but testament to the forward's class and composure, his second touch was to bring the ball inside of Roberto Ayala. Gaining vital space in the box, Bergkamp would lash the ball past the stranded Carlos Roa with the outside of his boot to win the game for Holland.

Barry Davies, commentating for the BBC, summed the moment up perfectly, 'Beautifully pulled down by Bergkamp… OHHHH WHAT A GOAL! Dennis Bergkamp has won it for Holland!' [407]

Commentators around the globe were in awe of the goal. Davies's line has since gone down in legend among nostalgic football fans. Perhaps taking celebration to the next level was Dutch commentator Jack van Gelder's screaming of Bergkamp's name, accompanied by a final howl of exultation. Bergkamp reacted to the goal by covering his face in shock as the realisation

---

406 Laurent Dubois, *Soccer Empire: The World Cup and the Future of France* (Los Angeles: University of California, 2010)

407 Barry Davies, *BBC Sport* commentary

of the moment instantly hit him. The magnitude of the goal meant even more to the Dutch striker.

In his 2013 autobiography, he wrote that the goal took him back to his childhood when he could only imagine and dream of scoring such important goals for Holland, 'After the first two touches… that moment… you give absolutely everything, like your life is leading up to this moment.'[408]

408 Dennis Bergkamp, *Stillness and Speed: My Story* (London: Simon and Schuster, 2013)

When The Clock Passes 90

ALTHOUGH A football match is meant to last for 90 minutes, it never does for so many reasons – and sometimes it can run for as long as 120 minutes.

Football has been littered with great moments occurring once the 'regulation' 90 minutes has been completed, either coming in stoppage time or in the additional 30 minutes available in cup ties.

The amount of stoppage time played at the end of the 90 has always been under the control of the referee, who will add on as much time as they see fit.

This can be for a multitude of reasons – injuries, substitutions, goals, time-wasting tactics – the list is really endless.

And for the majority of football's existence, stoppage time had been something of a mystery to supporters and players. Matches would continue beyond the scheduled finish with only the referee and their two assistants knowing for sure how long was still to play.

It wasn't until the latter part of the 1990s that this situation began to change with the implementation of the fourth official holding up a board displaying the amount of time to be added on. That number would also be read out by the stadium announcer. More often than not, stoppage time passes without incident and the revealing of the time left is just the prompt for some fans to leave early and 'beat the rush'.

But when the outcome of the match is on a knife-edge, the moment the board goes up is hotly anticipated and can lead to quite the change in atmosphere.

The supporters of the team chasing the game can get a second wind, urging their players on for one final push, while for those defending a lead it can become a time of increasing nerves as they know just how long they have to hold on for.

Equally, when the amount of time to be played is surprisingly short or long, those respective emotions can change to anger and frustration – that not enough time has been added for the chase, or that those clinging on feel that they are being asked to do so for too long.

Those aforementioned reasons for time to be added on should also apply during the allotted stoppage time. The minutes announced are, after all, 'a minimum of' to be played.

This can lead to game-changing moments occurring with the clock reading more time played than had been indicated. Michael Owen's late, late winner for Manchester United in a 4-3 classic against Manchester City in 2009 is one famous example.

The outcome enraged City boss Mark Hughes but the additional stoppage time was correct as his side had equalised early on during the extra period.

So stoppage time has often been the location for many of football's greatest moments – as has extra time.

Throughout football's history, extra time has brought with it some of the most dramatic and glorious passages of play. In cup matches, when teams are tied after 90 minutes, an extra 30-minute period is called to help decide the winner.

For some, this provides an additional period to help establish their dominance, with others using the 30 to psychologically wear away at the opposition in order to gain an advantage before the dreaded penalty shootout. It comes as a relative surprise to see that extra time is nothing new to football. Indeed, the 1875 FA Cup Final was the first major game to feature an additional 30 minutes, as the Royal Engineers searched for a maiden cup triumph over the Old Etonians. Even this wasn't the first example of its use, or potential use in football. The first season of the FA Cup saw a semi-final tie between eventual winners the Wanderers and Queen's Park level at full time. Wanderers' suggestion of an additional period was refused by the Scottish club, who wanted a replay instead. Citing the astronomical costs of another trip down to London, Queen's Park didn't attend the replay and the Wanderers progressed to the final.

The first major competition to be won in extra time came in 1877, as once more the Wanderers prevailed to win their fourth FA Cup in just six seasons. After 'it was arranged to continue for half-an-hour, 15 minutes each play', William Lindsay made football history by scoring 'under the tape' in the 97th minute.[409]

Despite remaining in the rules after this match, it comes as quite a surprise to see that only three finals (excluding replays) went to extra time between 1877 and 1930. The 1886 encounter was the first to end the game as a draw after 90 minutes before a replay was arranged a week later. The draw was regarded as a 'real boon to the association' bringing a considerable amount of 'grist to the mill'.[410] It is unclear why extra time wasn't arranged, but the *Glasgow Herald* wrote that the association conferred in the pavilion after the game to end it after 90 minutes.[411]

Extra time would therefore only be rarely used if the replay were also drawn. Although offering supporters another chance to watch the final, attendances could drop dramatically for replays. In 1901, the FA Cup Final between Tottenham and Sheffield saw over 110,000 fans cram into the Crystal Palace sports ground, but just 20,000 returned for the replay in Bolton. In 1902, 1910, 1911 and 1912, similar trends could be seen.

Three consecutive drawn finals irritated many fans as negative football began to creep into the game. 'Bored and made tired' from what they saw from Barnsley and West Bromwich Albion in 1912, spectators and journalists alike demanded a higher standard of football in the game's showpiece event.[412] *The Sportsman* agreed and called for the return of extra time in

409 *Nottinghamshire Guardian*, 31 March 1877
410 *Manchester Courier,* 5 April 1886
411 *Glasgow Herald*, 5 April 1886
412 *Sporting Life*, 22 April 1912

the first match and asked why indeed it had been removed in the first place.[413]

Following the end of World War One, FA Cup Finals would indeed include extra time from the first match. William Kirton would win the trophy for Aston Villa in the 110th minute in 1920. International football would follow suit with the 1920 Olympics featuring an additional 30 minutes to separate the Netherlands and Sweden after a 4-4 draw in Antwerp. The World Cup would also require extra time from 1934. Italy defeated Czechoslovakia 2-1 with a 95th-minute winner from Angelo Schiavio to delight the host nation.

With extra time now secure in its role in the laws of the game, little would alter its use until the 1970s, when penalty shootouts were introduced into the game.

In recent years, it has been argued that the promise of a penalty shootout at the end of a dramatic 120 minutes of football is enough for many teams to resort to negative tactics and indeed 'play for penalties'. The first World Cup to utilise the 'lottery' of the shootout was in 1974. Although not needed, the third-place play-off was to be decided by five spot kicks if no definitive result could be found after extra time. Two years later, the European Championships would be decided by an incredible chipped penalty by Czech forward Antonin Panenka in a shootout with West Germany. Remarkably, all four knockout games in the Euro 76 tournament went to extra time with 19 goals scored in total. Perhaps the lottery it brought meant sides would often go all out for the win to avoid their use.

The World Cup Final would require extra time in 1978 to determine its winner as Argentina overcame the Dutch challenge and condemned them to successive final defeats. Then the World Cup saw its first shootout in 1982, when West Germany controversially beat France in Seville. By the end of the decade, however, football had resorted to negative styles once

413 *The Sportsman*, 22 April 1912

more with Italia 90 being a distinctly dull tournament. Despite new rules being introduced to promote attacking football, the 1994 World Cup Final between Brazil and Italy was drawn 0-0 after extra time and penalties once more gave us the most diverse of emotions as pure ecstasy met utter heartbreak. FIFA's new innovation, 'golden goal', was sure to find the glory of extra time once again.

Golden goal was theoretically a sudden death situation, similar to 'overtime' in other sports. The next goal wins. The 1994 Caribbean Cup had been the first to trial its use with it then counting as 'two goals'.[414] Such a law caused its own controversy and thus meant it was later simplified in time for the 1996 European Championships when Oliver Bierhoff's 95th-minute goal ended the game and won the tournament for Germany. The rest of this book will feature some of the most dramatic golden goal moments from its short-lived use between 1994 and 2003.

Indeed, in 2001, a meeting between 12 elite coaches decided that golden goal had meant players and officials were being 'gripped by a fear factor' and that the response of a team going behind in extra time was 'part of the excitement of the game'.[415] After a World Cup littered with golden goals in 2002, FIFA decided to remove its use in 2003 following its final appearances in both the Confederations Cup and Women's World Cup. European football's governing body had, in the meantime, introduced a new system dubbed 'silver goal' where the goal was only 'golden' if the side who scored was still leading after the first 15 minutes of extra time. Confusing, clunky and useless, the new rule was abandoned after just a year and few examples of its actual use ever came into fruition.

---

414 Robert O'Connor, 'The Golden Goal: Remembering Football's Failed Attempt at Self-Improvement', *Vice*, 28 October 2015 https://www.vice.com/en_uk/article/z4djnj/the-golden-goal-remembering-footballs-failed-attempt-at-self-improvement

415 'Coaches oppose golden goal', BBC Sport, 30 August 2001 http://news.bbc.co.uk/sport1/hi/football/1517229.stm

Ever since, football has reverted back to its use of extra time and later penalty shootouts. The future for football's additional period is indeed uncertain, however. The increase in competitions and the amount of games needed for squads to play over a season has led to calls for cup matches to go straight to penalties. Since 2018, the English League Cup has removed extra time in all matches before the semi-finals, much to the delight of managers around England. Even the FA Cup is beginning to remove replays after the fourth round with the modern game and its mega clubs constantly dictating the way in which the sport is played.

For us at *The Football History Boys*, we hope the use of extra time isn't removed completely from the game. It is with dramatic and incredible 30-minute periods, like the 2020 Champions League match between Liverpool and Atlético Madrid,[416] that some of football's greatest stories are offered.

---

416 Played on 12 March 2020 – Liverpool 2-3 Atlético. Four goals were seen in extra time in the last Champions League match before the COVID-19 outbreak halted European football (Minute 85).

91

'It's up for grabs now!' – Michael Thomas's title winner (1989)

ARSENAL ARE a club steeped in a proud history. The 1930s saw five league titles and two FA Cups secured, and under the guidance of the legendary Herbert Chapman (1925–34), the club would step up to a new level of greatness. However, by 1989, the Gunners were on a titleless run stretching back to 1971. In the 91st minute of the last game of 1988/89, Michael Thomas's goal finally gave Arsenal a new reason to celebrate.

The 1988/89 season had been a battle between defending champions Liverpool and Arsenal. Sadly, tragedy struck on 15 April 1989 to overshadow the whole season in the shape of the Hillsborough disaster (Minute 6), as Liverpool took on Nottingham Forest in the abandoned FA Cup semi-final. After the horrific scenes, Liverpool next took to competitive action on 3 May, leaving them with a fixture pile-up that saw them play eight games in 23 days.

Unbelievably, Liverpool would win the FA Cup in the wake of the disaster, beating Forest in the rearranged semi-final before defeating city rivals Everton 3-2 in a thrilling final on 20 May. In the league, the final game of the season was perfectly poised – Liverpool versus Arsenal at Anfield for the First Division crown on 26 May. A draw would hand Liverpool the double, meaning Arsenal needed to win the match by two clear goals to overturn the Reds' superior goal difference. Anything else and the championship would remain at Anfield.

Alan Smith broke the deadlock in the 52nd minute on that Friday evening. His header was his 22nd goal of the season and wrapped up the Golden Boot. The single goal was not enough, though, and Liverpool were set to retain the title if it stayed at 1-0. As the clock was hitting 90, Liverpool's John Barnes decided to take on midfielder Kevin Richardson rather than kill the tie by the corner flag. Barnes recalled how the decision 'cost Liverpool the championship' as Richardson dispossessed him and played a (then-legal) back-pass to his goalkeeper John Lukic.[417]

Now into injury time, Lukic passed to defender Lee Dixon, whose long ball over the top found Smith. Smith controlled it and played a neat, chipped through ball to Thomas 30 yards from goal. As Thomas took the ball past defender Steve Nicol, it rebounded off him and left his path to Bruce Grobbelaar's goal clear. ITV commentator Brian Moore raised his voice in now-famous excitement, 'Thomas, charging through the midfield! Thomas! It's up for grabs now!'[418]

Thomas hit the back of the net and had his career moment; Arsenal had their league title. The side that needed a two-goal win had done it with less than 60 seconds left of the season. Liverpool boss Kenny Dalglish lamented 'three big, tense games in six days' that 'took it out of the players', but in north London, 26 May would be declared 'St Michael's Day'.[419] Arsenal manager George Graham would comment that 'only people at Highbury actually felt we were capable of doing it',[420] and perhaps he was right. Arsenal had pulled off the most amazing finish to a title race of all time – or at least until 2012 (Minute 94).

---

417 Louis Massarella, 'Football's greatest-ever title finish? Arsenal's 1989 triumph over Liverpool, told by the players', *FourFourTwo*, 3 March 2017 https://www.fourfourtwo.com/features/footballs-greatest-ever-title-finish-arsenals-1989-triumph-over-liverpool-told-players

418 Ibid

419 *The Independent*, 24 December 2006

420 *Sandwell Evening Mail*, 27 May 1989

92

Bill Perry wins the
Matthews Final (1953)

IN 1953, the FA Cup was edging past its 80th birthday. Over the decades, it had emerged as British sport's most popular competition and boasted incredible numbers of spectators to its showpiece event – the FA Cup Final, which had been held at Wembley since 1923. The stadium had witnessed some of football's finest moments before and after World War Two. As the war ceased and football was once more introduced back to the British public, six different sides won the competition in the first six seasons, before Newcastle United retained their title in 1952. Their opponents a year earlier had been Blackpool, a side littered with talent but yet to win a major trophy.

Central to the Tangerines' success was the 'wizard of the dribble', Stanley Matthews. At 38, Matthews had endured a discontinuous career with the intervention of World War Two robbing him of his playing peak. In 1938, he would be described by a Stoke supporter in the *Staffordshire Sentinel* as a 'football genius' following his five-goal performance against Ireland.[421] Throughout the war, alongside his wider role in the RAF, Matthews would be a frequent performer in wartime friendlies, featuring for a number of different sides after receiving permission from Stoke (his club at the time). The finest player

---

421 *Staffordshire Sentinel*, 23 November 1938

in world football at the time, his presence would help clubs to record impressive gates.

By 1953, Matthews was still going strong. Despite reaching the FA Cup Final for the third time in six seasons, he was still yet to win a major trophy and pre-match conversation was focused entirely on the winger's fortunes. The *Western Mail* ran with the headline 'Will Stanley Matthews win medal at last?'[422] and the *Coventry Evening Telegraph* stated that neutrals were well and truly on the side of the 'greatest player of the age'.[423]

The final itself saw Blackpool face northern rivals Bolton Wanderers. Widely considered to be favourites before the game, Bolton would race to a 3-1 lead in the opening 55 minutes. 'Shimmering in the brilliant sun,' Matthews would take matters into his own hands in the 68th minute when his cross was met by Stan Mortensen, who scored his second of the match. The crowd were beginning to purr at Blackpool's and indeed Matthews's resurgence with the *Yorkshire Post* claiming, 'Never in his 21 years of football has he played better.'[424]

With just a minute to play, Mortensen would notch a brilliant third before Bill Perry completed the comeback in the 92nd minute. Once more, incredible wing play from Matthews saw a brilliant dribble and an excellent cross which was diverted into the net. The second half had seen arguably the greatest FA Cup Final to date, helped into legend by the watching TV audience at home who had been granted access to watch a live broadcast. At the final whistle, Matthews was held aloft by his team-mates in tangerine and the nation's neutrals cheered for the success of their greatest player. Decades of effort, near-misses and war had paid off for the 'unassuming' Matthews who was reluctant to take personal credit for the victory, instead dedicating it to the team.[425]

422 *Western Mail*, 2 May 1953

423 *Coventry Evening Telegraph*, 1 May 1953

424 *Yorkshire Post*, 4 May 1953

425 *Yorkshire Evening Post*, 4 May 1953

Matthews had come to represent the 'English' game. A working-class player who seemed to just 'get on with it', he had a deferential attitude to the authorities. Winning at 38, he had symbolised the traditions of British sport in a decade of immense wider social change.

Matthew Taylor wrote that Matthews somewhat reflected the mood of wider British society – 'proud of its traditions but optimistic about the future'.[426] However, such sporting feelings were to come crashing down six months later (Minute 1).

---

426 Matthew Taylor, *The Association Game* (London: Routledge, 2008) p.238

93

'And Solskjær has won it!' – Manchester United seal the treble (1999)

SIR ALEX Ferguson is arguably the greatest British manager of all time, and in 1999, his crowning glory was achieved as Manchester United clinched a marvellous treble – the Premier League, the FA Cup and the UEFA Champions League. The 'continental' treble was the first by an English club and just the fourth in European history, following Celtic (1966/67), Ajax (1971/72) and PSV Eindhoven (1987/88). This moment was secured deep into injury time by Ole Gunnar Solskjær's 93rd-minute strike in the Champions League Final.

Under Sir Alex, Manchester United were no strangers to success. They enjoyed four Premier League titles prior to 1998/99, the league and FA Cup double coming first in 1994 and again in 1996. Much of the success was built upon the now-famous Class of '92, the youth cohort that featured David Beckham, the Neville brothers, Paul Scholes, Ryan Giggs and Nicky Butt. Alongside this, Ferguson was the master of bringing in the right player to United, and perhaps more importantly, knowing when to let players leave.

United lost just three games en route to winning the Premier League, remaining unbeaten from Boxing Day until the end of the season to top the table ahead of Arsenal. In the FA Cup, rivals Liverpool were one of those dumped out as they headed to a semi-final versus Arsenal. The 0-0 draw was followed by a replay three days later and with the scores at 1-1, Ryan Giggs would net a stunning extra-time winner (Minute 109) to send the Red Devils to Wembley. On 22 May 1999, Newcastle were beaten 2-0 thanks to goals from Teddy Sheringham and Paul Scholes.

That fourth-round victory over Liverpool, earned from a losing position with two goals in the last couple of minutes, foreshadowed what was to follow.

Wednesday, 26 May provided Ferguson's men with a chance to grab that last trophy, the hallowed Champions League. Despite drawing four times with Bayern Munich and Barcelona, they had escaped their group after two decent wins against Danish side Brøndby. A progress-deciding 1-1 draw with group winners Bayern at Old Trafford was enough to see them reach the knockout rounds. Ferguson described 'nervy moments',[427] but was delighted to maintain the pursuit of the trophy into the knockout rounds. Italian teams Inter Milan and Juventus were beaten by United as they booked a place at Barcelona's Camp Nou for the final and a rematch with Bayern Munich.

Even the *Liverpool Echo* built the fixture up, calling it a 'massive night for United and English football',[428] as they attempted to make history. For United, central midfield pair Paul Scholes and captain Roy Keane were absent from the squad, both through suspension. Ferguson called Keane's decision to take a yellow card in the semi-final the 'most emphatic display of selflessness I have seen',[429] as he prevented Zinedine Zidane's dangerous counter attack. The blow of missing two key men was seemingly instant in Spain as Bayern's right-winger Mario Basler opened the scoring for the Germans after just six minutes.

United looked well beaten but in the 90th minute they earned a corner kick. Goalkeeper Peter Schmeichel ventured

427 *Irish Independent*, 10 December 1998
428 *Liverpool Echo*, 25 May 1999
429 *The Guardian*, 25 April 2012

up the pitch as United fought for an equaliser and as Giggs's poorly struck shot found Sheringham, the Englishman was able to tuck the ball home from the six-yard area, making the score 1-1 and setting up extra time.

United's goal had given them hope of even winning the game before extra time was needed and in the 93rd minute Beckham would stand over another corner. His delivery found Sheringham, who was able to flick the ball towards the back post. Substitute Solskjær was there waiting and poked the ball across the line, and United had the lead in dramatic style.

Stunned ITV commentator Clive Tyldesley shouted, 'And Solskjær has won it!'. From the treble slipping away, to seizing the trophy in a matter of minutes. Midfielder Jesper Blomqvist recalled the scenes of 'euphoria' as United attempted to process that 'something impossible had just happened'.[430] The best comeback in Champions League Final history? That is something for United and Liverpool (Minute 54) fans to debate.

430 Jesper Blomqvist in Ben Lyttleton (ed.), *Match of My Life: European Cup Finals* (Studley: Know The Score Books Limited, 2006) p.149

94

'Agüeroooooo' – Manchester City snatch the title (2012)

'I swear you'll never see anything like this ever again. So watch it, drink it in! Two goals in added time for Manchester City to snatch the title away from Manchester United. Stupendous!' [431]

SERGIO 'KUN' Agüero's move to Manchester City in the summer of 2011, for a reported £38m, was one that came with the promise of 'major trophies'.[432] The 23-year-old had already proved himself a goalscorer in Spain with Atlético Madrid, and his signing signalled the continued investment of City chairman Khaldoon Al Mubarak. Kun immediately proved himself a prolific addition, claiming 23 Premier League goals and the club's Player of the Year award in his debut campaign.

Manager Roberto Mancini was hunting City's first Premier League title, the blue half of Manchester having gone without a top-flight championship since 1967/68. They had only won it once prior to that, 1936/37. Manchester United's legendary

431 Martin Tyler's commentary on Sky Sports on 13 May 2012
432 *The Guardian*, 28 July 2011

Sir Alex Ferguson had nicknamed City the 'noisy neighbours' back in 2009,[433] believing the Red Devils would always be the greater club. In October 2011, City routed United 6-1 at their Old Trafford home (Minute 22), stunning the watching world – perhaps they were more than noisy neighbours?

City would remain unbeaten in the top flight until 12 December 2011, showing their credentials as genuine challengers. Both Manchester clubs fought throughout the season but a goal-filled run of five wins in five matches before the final game put City in pole position. This run included a vital 1-0 victory over United on 30 April 2012, captain Vincent Kompany scoring on the brink of half-time to win at the Etihad Stadium.

On 13 May 2012, the Premier League crown would be decided with United away to Sunderland while City hosted QPR, the latter needing to equal the result of the former to secure the title as both fixtures played out simultaneously. The first half saw Sunderland fall behind to a Wayne Rooney strike in the 20th minute for United, before Pablo Zabaleta gave City a 1-0 lead at the break – so far so good for the Citizens.

The drama kicked up a notch in the second half at the Etihad as Djibril Cissé netted for QPR (48) and Jamie Mackie then made it 2-1 to the visitors in the 66th minute. Despite Joey Barton earning himself a ridiculous red card between the goals for the side battling to avoid relegation, it appeared that they were sending the league to Old Trafford. With time slipping away, in the 92nd minute, striker Edin Džeko gave City hope as he levelled the match at 2-2. For viewers watching at home, the full-time whistle blew in Sunderland to confirm United's win and seemingly confirm their title too.

Then came the moment. With City's game still playing, they threw everybody forward and Agüero picked up the ball 30 yards out. His pass found Mario Balotelli, who slipped, but still managed to return it to Agüero who had continued his run. The Argentine beat his defender inside the box, and as

433 *Metro*, 20 September 2009

the clock struck 93:20, he smashed it beyond keeper Paddy Kenny. Commentator Martin Tyler screamed his now-famous 'Agüeroooooo!' line. City led 3-2 and with two injury-time goals, they had stolen the title from their neighbours' hands. The most incredible way to settle a season in the very last seconds of action.

Tyler's iconic commentary is now remembered as much as Agüero's goal itself, the moment apparently leading to the City stadium shop running out of the letter O due to all the 'Agüeroooooo' shirts fans were clamouring for.[434] Tyler felt the finish was a perfect one for a commentator, 'The trigger for that level of excitement in a commentator's voice is rooted in a passion for football and love of the moment.'[435]

434 *The Telegraph*, 20 December 2012
435 *Manchester Evening News*, 24 June 2017

95

Oliver Bierhoff's golden goal
wins Euro 96 (1996)

THE INTRODUCTION of the 'golden goal' in the mid-1990s split opinions on its success and indeed its use in modern football. Designed to make extra time more attacking and, therefore, more exciting, its first major use at the 1996 European Championships was intended to highlight its appeal. Following a draw in the knockout rounds, the sudden death system would see a 'next goal wins' scenario played out over the course of the additional 30 minutes. Contrary to expectations, two goalless quarter-finals and two drawn semi-finals failed to break a stalemate after 120 minutes with sides almost scared to make the sucker punch in extra time. The new rule would have to wait for its gloriously devastating introduction.

As if hanging on for the grandest stage of all, its first use would come in the Euro 96 final at Wembley. Before the game, the golden goal rule had caused some debate. The excitement of the group stage had dwindled, and were it not for dramatic penalty shootouts, the knockout rounds would have been starved of real drama. The *Liverpool Echo* was quick to voice its frustration at the 'so-called and so far fruitless' golden goal as the Czech Republic and France played out 'quite frankly, the worst match I have ever seen'.[436] Adding to the reporter's annoyance

436 *Liverpool Echo*, 27 June 1996

that *Neighbours* had been cancelled to accommodate the semi-final, it is clear that golden goal was not offering the impact envisioned upon its ratification by FIFA in 1994.

The negative air around the innovation was reflected further by Irish paper the *Daily Herald*, which questioned its future if it failed to be used in the final. Believing it 'closes down play in extra time', the final between Germany and the Czech Republic may have been its last chance to impress.[437] According to the script, Oliver Bierhoff's 73rd-minute equaliser to cancel out Patrik Berger's 59th-minute penalty sent the final into extra time.

After two hours of goalless extra time periods across the semi-finals and two of the quarter-finals, it took just five minutes for Oliver Bierhoff to shatter Czech dreams of victory. Turning sharply on the edge of the Czech box, he unleashed a powerful yet deflected shot towards keeper Petr Kouba. Kouba failed to hold on to the shot and watched it drop tamely into the net to send the Germans into raptures.

The *Aberdeen Press and Journal* dissected the successes and failures of the new system in an article a day after the final. Described as both cruel and entertaining, it was clear that golden goal would divide opinion in the coming years, with the lack of goals before Bierhoff's intervention making most see it as a negative innovation.[438]

As a tournament, Euro 96 is viewed today through rose-tinted glasses, especially in England where it holds a certain nostalgic resonance akin to Italia 90. England's success in reaching the semi-finals and the sense of 'Englishness' the tournament reintroduced to society is perhaps to blame for its modern-day reverence. Its promotion of historical victories both in war and sport, and the popularity of the Lightning Seeds' single, 'Three Lions', make many today believe it to be a sporting success story. In fact, opinions were generally negative in the

437 *Daily Herald*, 27 June 1996
438 *Aberdeen Press and Journal*, 2 July 1996

immediate aftermath with the *Daily Telegraph* even describing the competition as a 'tactical grind' which lacked the 'buccaneer spirit' of the 1994 World Cup.[439]

Perhaps what Euro 96 should be remembered for, above all else, is a history-making and era-defining golden goal from Bierhoff ...

439 *The Telegraph*, 2 July 1996

96

Ajax stunned by Lucas Moura's last-gasp winner (2019)

THE UEFA Champions League is club football's most desirable modern-day prize. The competition born as the European Cup in 1955/56 (Minute 14) has provided some major moments in its history. The 2018/19 season, though, featured two jaw-dropping semi-finals – Barcelona v Liverpool (Minute 56) and Tottenham Hotspur v Ajax. In the 96th minute of Tottenham's second leg, a late, injury-time goal put Spurs into their first Champions League Final.

Spurs' route to that final was less than straightforward, the English club sitting on just one point after their first three group matches. Two big home wins against PSV Eindhoven and Inter Milan left them needing an unlikely result away to Barcelona, with Inter home to PSV. Trailing 1-0 and with Inter Milan at 1-1, Spurs were heading out of the competition until Lucas Moura popped up in the 85th minute to equalise. The result levelled Spurs and Inter on points, goal difference and head-to-head record, meaning head-to-head away goals would be needed to separate the two. Spurs were the beneficiaries of that rule.

In the last 16, Spurs decimated Borussia Dortmund 3-0 in London, winning the away fixture 1-0 and setting up an all-English quarter-final against Manchester City. Spurs would win 1-0 at home, leaving them in pole position heading to the Etihad Stadium. A rip-roaring clash ensued and saw five goals in the first 21 minutes, Raheem Sterling (4 and 21) and Bernardo

Silva (11) for City, with Son Heung-min netting twice for Spurs (7 and 10).

The second half saw City take a 4-2 lead on the night through Sergio Agüero, but in the 73rd minute substitute Fernando Llorente scored from a corner. The ball appeared to flick off his arm on the way to goal, but a VAR check would not rule it out – Spurs were heading through on away goals. City fans' fury with VAR would double in injury time as Sterling's 92nd-minute hat-trick was ruled out by VAR due to an incredibly tight (but correct) offside call against Agüero, who had provided the assist. Spurs were into the semi-finals in the 'most dramatic of circumstances'.[440]

Spurs lost 1-0 at home to Ajax in the first leg, leaving themselves with it all to do in Amsterdam. Things would go from bad to worse on 8 May, Ajax taking a 2-0 half-time lead and requiring Spurs to score three to make the final. With talisman Harry Kane missing, Spurs looked to Lucas to turn things around. His goals in the 55th and 59th minutes saw Spurs needing one more to progress. With time seemingly running out, Moura would earn his hat-trick. In the 96th minute, the ball fell to him just inside the box, where he hit it first time and found the net – Spurs had their third, the tie-winning goal to settle the semi-final and stun Ajax with seconds remaining.

Ajax captain Matthijs de Ligt told journalists, 'It's a nightmare, like a dream that went bad.'[441] The Dutch missed out on a place in the final, but Spurs would face Liverpool, who themselves had rocked Barcelona. Despite losing the game in Madrid 2-0, Spurs' run had been a brilliant, drama-filled affair marked by significant late moments.

The current financial reward of UEFA's premier tournament is immense. Should the victorious Champions League side win all six group games too, they will earn a staggering £72.6m in prize

---

440 *Manchester Evening News*, 17 April 2019
441 *London Evening Standard*, 9 May 2019

money alone, and that is before television money is included.[442] This set-up, however, is only protected until 2024. The future of the competition is up for grabs with many observers believing that a new 'European Super League' is coming.

One suggestion in 2019/20 was a 32-team league where sides play at least ten matches but can guarantee their qualification through their performance in this tournament, rather than domestically.[443] This has led to fears about clubs breaking away from their domestic leagues, with more riches and rewards to be gained in a continental division. While it has been initially rebuffed, our future football history books are likely to write about a European competition vastly different from the Champions League so many know and love.

442 *Daily Express*, 12 December 2019
443 *Daily Mail*, 13 December 2019

97

Troy Deeney punishes Anthony Knockaert's penalty miss (2013)

'That is the nature of the beast. It can be a very cruel game at times.'[444]

THE CHAMPIONSHIP play-off final is known as the 'richest game in football'. The winners, by earning promotion to the Premier League, have access to the riches and extravagance of the top flight. By 2019 the value of that game had grown to a staggering estimated £170m.[445] In 2013, Watford faced Leicester City in the semi-finals with a place at Wembley at stake. In the 97th minute, the game was won by Troy Deeney in an insane finish at Vicarage Road.

With Cardiff City winning the league, followed by Hull City in the second automatic promotion place, it was left to four clubs to fight it out in the play-offs. Watford, who finished third, played Leicester City, who had finished sixth, nine points adrift of their opponents. The first leg of their tie saw Leicester take a 1-0 home victory thanks to an 82nd-minute goal from David Nugent, leaving the Hornets with it all to do three days later.

On 12 May, Watford hosted the Foxes at Vicarage Road. After 15 minutes, prolific Championship goalscorer Matěj

---

444 Leicester City manager Nigel Pearson in the *Watford Observer*, 13 May 2013
445 *Irish Independent*, 24 May 2019

Vydra netted his 21st strike of the campaign, to level the tie on aggregate. However, just four minutes later, Nugent scored again to make it 1-1 on the day and 2-1 Leicester overall – Wembley beckoned.

Vydra, the Championship Player of the Year, would again equalise, playing a neat one-two with Deeney before slotting into the bottom corner. Extra time loomed until a minute of football that will not be forgotten in play-off history. Firstly, deep into injury time, Marco Cassetti was penalised in a seemingly dubious decision on Leicester's Anthony Knockaert. Referee Michael Oliver awarded a penalty that could have seen Leicester heading to the final.

Knockaert, who had certainly hit the ground easily, stepped up to take the spot kick. Attempting to calmly put it down the middle, his soft shot was saved by keeper Manuel Almunia's legs and Knockaert's rebound was also smothered. Cassetti, presumably delighted his error had been redeemed, hoofed the ball upfield.

The clearance found Watford's Ikechi Anya who saw a chance to break and steal the game for the Hornets instead. Anya played in forward Fernando Forestieri on the right-hand side of the box, from where he delivered a superb cross to midfielder Jonathan Hogg. Hogg cushioned a header back to Deeney on the penalty spot and the striker buried the 97th-minute opportunity.

Watford had gone from Almunia's save to Deeney's goal in just 20 seconds and fans understandably rushed the pitch in celebration. The final whistle blew seconds later, and Vicarage Road erupted in joy. While Watford went on to lose in the final to Crystal Palace, that finish at Vicarage Road is still fondly remembered.

Deeney perhaps summed the moment up best himself, 'That goal shows the magic and beauty of football. It's why we love it, for moments like that.'[446]

98

Germany's golden goal snatches the Women's World Cup (2003)

TWELVE YEARS into its short life, the Women's World Cup had grown remarkably since its inaugural competition in 1991 (Minute 20). The successes of the US in both 1991 and 1999 had promoted a boom in female football participation across the continent and had helped to cement the USWNT as the world's finest squad. By 2003, Mia Hamm, Kristine Lilly and Brandi Chastain had become household names and the second successive Women's World Cup to be held in the US was sure to be popular once more among supporters.

Originally to be held in China, the outbreak of SARS in 2003 forced the competition to be moved to the US. FIFA president Sepp Blatter insisted the decision had been a reluctant but necessary one. Citing the immense spectatorship and success of the US-held tournament in 1999, it was an easy decision to take.[447] It is an incredible scenario which draws direct comparisons with the 2020 coronavirus outbreak (Minute 85), which saw the postponement of major sports and indeed football tournaments.

For all of the Women's World Cup's accomplishments, another of FIFA's recent initiatives, the 'golden goal', had ultimately failed to impress. Most believed it to encourage negative football with

---

447 'Women's World Cup moved to US', BBC Sport, 26 May 2003 http://news.bbc.co.uk/sport1/hi/football/2998291.stm

teams 'too afraid to concede'.[448] Further confusion in stadiums as to when the game would end also prompted its removal or downgrading to the 'silver goal'. The 2003 Women's World Cup would therefore be the final chance to see the rule in action.

The tournament itself saw lower attendances than the 1999 edition, which had recorded over 90,000 fans for the final. The limited time to organise such a competition on the same scale proved impossible, yet a decent 21,000 average still attended. With the US and China underperforming, it came as quite a surprise to the footballing world to see Germany and Sweden reach the final at the Los Angeles Home Depot Center. Germany had been helped by the immaculate form of striker Birgit Prinz, whose seven goals had brought them within reach of the trophy.

In a tournament of surprises, Sweden took the lead in the final through Hanna Ljungberg. Immediately after half-time, Germany equalised with a strike from Maren Meinert before no further goals were scored, sending the game to extra time and activating the 'golden goal'. In the 98th minute, a free kick was awarded to Germany and sent into the box dangerously by Renate Lingor. Rising highest to meet the ball with a powerful header, Nia Künzer struck to win the trophy for the Germans and break Swedish hearts.

The final golden goal in football history had been scored. Künzer's header had brought a last piece of gloriously bittersweet drama to the fore and given FIFA's mid-90s experiment a fitting end. Germany's win and indeed Sweden's shock run to the final had been good for the women's game, ending the US dominance and bringing success to wider nations. The positive performances of Canada and France had promoted participation in their respective countries, with Ghana recording a first World Cup win and disseminating the game across the African continent.

The 2003 Women's World Cup is often forgotten in comparison to the tournaments on either side of it in 1999 and 2007, but it proved 'golden' in promoting the wider global game.

448 *The Guardian*, 28 April 2003

99

Bobby Charlton completes United's remarkable journey back from the brink (1968)

IT'S FAIR to say that 1958 is a year etched into British footballing history. Manchester United's superb side, led by manager Matt Busby, was decimated by the Munich air disaster (Minute 2). The devastation was followed by a decade of rebuilding the club, a process victoriously completed in 1968 as United lifted the European Cup against Benfica at Wembley, Bobby Charlton netting the final goal in the 99th minute.

The European Cup was not something British teams had enjoyed success in since its launch in 1955/56. Celtic's Lisbon Lions would become the first British club to raise the crown in 1967 (Minute 62) but still no English side had achieved the feat. Manchester United's opportunity was so cruelly ripped away in 1958 but ten years later, Busby had the chance to complete his 'long-standing and burning ambition'.[449]

Portuguese side Benfica had twice lifted the title in the early 1960s, but upon departing in 1962, legendary manager Béla Guttmann had cursed the club. He promised they would not win another European Cup for 100 years (Minute 69) and following this, As Águias had lost in the 1963 and 1965 finals. In 1966, United drew Benfica in the quarter-finals of the

449 *Reading Evening Post*, 29 May 1968

European Cup. They put them away 3-2 at Old Trafford and were 5-1 winners away at Estádio da Luz. Yugoslav side Partizan ended United's 1966 dream in the semi-finals, allowing Celtic to take the first British glory a year later.

On 29 May 1968, United would get another shot at Benfica after a run to the final that had seen them beat the Maltese side Hibernians, Sarajevo, Górnik Zabrze and Real Madrid. Benfica, meanwhile, had beaten Northern Ireland's Glentoran, Saint-Étienne, Vasas and Juventus as they sought to break Guttmann's curse.

The final at Wembley featured two superstars, Benfica's Eusébio and Manchester United's George Best. United's goalkeeper Alex Stepney reminisced about the 'incredible' Best, summarising him simply, 'His surname said it all.'[450] After a goalless first 45, captain Charlton opened the scoring for the Red Devils in the 53rd minute with a superb header. Eleven minutes from time, Jaime Graça levelled and sent the game to extra time.

Just two minutes into the extra half hour, Best scored after dribbling past keeper José Henrique, and Brian Kidd made it 3-1 after 94 minutes, heading in from close range at the second attempt. The fixture was wrapped up in style in the 99th minute by Charlton, sweeping the ball home to seal the tie. Charlton had miraculously survived Munich with minor injuries along with centre-half Bill Foulkes, and perhaps it was the perfect end to the story for him to raise the trophy that night.

Busby had experienced his fair 'ration of success and tragedy' during his tenure at Old Trafford.[451] Now finally triumphant in Europe, he declared, 'This is the greatest night of my life, the fulfilment of my dearest wish.'[452] Manchester United's redemption from the darkness that enveloped them in 1958 was completed with a stunning 4-1 demolition – a night that the Red Devils will never forget.

450 Alex Stepney in Ben Lyttleton (ed.), *Match of My Life: European Cup Finals* (Studley: Know The Score Books Limited, 2006) p.59

451 *Birmingham Daily Post*, 30 May 1968

452 Scott Murray and Rowan Walker, *Day of the Match: A History of Football in 365 Days* (London: Boxtree, 2008) p.155

100

Shannon MacMillan's Olympic golden goal sends USA to the final (1996)

THE OLYMPIC Games offered the first opportunity for men's football to be played on the world stage. After trials in 1896, 1900 and 1904, it debuted at the London 1908 Olympics. Historian Richard Holt described how the 'London Games of 1908 glorified the amateur athlete',[453] and this was how Olympic sport continued to be seen, with no professional competitors allowed. As well as this, the Olympics continued to be dominated by male athletes and events as the Games grew. The percentage of women competitors rose from '4.4 per cent in 1924 to 8.1 per cent by 1936', but the events included for women 'remained severely restricted'.[454] One of those events that did not feature was football.

Incredibly, it would be the 1996 Games in Atlanta, USA, before women footballers were welcomed to the Olympics, 100 years after the introduction of the event by Frenchman Pierre de Coubertin. The first Women's World Cup in 1991 (Minute 20), had seen the game grow in popularity and in 1993, it was announced that the Atlanta Games would feature a women's tournament. The eight teams invited were those who had finished in the top eight of the 1995 Swedish World Cup,

453 Richard Holt, *Sport and the British: A Modern History* (Oxford: Oxford University, 1989) p.185
454 Ibid, p.130

with Brazil taking the place of England. The USA's success at the first World Cup was followed by a third place in 1995, with Norway taking the crown. For the Olympics on home soil, the pressure was placed upon the USA. The US Olympic Committee had declared the women 'potential gold medal winners' and 'invested a lot of money in their preparation' for the competition.[455]

The tournament was split into two groups of four, with two sides from each progressing to the semi-finals. The USA started with a 3-0 win over Denmark before beating Sweden 2-1 and drawing 0-0 with China. China, meanwhile, would top the group on goal difference, having beaten Sweden 2-0 and Denmark in style 5-1. In the other group, Norway and Brazil would make the knockout stages, having seen off Japan and Germany.

With World Cup holders Norway taking on the USA in the semi-finals, it was set to be a fine encounter on 28 July. Eighteen minutes in, Linda Medalen (who would eventually earn 152 caps and score 64 goals) struck to take the lead for Norway. With defeat on the cards, the US earned a late penalty. Michelle Akers (career record of 153 appearances and 105 goals), who was playing through injury for her country, stepped up and levelled the match to send the game to extra time.

Thirty minutes of additional football would be played, unless a team could find a winner with the 'golden goal' rules applying. In the 96th minute, Shannon MacMillan was substituted into the game and less than four minutes later she made her impact. As the clock hit 100, MacMillan picked the ball up from team-mate Julie Foudy 12 yards from goal. Her shot beat the Norwegian keeper and USA had their golden goal. They had 'dethroned the world champions' and set off in 'rapturous' celebrations.[456]

455 FIFA website, 'Women's Olympic Football Tournament Atlanta 1996', *FIFA* https://www.fifa.com/womensolympic/archive/atlanta1996/

456 Clemente A. Lisi, *The U.S. Women's Soccer Team: An American Success Story* (Plymouth: Scarecrow Press Inc., 2010) p.49

After the first golden goal in the first Olympics to feature a women's tournament, interest in the gold medal match built. Incredibly, though, American broadcaster NBC did not show coverage of the game across the country. This led to the US Soccer Federation's executive director, Hank Steinbrecher, 'blasting the network' for the decision, especially with the final's attendance hitting 76,481, the biggest ever crowd to watch a women's football fixture.[457]

On 1 August, China were the opponents after their 3-2 victory over Brazil. A 'charged-up' MacMillan,[458] now starting, would net the opener after 19 minutes and despite an equaliser from China in the first half, the gold medal was secured in the 68th minute. Forward Tiffeny Milbrett, who would record 100 goals in 206 caps, was assisted by Joy Fawcett as she finished off an American break to give the hosts the lead again and secured a 2-1 win that gave the USA a well-deserved first Olympic title.

---

457 *New York Times*, 2 August 1996
458 *Washington Post*, 2 August 1996

101

Pipo Rodríguez's winner sparks the Football War (1969)

'The imagined community of millions seems more real as a team of 11 named people.'[459]

IF PROOF was ever needed to exemplify just how important football is to entire nations, the aftermath of Maurcio 'Pipo' Rodriguez's 101st-minute winner for El Salvador against neighbours Honduras surely lays any scepticism to rest. Played in neutral Mexico City, the 1970 World Cup qualifier would see one of the two nations qualify for the following year's competition and represent their wider country on the grandest stage of all. Following months of diplomatic tensions between El Salvador and Honduras, the Estadio Azteca had become a battleground in which the players carried the hopes of the entirety of their respective nations.[460] The match was to be decided in Mexico following an inconclusive two-legged play-off. FIFA rules at the time did not pay attention to aggregate score and with both sides winning their home ties, a one-off match was needed to settle the tie. The two previous games had indeed been eventful

---

459 Eric Hobsbawm, *Nations and Nationalism Since 1780: Programme, Myth, Reality* (Cambridge: Cambridge University, 1992) p.143

460 Ben Jones and Gareth Thomas, *Football's 50 Most Important Moments* (Worthing: Pitch Publishing, 2020) p.99-101

and Honduran persecution of Salvadoran immigrants had been central to a rise in animosity between the two.

Following Honduras's 1-0 first-leg victory in Tegucigalpa, clashes between supporters erupted. Prior to the game, the home support had been intent on disrupting the sleep of the El Salvador visitors, singing loudly into the night. Already vexed by the unfair treatment of the El Salvadoran immigrant population in Honduras, violence would spark a response in the second leg. Displaying a dirtied rag in place of the Honduran flag when the two sides met in San Salvador, the away side, and their intimidated support, were further antagonised.

Worryingly, the 3-0 scoreline in favour of El Salvador only led to that further play-off in Mexico. With the two nations already teetering on the edge of war, another game was the last thing either country needed or indeed wanted.[461] The match itself was a brilliant example of competitive football and on the muddy turf of the Azteca, both sides traded goals. With the scoreline locked at 2-2 at full time, an additional 30 minutes was arranged to decide who would represent their nation at the 1970 World Cup. In the 101st minute, Pipo Rodríguez slid the ball beneath Honduran goalkeeper Jaime Varela and into the net.

Holding out to secure victory and qualification, the Salvadoran players celebrated euphorically while the Hondurans 'threw themselves on the muddy field and wept like children'.[462] In Honduras, irate supporters immediately focused their ire once again on El Salvadoran immigrants, often violently, prompting a mass exodus across the border. With their nationals under threat, El Salvador would declare war days later and even invade Honduras. Lasting for just 100 hours, the war saw 6,000 dead and a complete breakdown in diplomatic relations which are still yet to be fully restored. The match had highlighted football's role in promoting incredible levels of national identity and Eric Hobsbawm's words were put into brutal practice.

461 Jim Murphy, *The 10 Football Matches That Changed The World: And The One That Didn't* (London: Biteback, 2014)

462 *Liverpool Echo*, 28 June 1969

102

Injuries take their toll in 'the most brutal game in English football history' (1970)

THE 102ND minute proved the most difficult to find a distinctive moment for. After trawling through a seemingly endless amount of match reports, newspapers archives and secondary texts for references to the 12th minute of extra time, few goals, red cards or events could be found. However, upon reading up on the infamous FA Cup Final replay in 1970 we noticed that in this minute two injuries began to hinder the advance of Leeds as they searched for a cup triumph over Chelsea.

The later 1960s and early 1970s would see Leeds become one of the dominant forces in not only the British game, but across Europe. Built from the bottom up by the enigmatic Don Revie, the side had won little favour with neutrals due in part to their industrious nature and combative style of play.[463] Leeds had been perceived as 'dour, gritty northerners' and in some ways the antithesis of Londoners Chelsea. Chelsea reflected the flashy southerner, used to the finer things on the Kings Road. Of course, perceptions are often false with the two sides actually being remarkably similar in terms of their approach to

463 Sebb Stafford-Bloor, 'The Story of Don Revie and "Dirty Leeds", Tifo Football on YouTube, 10 February 2020, available at: https://www. youtube.com/watch?v=f2nmgf_z60k

the game. For all their aggression, they could also play some beautiful football.[464]

The 1970 final saw the sides draw 2-2 at Wembley before meeting once again in a replay held at Manchester United's Old Trafford. It was no secret that the two teams took a respectful dislike to their opponents. Earlier in his career, Leeds player Billy Bremner had described Chelsea as a side 'who would stoop to any level to intimidate and bully'.[465] Chelsea forward Peter Osgood, who scored the equaliser in the replay, would later write that there was no club he enjoyed beating more than Leeds, citing their arrogance as the main reason for such animosity.[466] Watched by a record 28 million people on British television, the game would live up to its billing.

The match was incredibly feisty. Described as 'the most brutal match in English football history' by the BBC in 2020,[467] its tempestuous nature is evident for all to see in the footage available. Perhaps even more astounding is the lack of discipline shown by referee Eric Jennings as tackle after tackle went unpunished. The match's antagonists were Chelsea's Ron 'Chopper' Harris and Leeds pair Bremner and Norman 'Bites Yer Legs' Hunter. It was Bremner, however, who fell victim to the game's most unseemly challenge. As the ball looped high into the Chelsea box, Bremner was caught in the head by a reckless, kung fu-style kick from Chelsea's centre-back Eddie McCreadie.

Watching Bremner crashing to the turf, it is hard to believe that Jennings insisted on playing on. After the score was still locked at 1-1 at full time, extra time saw no let-up in the

464 Phil Dawkes, '1970 FA Cup Final: The most brutal game in English football history', BBC Sport, 27 April 2020 https://www.bbc.co.uk/sport/football/52416192

465 Billy Bremner in Paul Harrison, *Keep Fighting: The Billy Bremner Story* (Black and White Publishing, 2010)

466 Peter Osgood, Martin King and Martin Knight, *Ossie: King of Stamford Bridge* (London: Mainstream, 2002)

467 Phil Dawkes, '1970 FA Cup Final: The most brutal game in English football history', BBC Sport

physicality with challenges starting to take their toll and even the usually unbreakable Hunter and Jack Charlton would begin to struggle in the 102nd minute.[468] Just two minutes later, a long throw from the left was flicked on and then bundled home at the far post by David Webb. Chelsea would go on to win the final and lift the cup for the first time.

The game's physical nature has led to it earning iconic status. Widely criticised in the immediate aftermath by fellow professionals and commentators, it is perhaps a match which perfectly encapsulates the British game as it headed into a decade of turbulence off the pitch.

Some 27 years after the final, top-flight official David Elleray would 're-referee' the game, stating that he would have issued six red cards throughout the 120 minutes. Even more recently, in 2020, Michael Oliver looked at the game with his modern views, deciding that, in total, 11 players should have been sent for an early bath.[469] This would of course have led to the game being abandoned.

Staggeringly, replay referee Jennings only issued a single booking as Chelsea and Leeds went to war at Old Trafford ...

468 *The Guardian*, 21 March 2020
469 *The Telegraph*, 15 April 2020

103

Thierry Henry's handball sets it up for William Gallas (2009)

ASK AN Irishman about their biggest injustice in football history and they are likely to say Thierry Henry ruining their World Cup hopes in 2009. The Republic of Ireland had drawn France in a World Cup play-off, with the winner earning a place at South Africa the next summer. On 18 November 2009, in the second leg, Henry's handball allowed him to assist team-mate William Gallas and book France's plane tickets.

The Republic of Ireland's 18 points in ten qualification matches had secured the Green Army a play-off place, with Italy topping their group. France, meanwhile, had finished second with 21 points, behind Serbia's 22. The two were drawn together to fight for one qualification spot, with the first leg in Dublin and the second in Saint-Denis.

On 14 November, at Croke Park, France won the first clash in the 72nd minute thanks to a Nicolas Anelka strike. This left the Irish needing a victory at the Stade de France four days later to keep their World Cup dream alive. In the 33rd minute Robbie Keane levelled the aggregate score at 1-1 and increased the belief that Ireland could make it to a fourth World Cup tournament.

After no further goals in the remaining hour, extra time would be required to decide the fate of the two nations. Then, in the 103rd minute, the travesty came. Florent Malouda delivered a deep free kick from near the halfway line and with the set piece heading out of play, Henry seemingly managed to bring it under control and slip it across to defender Gallas who headed the ball into the Irish net. Immediately, the Irish players erupted in furious protest and the television replays made it clear why. Henry used his hand not once, but twice, to keep the ball in play, enabling him to set up Gallas. The officials, not seeing this, gave the goal and with the final score ending 2-1 on aggregate, France were heading to South Africa.

French newspaper *L'Equipe* led with the headline 'The Hand of God',[470] taking inspiration from Diego Maradona's famous moment in 1986 (Minute 51), leading to the incident being remembered by some as 'Le Hand of God'. Henry himself claimed that 'it was a reflex', and that he immediately admitted the misdemeanour, saying the Irish players responded with, 'We don't blame you.'[471] The outpouring of anger though, was clear, with even French commentator Thierry Roland labelling it 'a scandal, a disgrace with a capital D'.[472]

At the 2010 World Cup, France would waste their gifted opportunity. A squad implosion in Africa saw Les Bleus finish bottom of their group, drawing 0-0 with Uruguay before losing to both Mexico and hosts South Africa. French president Nicolas Sarkozy described the behaviour of some of the national team as 'unacceptable'.[473] The early French exit perhaps compounded Irish disappointment, 2009 remaining a question of 'what if?' for the country to this day.

470 *L'Equipe*, 19 November 2009
471 *Daily Mirror*, 18 November 2018
472 *The Guardian*, 19 November 2009
473 *Daily Mail*, 24 June 2010

104

Henri Camara wins the 'best golden goal period ever' (2002)

'This is the best golden goal period I've ever seen, although there's not much in the way of competition because the rest have been dull as hell.'[474]

FOR ALL its negative press, there is no doubt that the golden goal rule left a memorable legacy on the beautiful game. Despite not fulfilling its ambition, it had created some of modern football's most infamous moments. Its final three uses, at the men's World Cup, would come in 2002 with the eventful last-16 tie between Senegal and Sweden offering a golden goal passage 'clearly not for the faint-hearted'.[475] Full of drama, in just 14 minutes, the two sides had at last brought FIFA's initial aim of attacking football to fruition.

Senegal had shocked the football world by winning the tournament's opening match against world and European champions France. The 1-0 scoreline in favour of the Lions of Teranga had symbolised the emergence of Africa, not just in

474 *The Guardian*, 16 June 2002

475 'Clockwatch: Sweden 1-2 Senegal (aet)', BBC Sport, 16 June 2002
     hhttp://news.bbc.co.uk/sport3/worldcup2002/low/matches_wallchart/
     sweden_v_senegal/newsid_2045000/2045497.stm

football, but as a wider continent. Defeating its former colonial power in South Korea, the victory prompted widespread rejoicing and jubilation in Senegal.[476] Spurred on by the triumph, the side managed by Bruno Metsu would progress from a difficult group which included Euro 92 winners Denmark and two-time world champions Uruguay.

Sweden, like Senegal, had also progressed from a troublesome group. Alongside Argentina, England and Nigeria, it had been regarded as the tournament's proverbial 'group of death'. Sweden would stun the watching world by winning the group and grew into each of the opening three games. Unfancied but respected, the squad could call upon the likes of Henrik Larsson and Freddie Ljungberg to provide moments of class. Going into the knockout fixture against Senegal, they had been regarded as narrow favourites to reach the quarter-finals.

According to the script, Larsson put the Swedes ahead in the 11th minute. However, a lesson which would be learned by most upon watching the 2002 World Cup was that matches rarely stuck to pre-written plans. Equalising in the 37th minute, Henri Camara helped the Senegalese send the tie into extra time. With only one previous example of a golden goal in World Cup history (Minute 114) the odds of a goal between Sweden and Senegal seemed incredibly unlikely with many fearing the additional period from the tournament's start.

During a 14-minute spell of attacking, end-to-end football, both sides came close to winning the match. First, Anders Svensson struck the Senegalese post with a powerful shot that was 'worthy enough to win the tournament itself, never mind this game'.[477] Emerging star El Hadji Diouf had caused the Swedish defence problems with his mazy runs and the man-mountain Papa Bouba Diop had fired over the bar from range. With Swedish legs growing tired, Senegal found another gear leading to Camara scoring past goalkeeper Magnus Hedman in

---

476 Robert Aldrich and Kirsten McKenzie, *The Routledge History of Western Empires* (London: Routledge, 2013) p.405

477 *The Guardian*, 16 June 2002

the 104th minute to seal the West African nation's place in the quarter-finals. As if to add further evidence to the bittersweet nature of the golden goal, Senegal would bow out in the following round to an extra-time strike by Turkish forward İlhan Mansiz.

105

Traianos Dellas scores football's only 'silver goal' (2004)

THE TRIALS and tribulations of the golden goal are well documented in this book and although not favoured at the time, it has seen a wealth of nostalgic sentiment in recent years. Its short-lived successor, the 'silver goal', however, has seen nothing of the sort. Only in existence for a year, the innovation by UEFA was designed to 'encourage positive football' and 'produce a sensible and fairer ending to a game'.[478] Used just once in a major international competition, the result of the experiment was a confusing, complicated and calamitous exercise from which football was quick to distance itself.

The silver goal would effectively limit extra time to 15 minutes. If a deciding goal was scored in the first period, then the game would end at half-time in extra time. This theoretically gave losing sides an opportunity to come back and provide stadiums with a definitive finishing time to ease and combat safety and security concerns.[479] If opposing teams were still level after the first period, then the rule would apply again in the second period before a penalty shootout would decide the winner if none could be found earlier.

478 *Irish Independent*, 29 April 2003
479 *Irish Independent*, 29 April 2003

Its most significant usage came in the 2004 European Championships, hosted in Portugal. Greece's run to the final, which they eventually won (Minute 57), was certainly eventful and their triumph was mainly thanks to a staunch defensive unit headed by centre-back Traianos Dellas. Withstanding attacking onslaughts from Portugal, Spain, Russia and France, the defence seemed unbreakable with another clean sheet against an impressive Czech side in the semi-final, taking the tie into extra time.

In the 105th minute, a corner from the right was swung in dangerously towards the front post. Amid a cluster of players, Dellas managed to flick a header goalwards and past the flat-footed Petr Čech. 'A silver goal worth its weight in gold,' wrote *Telegraph* journalist Henry Winter after the game, for Dellas's silver goal had indeed proven to be as valuable as its predecessor.[480] With just seconds left on the clock, there was no time for the Czechs to offer up a response to falling behind and the game was almost immediately brought to an end by referee Pierluigi Collina.

As if premeditating the law's future discrepancies, FIFA chose to remove the silver goal rule earlier in 2004 at an IFAB meeting in London. Its eradication was met with little contention and the game reverted back to the tried-and-tested extra-time method after the 2004 Euros.

480 *The Telegraph*, 2 July 2004

106

Roger Milla dances around the corner flag (1990)

AFRICAN FOOTBALL has boomed over the last 30 years. For decades, its nations were unfairly forgotten from international competition. From 1930–90 CAF (Confederation of African Football) countries had only been represented at the World Cup eight times. Indeed, until 1970 there was no certainty that African nations would be represented at all, with a 1966 continental boycott vehemently expressing their concerns. Adding to the detriment was the fact that when sides did qualify, like Zaire in 1974, a thrashing was just around the corner. African football needed revival.

Indeed, in 1990 the continent was only at the end of its post-war decolonisation. The late 1970s and early 1980s had seen FIFA, under the leadership of João Havelange, undertake sweeping changes to promote football in underdeveloped countries. International academies, of which six were in Africa, aimed at promoting both coaching and officiating before attention eventually switched to youth football.[481] Africa was being noticed, perhaps for the first time in the game's history.

Representing Africa at the 1990 World Cup were Egypt and Cameroon. Both sides had previously qualified for the finals, but neither had won a match. Egypt crashed out in a

481 Paul Darby, *Africa, Football and FIFA: Politics, Colonialism and Resistance* (London: Frank Cass, 2002) p.90

first knockout round in 1934, with Cameroon drawing all three group matches in 1982. There would be no tougher test then for Cameroon's Indomitable Lions than an opening meeting with defending champions Argentina. Played at the impressive San Siro in Milan, the game would open one of the sport's most revered tournaments – Italia 90.

With the odds stacked against them, it came as a shock when François Omam-Biyik put his side ahead in the 67th minute. A towering, yet relatively tame header squirmed underneath goalkeeper Nery Pumpido and over the line. Cameroon held firm until the end of the game and showed incredible grit and determination until the final whistle, and would ultimately qualify for the knockout stages where they faced a strong Colombian side in the last 16. After 90 minutes, the 0-0 scoreline had reflected, in its low scoring and negative play, the wider tournament's general standard. In extra time, however, the game would burst into life.

At 38 years old, Roger Milla had started his career in 1970 and helped to spread the African game to European shores through his goalscoring exploits in France's Ligue 1. At the 1990 World Cup he had found himself predominately on the substitutes' bench but was still able to make a positive impact when he came on. In the 106th minute against Colombia a long ball forward was poorly dealt with by Luis Fernando Herrera, allowing Milla through on goal with only goalkeeper René Higuita to beat. Striking left-footed into the net, Milla had sent the Cameroon supporters wild.

The image of Milla's celebration, dancing a 'jig of delight' at the corner flag, has arguably created a stronger legacy than the goal itself.[482] Milla's actions had indeed 'opened up new directions regarding how to celebrate a World Cup goal', with his dancing arguably having a greater symbolic meaning.[483]

482 *Newcastle Journal*, 25 June 1990

483 Susann Baller, Giorgio Miescher and Ciraj Rassool, 'Global Perspectives on Football in Africa: Visualising the Game', *Soccer and Society*, Vol. 13, Issue 2 (March 2012) pp.139–155

Upon his celebration, the promotion of wider African culture was clear. Its subsequent use by a multitude of African nations at the World Cup, like Senegal in 2002 or South Africa in 2010, seems to prove this.

Providing arguably the greatest shock in World Cup history since North Korea in 1966 (Minute 42), Cameroon's run to the quarter-finals, where they were eventually beaten by England after extra time, was one for the entirety of African football. Played among an 'irresistible narrative', it provided the impetus for the continental game to make dramatic improvements over the coming decades.[484] Culminating in the 2010 South African World Cup, Cameroon's role in the reinvention and reimagining of African football cannot be understated.

484 *The Guardian*, 13 March 2018

107

Blackburn Olympic provides football's early rebirth (1883)

TWENTY YEARS after the formation of the FA and the codification of the modern game, football was encountering its greatest challenge to date. The introduction of 'veiled' professionalism had caused a schism which tore through the heart of the game.

Described by some as a 'disease', it brought wider issues surrounding class and identity to the forefront of football discussion. In 1883, on the then grandest stage of all, the FA Cup Final, a meeting between Blackburn Olympic and Old Etonians would change the sport forever.

Football had been introduced as an amateur venture. Indeed for those playing, doing so for 'the love of the game' was to outweigh any other reason for competing. Taken up in great numbers midway through the 19th century, football's main participants had been wealthy, upper-class public schoolboys and alumni. Amateurism reigned supreme and the eventual success of the Football Association led to a 'sporting revolution' with each new game also promoting 'playing for the sake of playing'.

By the late 1870s, a shift in the game was clear. A result of increased leisure time for the working classes, athletic exercise became prevalent in British society. Football, with its simplistic rules and lack of violence (in comparison to rugby), seemed a natural sport for the emancipated workers to undertake.[485] The game began to shift northwards and into the industrial heartlands of the country, making significant inroads in the Midlands and Lancashire. Nottingham Forest's run to the semi-finals of the FA Cup in 1880 raised a few eyebrows, particularly after 'beating' one the game's great amateur sides, Sheffield FC. The latter had refused to play on after drawing 2-2 at full-time leading to a 'monstrous departure from the line of justice and fair play'.[486]

If eyebrows had been raised in 1880, 1882 finalists Blackburn Rovers would cause an influx of snobbery and condescension from the southern-based media. Rovers would lose the game to the Old Etonians 1-0 at the Oval, but their sheer presence in the latter stages of the competition brought reports of 'patricians vs plebeians' in the *Athletic News*.[487] Etonian victory over the 'northern horde of uncouth garbe' had been welcomed by many and the following year, they would reach the final once again. This time it would be another Blackburn side meeting them – Blackburn Olympic.[488]

Olympic would win the tie, defeating their southern rivals 2-1 after extra time. A powerful shot in the 107th minute from James Costley had proven to be the difference in front of one the game's largest ever gates.[489] Consistently regarded as 'northerners', the FA Cup victory was immediately recognised as a significant one. For many commentators, the game between Blackburn Olympic and the Old Etonians is significant for its role in shifting the game from the south of England to the north. Matthew Taylor disagreed with this sentiment, arguing that such a trend was already firmly under way.[490] Looking

---

485 Derek Birley, *Sport and the Making of Britain* (Manchester: Manchester University Press, 1993) p.270

486 *Nottingham Evening Post*, 21 February 1880

487 *Athletic News*, 21 March 1883

488 Matthew Taylor, *The Association Game* (London: Routledge, 2008) p.47

489 *Manchester Guardian*, 2 April 1883

490 Matthew Taylor, *The Association Game*, p.43

deeper into the victory for Olympic, the most important element to draw from their success was their new 'professional' attitude to the game. The side had prepared for weeks before the final, even enduring strict 'training' at Blackpool.[491] The impact of such measures were clear to see, according to the *Manchester Guardian,* as the newspaper noticed the 'superb condition' and 'fresh vigour' of Olympic, even in extra time.[492]

Introducing professional approaches is of course different to actual professionalism. Financial backing had been present in Olympic's victory but whether the players themselves were being paid to play the game is unclear. However, in 1883, football would see paid players begin to surface, most notably with Accrington's expulsion from the FA for 'having employed and paid a professional player'.[493]

Despite being later reinstated to the relief of enthusiastic crowds, the debate around professionalism would dominate discussion and debate for the next decade. Blackburn Olympic's victory had helped cement the game's shift northwards and open football to a new standard of play through their professional approach.

Blackburn Olympic 2 Old Etonians 1 – football's most important game? It just might be.

491 *Sporting Life*, 31 March 1883
492 *Manchester Guardian*, 2 April 1883
493 *North British Daily Mail*, 28 November 1883

108

Klaus Fischer equalises for West Germany against France (1982)

THE 1982 FIFA World Cup, held in Spain, has been regarded by some admirers of the beautiful game as the 'best ever'.[494] Italy would lift a third world crown with Juventus striker Paolo Rossi taking home the Golden Boot. For many, the epic semi-final clash between West Germany and France will be considered one of their favourite games of the whole competition.

The 1982 tournament was the first that was expanded to 24 teams. This enabled Algeria, Cameroon, Honduras, Kuwait and New Zealand to all make their World Cup debuts. With two scheduled group stages, countries would have to navigate five fixtures to earn themselves a place in the last four. Home nations England and Northern Ireland fell in the second group stage, while Scotland were sent packing after just three games.

West Germany's progress was secured via the controversial 'Disgrace of Gijón'.[495] Having shockingly lost to Algeria 2-1 in their opening match, the 4-1 victory over Chile still meant they needed to beat Austria to stay in Spain. However, with Algeria's final game win against Chile being played the previous day, Austria knew that they could lose narrowly to West Germany

494 Ben Jones, 'The 1982 World Cup: The Best Ever?', *The Football History Boys*, 9 April 2019 https://www.thefootballhistoryboys.com/2019/04/the-1982-world-cup-best-ever.html

495 Ibid

and they would be safe too. With Horst Hrubesch giving the Germans an early lead, what followed was an incredibly tame affair with the neighbours seemingly protecting each other. West Germany made just eight tackles in the second half as both sides boasted pass-completion rates of over 90 per cent. It was a 'terrible' match.[496]

With both sides controversially through, the West Germans would then draw with England and beat Spain to make the semi-finals. France's route, meanwhile, was also less than straightforward. An opening loss to England saw them bounce back to see off Kuwait 4-1, before their 1-1 draw with the Czechs gave them second spot in Group Four. They began to peak at the right time in the second stage, beating the Austrians 1-0 and putting four past Northern Ireland, both at Madrid's Vicente Calderón Stadium.

On 8 July, West Germany and France would meet in Seville with a place in the final on the line. West Germany were missing their captain Karl-Heinz Rummenigge, a hamstring injury limiting him to the bench only, but they would strike first with Pierre Littbarski making it 1-0. After 26 minutes the match was level again, German defender Bernd Förster giving the French a penalty that Michel Platini slotted home.

The second 45 was marked by an injury to French substitute Patrick Battiston. As he raced to connect a toe with a bouncing through ball, German keeper Harald Schumacher charged the Frenchman on the edge of the box. The ball sailed wide but Battiston took the brunt of Schumacher's hip, knocking him unconscious and leaving him needing a stretcher to leave the field. The unpunished incident enraged the French, but despite a host of good chances for both countries, the scores remained 1-1 after 90 minutes – extra time would be required.

Two minutes into the additional half-hour, France scored. Defender Marius Trésor smashed a volley in from the penalty spot from a wide free kick. Les Bleus quickly added a third,

496 *Irish Times*, 23 May 2018

Alain Giresse surely making the lead unassailable. But then the West Germans came roaring back as the risked substitute Rummenigge breathed life into the German fans. Then, after 108 minutes, Klaus Fischer completed the comeback with a bicycle kick from the six-yard line making it 3-3.

Two hours of football had left the players 'exhausted and drained' but equal.[497] This meant the first World Cup penalty shootout would take place. French misses from Didier Six and Maxime Bossis meant that Hrubesch's successful spot kick would take the West Germans into the final with a 5-4 victory. The tournament had enjoyed a 'pot pourri of scoring, strength and stamina' in this tie,[498] while Platini would later reminisce that this was his 'most beautiful game', poetically recalling, 'What happened in those two hours encapsulated all the sentiments of life itself.'[499]

The Italians would lift the trophy as 3-1 victors against West Germany, perhaps the toll of the semi-final playing a part. This game, though, should rightly be remembered as one of the best.

497 *Reading Evening Post*, 9 July 1982

498 Clemente A. Lisi, *A History of the World Cup: 1930–2010* (Plymouth: Scarecrow Press Inc., 2011) p.184

499 *The Guardian*, 26 October 2008

109

Substitute Ryan Giggs weaves through the entire Arsenal defence (1999)

SIR ALEX Ferguson and Ryan Giggs both had long and incredibly successful careers with Manchester United. The pair boast a personal trophy cabinet that most footballers, managers and fans could only dream of. There is little doubt though, that their greatest campaign was the 1998/99 treble season as United brought the Premier League, Champions League and FA Cup to Old Trafford. The Champions League win is remembered for late drama (Minute 93), but the FA Cup, too, was only secured with a semi-final extra-time beauty.

Under Ferguson and Arsène Wenger, United and Arsenal had some fiery, intense and brilliant battles. In 1999, Arsenal were playing their part in attempting to prevent a first English domestic and European treble, scrapping with United in both the league and the FA Cup. On 18 May 1999, David Beckham and Andy Cole scored in the 2-1 defeat of Tottenham Hotspur to win the league title ahead of Arsenal by just a single point.

A month previous, in April 1999, the two had met in FA Cup semi-final action. At neutral Villa Park, United and Arsenal drew 0-0 and as was the case back then, a replay would be required. Three days later they came face to face again and just 17 minutes in Beckham broke the deadlock with a fine, first-time strike from 25 yards. In the second 45, the scores were levelled by Arsenal forward Dennis Bergkamp. Picking the ball up in the middle of the Manchester United half, the Dutchman turned and drove towards goalkeeper Peter Schmeichel, hitting it from 30 yards. The ball struck defender Jaap Stam, Bergkamp's international team-mate, deflecting off his knee and passing the giant Dane.

Momentum shifted in the Gunners' favour: Nicolas Anelka had a potential match-winning goal ruled out for offside minutes later, before United's midfield hard man Roy Keane was dismissed for a second yellow in the 74th minute. Then, in added time, Phil Neville brought down Arsenal's Ray Parlour inside the box and a penalty was awarded. Arsenal were a kick from the FA Cup Final as Bergkamp confidently stepped up. The penalty, struck to Schmeichel's left, was saved, United too were saved and extra time beckoned.

In the 109th minute of the tie, as was reported in the media, 'just when it seemed as if there was nothing else which this compelling match could produce to shock or thrill',[500] Giggs's stunner came. Intercepting the ball ten yards inside his own half, the Welshman surged towards goal at pace. Beating four players, including defender Lee Dixon twice, Giggs burst into the Arsenal penalty area and hit his shot high past the helpless David Seaman to put United 2-1 up.

The winger ripped his shirt off and spun it around his head in a now-famous, bare-chested celebration, keeping United's 'dreams of the treble firmly on course'.[501] With the FA Cup lifted on 22 May 1999 with a 2-0 victory over Newcastle, the treble was then achieved at the Camp Nou, Barcelona. In remarkable circumstances against Bayern Munich, a Red Devils late show wrote Manchester United 1998/99 into English footballing history.

Upon Giggs announcing his retirement in 2014, the *Daily Mirror* paid tribute to him, recalling 'one moment from 15 years ago that stands above the rest'.[502] This FA Cup semi-final goal really is one of the competition's best.

500 *Aberdeen Press and Journal*, 15 April 1999
501 Ibid
502 *Daily Mirror*, 19 May 2014

110

Zinedine Zidane headbutts his way into retirement (2006)

ZINEDINE ZIDANE. The name alone provokes a wealth of superlatives, each justifiably used to describe the Frenchman's remarkable career. There is, however, one word above all else for which he will be forever remembered – headbutt. Zidane's time at the top of the world game had seen him rise to superstar status in the late 1990s. His demonstrations of outrageous skill and unbelievable goals, like that which won the Champions League in 2002, helped him to become the 'greatest player of his era'.[503]

Zidane had retired from international football after France's failed title defence at Euro 2004. Adamant that this was 'the end of the story', the Real Madrid midfielder was sure in his decision.[504] However, just a year later, French coach Raymond Domenech had convinced Zidane to return to the international fold in time for his nation's final World Cup qualifiers. The 2006 World Cup in Germany was to be his swansong with the weeks prior to the tournament's start dominated by Zidane's announcement of complete retirement after the competition's finale.

503 Tim Hill, *Encyclopedia of World Football: From the Origins of the Game to 2007: The Essential Fans' Guide* (Bath: Parragon, 2007) p.92

504 CNN, 'Zidane quits French national team', *CNN*, 12 August 2004 https://edition.cnn.com/2004/SPORT/football/08/12/zidane.retirement/

Claiming that his form had dropped, and that each year football was becoming more and more difficult, this retirement would be definitive.[505] After the announcement, Zidane took little time in imposing himself upon the tournament. *The Times* reported that the midfielder was 'making a late run for immortality' after his virtuoso performance against Spain in the first knockout round.[506] Four days later, the superlatives were out once again after Zidane produced one of the greatest individual performances of all time to help knock out favourites Brazil in the quarter-finals. Described by *The Guardian* as a 'second coming', the performance was akin to an act of divine intervention.[507] Neutral support was well and truly behind Les Bleus following victory over Portugal in the semi-final. Italy was all that stood between the number ten and footballing immortality.

Just seven minutes into the final in Berlin a clumsy challenge from Marco Materazzi on Florent Malouda gave Zidane a chance from the penalty spot. As if exemplifying the undoubted class and elegance of the French captain, a cheeky Panenka was chipped to Gianluigi Buffon's left before caressing the underside of the bar and bouncing in. France led 1-0. The footballing gods, it seemed, were smiling down on Zidane. Just 11 minutes later, however, a header from Materazzi levelled the final at 1-1. Despite an entertaining game, the scoreline would remain the same until full time, offering Zidane 30 extra minutes to win his second World Cup title.

Zidane had gone close to putting France ahead in extra time after his fine header was stopped by an even better save from Buffon. In the 110th minute, with the game heading towards penalties, a coming together between Zizou and Materazzi resulted in the Italian centre-half launching into a tirade of

505 Alex Livie, 'Zidane announces retirement', *Sky Sports*, January 2006 https://www.skysports.com/football/news/11835/2374656/zidane-announces-retirement

506 *The Times*, 28 June 2006

507 *The Guardian*, 2 July 2006

insults aimed at his opponent. Without a moment's hesitation, Zidane's head came crashing into the centre of Materazzi's chest, sending him unceremoniously down to the turf. After consulting with his assistant, Argentine referee Horacio Elizondo had no choice but to show Zidane a straight red card.

The dismissed Zinedine Zidane walking past the World Cup trophy with his head down has become one of the game's defining images.

To add further misery to the French, Italy would seal a fourth World Cup title in the resulting penalty shootout. Semi-final hero Fabio Grosso (Minute 119) scored the decisive penalty amid jubilant scenes.

For the neutral, the feeling at the final whistle was mixed – perhaps Brazilian legend Leonardo summed it up best on BBC Sport: 'I am really happy for the Italians; I think they deserved it. But it is hard to express total happiness because of Zidane. He is the symbol of the last generation of football. He scored the early penalty. But he deserved to be sent off. The world of football is very sad.'[508]

508 Leonardo in BBC, 'Italy 1-1 France (aet)', BBC Sport, 9 July 2006 http://news.bbc.co.uk/sport1/hi/football/world_cup_2006/5148796.stm

111

The 'Game of the Century' is settled by Gianni Rivera (1970)

THROUGHOUT RECENT history, the relationship between Germany and Italy has been often fractious, sometimes friendly and always full of football. At international level, the rivalry between the two is one of the most revered and renowned with numerous memorable encounters shaping the modern game. In 1970, the two sides both enjoyed successful runs to the World Cup semi-finals before meeting at the Estadio Azteca in Mexico. The resulting 120 minutes have been described, by a wealth of commentators, as the 'Game of the Century'.

The 1970 World Cup had seen both Germany and Italy progress to the knockout rounds as group winners. Germany had been free-scoring, with the talented Gerd Müller firing an impressive seven goals in three games. Italy, on the other hand, had emerged on top by demonstrating their tried-and-tested catenaccio style. With only one goal scored, but none conceded, their progression was secure. The watching world was surprised to see a tactical shift by the time the Azzurri faced hosts Mexico in the last eight. Scoring four in Toluca, Italy were determined not to let the ghosts of 1966 resurface (Minute 42) with captain Giacinto Facchetti stating he'd rather drop dead than let it happen again.[509]

509 *The Times*, 16 June 1970

Germany had beaten their 1966 conquerors England in the quarter-finals and entered the semi-finals as slight underdogs. Defeating England after a dramatic comeback meant they could now feel 'capable of anything', but *The Times* believed Italy 'just to have the edge'.[510] Roberto Boninsegna opened the scoring in the eighth minute before Karl-Heinz Schnellinger equalised in the final minute of the game. According to the script and with the score locked at 1-1, the two sides couldn't be separated after 90 minutes, leading to an eventful period of extra time.

The 30 minutes that followed was comfortably the greatest additional period in football's illustrious history. In spite of their aggravations at some contentious decisions towards their side and an injury to star man Franz Beckenbauer,[511] West Germany took the lead four minutes into extra time. Müller notched his tenth of the tournament before Tarcisio Burgnich levelled the scores. With the game flowing and the action moving from one end of the Azteca to the other, Luigi Riva would put the Azzurri ahead. The lead lasted just six minutes as Müller once again pounced on some circumspect Italian defending to make the score 3-3.

West German jubilation was short-lived. Straight from the kick-off, Italy attacked down the left. German legs were growing increasingly fatigued and after a burst of pace from Boninsegna, his fine cut-back was side-footed into the net by Milan midfielder Gianni Rivera. Italy had well and truly thrown off the shackles of catenaccio and utilised their attacking might to devastating effect. Upon the final whistle, both sides collapsed on the turf exhausted after their colossal efforts over 120 minutes in the Mexican heat.

The tie drew worldwide acclaim. The *Coventry Evening Telegraph* described the action as 'sensational' and took note of the reception both sides received at the end, with the players

---

510 *The Times*, 17 June 1970

511 Beckenbauer had been forced to play the remainder of the game with his arm in a sling.

applauded off the pitch for several minutes.[512] Despite losing the subsequent final to Brazil 4-1, the semi-final triumph has become legendary in Italy. John Foot wrote that the victory over West Germany has remained part of the nation's identity with books, films and numerous newspaper articles telling and retelling the story of '*the* game' in 1970.[513] Arguably the greatest game of all time – this was football at its best.

512 *Coventry Evening Telegraph*, 18 June 1970

513 John Foot, *Calcio: A History of Italian Football* (London: Harper Perennial, 2006) p.495

112

Johan Cruyff's Dream Team completes the set (1992)

FOOTBALL IN the 1970s was defined by Johan Cruyff. A player of elegance, skill and direction, he swept all aside with his attacking flair and incredible mentality. Developing his playing career under the stewardship of Total Football pioneer Rinus Michels, Cruyff's own coaching ideology would reflect that of his former mentor.[514] Michels's positive approach to man-management and his intention on developing a one-club mentality is clear to see in Johan Cruyff's own Barcelona side of the late 1980s and early 1990s. After a decade of decline, Cruyff would reinvent the Spanish team into Europe's 'Dream Team'.

The early 1980s had been turbulent for Barcelona. Two league titles in 28 years highlighted the once great Catalan club's dramatic fall from grace. For many, the club had become a fractured institution with problems both on and off the pitch. The Hesperia Mutiny in 1988 had highlighted the angst of senior players against the dictatorial style of club president José Luis Núñez.

Furthermore, the infamous Boixos Nois casuals group had caused a wealth of issues in the stands. As if to rub salt into the wound, Barça's great rivals, Real Madrid, were undergoing

---

514 Johan Cruyff, *My Turn* (London: Pan Macmillan, 2016) pp.13–14

a resurgence, spearheaded by the home-grown La Quinta del Buitre (The Vulture's Cohort).[515]

Unpopular and universally criticised, Núñez would appoint former fan favourite Cruyff as manager in 1988. A populist move, the capture of the Dutchman was aimed initially to deflect attention away from the president's incapability. Immediately, Cruyff began to make his presence known. Shrewd in his tactics and wholly committed to training, for the new Barcelona manager, football was about 'thinking through creatively but logically'.[516] Turning traditional thinking on its head, Cruyff would impose a new form of management. Constantly reinventing training drills and promoting youth from their relatively new academy, La Masia, the club's fresh image was reflected in their instant victories across multiple competitions.

Prior to 1992, Cruyff had led his side to the European Cup Winners' Cup in 1989, the Copa del Rey in 1990 and the La Liga title in 1991. The league was successfully defended in '92 and silverware was returning to the enormous trophy cabinet at the Camp Nou. Cruyff had worked tirelessly to change the whole mentality of the club and helped it to develop a backbone.[517] His adoption of a 3-4-3 formation was adapted from Michels's favoured 4-3-3 and disseminated into each and every Barça side. If the first team played that system, so would the reserves and youth teams. In that way, Cruyff could find players from across the club to immediately cover any empty first-team position.

Cruyff had assembled a side revered by the footballing world as the Dream Team. A mixture of world-class foreign talent and home-grown youngsters provided the catalyst for European domination in 1992. After reaching the European Cup Final at Wembley, the Italian side Sampdoria were all that stood in

---

515 Ben Jones and Gareth Thomas, *Football's 50 Most Important Moments* (Worthing: Pitch Publishing, 2020) pp.134–135

516 Johan Cruyff, *My Turn*, p.130

517 Graham Hunter, *Barca: The Making of the Greatest Team in the World* (Glasgow: BackPage Press, 2012) p.132

Cruyff's way of achieving what few believed possible upon his arrival just four years earlier. The game itself was poor with few chances in normal time, and the only goal would come in the 112th minute. A superbly struck free kick from Dutch sweeper Ronald Koeman flew past Gianluca Pagliuca and into the Wembley net. In the words of Cruyff himself, 'After four years, my mission had been accomplished.'[518]

518 Johan Cruyff, *My Turn*, p.132

113

The Soviet Union win the first European Championships (1960)

FIFTEEN YEARS after the end of World War Two, global tensions were yet to cease. The emergence of the communist USSR as a genuine superpower to rival the US was, to many, a threat which needed sorting. For all the wider conflicts during the immediate period in Korea, Vietnam and Central America, sporting arenas would also become battlegrounds in which opposing ideologies were brought to the centre of attention. The first European Championship (then called the European Nations' Cup) would bring the peculiar relationship of politics and sport into the forefront of popular discussion.

The founding of UEFA in 1954 had seen general secretary Henri Delaunay intent on promoting the idea of an international competition exclusive to Europe. Described by UEFA as a 'fascinating genesis', its origins can be traced back to 1927.[519] Three years before the World Cup, Delaunay and Austrian football pioneer Hugo Meisl had suggested the idea of a 'European Football Championships' to FIFA, but to no avail. Almost 30 years later, Delaunay succeeded, in spite of reservations from FIFA once again. The tournament was to be set in two stages with a two-legged knockout 'qualification' campaign before a final tournament comprising the remaining four sides.

519 UEFA Publication, 'UEFA's Euro: 60 years on', *UEFA Direct*, Issue 179, 1 July 2018, Available at: https://www.uefa.com/

As it seems with any new innovation in football, the introduction of the European Nations' Cup was not welcomed by everyone. West Germany, Italy, Switzerland and the home nations all refused to take part. Disappointingly, particularly with players, the home nations had believed their own four-team tournament to be of a higher standard with Gordon Banks describing their attitude as 'insular'.[520] For all British football's renaissance in the late 1950s, such a decision was frustrating.

Even the nations who took part were not short of grievances. Spain in particular caused a wealth of commotion by refusing to play their quarter-final tie with the USSR. The Spanish Civil War had seen tensions between the nations reach critical levels as the Soviet Union openly supported the Republican regime and was fiercely critical of Nationalist General Franco. Sport had been used to spread the propaganda of the dictator's regime and defeat to a communist nation would have proven detrimental to his power. The match's potential to ease relations had been clear as soon as the draw was made with newspapers claiming it offered the first chance 'to break the ice', but ultimately Spain was unmoved.[521]

The start of the competition would receive little recognition from the British press, perhaps due in part to the scepticism around the finalists. It is notable to see that three of the four nations that reached the final tournament were from the eastern side of the Iron Curtain. The USSR would go on to win the tournament. Led by the 'Black Spider' Lev Yashin in goal, they beat Czechoslovakia comfortably in the semi-final before taking on Yugoslavia in the final in Paris.

The final was surprisingly broadcast on the BBC with one writer from the *Belfast Telegraph* writing about how he was 'entranced by the skill of the players' and the 'gallant pronunciation of the players' names by commentator Kenneth

---

520 Gordon Banks, *Banksy: The Autobiography of an English Football Hero* (London: Penguin, 2003)

521 *Torbay Express and South Devon Echo,* 18 April 1960

Wolstenholme'.[522] The match had seen only 17,000 supporters in attendance but an exceptional performance from the Soviet Union. With the scores being level at full time it would take until the 113th minute for the winner to be found. Viktor Ponedelnik's header proved to be the difference and the first European Nations' Cup was heading to the USSR.

What makes this minute so decisive in football history? Firstly, it is a moment which summarises the immediate years after World War Two. It highlights the mistrust of communism from western Europe, the politicisation of sport under Franco's fascist dictatorship and the continued isolationism of British football towards the rest of Europe. Four years later, however, the tournament would see an improvement in participation as Spain even hosted the competition. Ironically, they beat the USSR in the final.

522 *Belfast Telegraph*, 11 July 1960

114

Laurent Blanc's golden goal puts the Rainbow Team on course for victory (1998)

TO HOST a World Cup is a great honour for a country, but more than that, it brings the pressure of home success. For France in 1998, the expectations were high that they would emulate Uruguay (1930), Italy (1934), England (1966), West Germany (1974) and Argentina (1978) by winning the ultimate reward on home soil. In the last 16 against Paraguay, however, the French had been held to a 0-0 deadlock, and in extra time, Laurent Blanc's golden goal in the 114th minute allowed them to progress.

The French squad of 1998, captained by Didier Deschamps, are remembered as the 'Rainbow Team'. It was a squad of 22 men not just from France but with 'ethnic backgrounds from North Africa, West Africa, the Caribbean, the Pacific islands, Armenia and the Basque country'.[523] The national team reflected the make-up of France itself, diverse and multicultural in nature. Glory in 1998 could bring these nationalities and ethnicities together, giving the football a far deeper societal importance.

In their group games, Les Bleus recorded a 3-0 win over South Africa in the opener before beating Saudi Arabia 4-0

---

523 Matias Grez, 'France's "Rainbow Team" looks back at historic World Cup triumph', *CNN*, 6 July 2018 https://edition.cnn.com/2018/06/08/football/france-1998-world-cup-win-anniversary/index.html

and then seeing off an excellent Denmark 2-1. The nine points secured them a last-16 clash with Paraguay. The South Americans had come through as the second-placed side in Group D, behind Nigeria, winning just once and drawing twice. France were clear favourites for the fixture on 28 June at Stade Félix-Bollaert, Lens.

French talisman and poster boy Zinedine Zidane was suspended, having been given a straight red card against Saudi Arabia. He was serving the second of a two-match ban but in his absence, Thierry Henry could have stolen the headlines in the 39th minute. Through on goal, the young Monaco forward had just Paraguay keeper José Luis Chilavert to beat but his shot struck the post.

After a 0-0 draw in normal time, extra time took place with the new World Cup 'golden goal' rule of 30 minutes of sudden death football where a single goal would settle the match. In the 114th minute, a half-cleared header from Paraguay fell to Robert Pires. The Metz midfielder delivered a delightful cross to striker David Trezeguet, whose cushioned header found Blanc at the back post. Blanc buried the opportunity and a first World Cup golden goal was scored.

France needed penalties in the quarter-finals to defeat Italy, but their 2-1 victory over Croatia in the semi-finals gave them a massive final on their home turf. On 12 July, Zidane seized the final for Les Bleus with a brilliant brace against Brazil. Emmanuel Petit made it 3-0 in injury time at the Stade de France and the French finally had a first World Cup crown.

'Merci, Zizou!' was projected on to the Champs-Élysées after the game in celebration of their star man,[524] and the *New York Times* the next day highlighted the importance of Zidane in the final. Wearing the hallowed number ten shirt, the 'most evocative in soccer', one that implies 'creativity' and 'leadership', Zidane lived up to the weight on his shoulders and the number

---

524 Thomas Dunmore and Scott Murray, *Soccer for Dummies* (Indianapolis: John Wiley and Sons Inc., 2013) p.313

on his number back on 'the most important evening in the history of French sport'.[525]

Defender Marcel Desailly, himself of Ghanaian descent, reflected on the impact of the Rainbow Team's victory, 'The fans, everybody was together. No racism, no discrimination, everybody was happy in France.'[526]

For Blanc too, his moment would go down in World Cup history. The first golden goal (and one of just four) on the grandest stage of them all had kept the dream alive.

525 *New York Times*, 13 July 1998

526 Matias Grez, 'France's "Rainbow Team" looks back at historic World Cup triumph', CNN, 6 July 2018 https://edition.cnn.com/2018/06/08/football/france-1998-world-cup-win-anniversary/index.html

115

Argentina win the most controversial tournament in history (1978)

TWO YEARS after Argentina had seen a ruthless military coup rise to power, it hosted the World Cup in 1978. Taking place during the Cold War, the tournament's preparations were overshadowed by the removal of president Isabel Perón by the right-wing Argentine military. Amid negative global reaction to the conflict, some of the qualified nations would publicly consider their involvement. Once again, football's intricate relationship with politics was to be thrust into the forefront of public debate. As the opening game approached, it was clear the competition was to be about far more than just football.

The tournament was to be littered with controversy. For all its initial positivity, negative sentiment surrounding the hosts' progression to the final was rife. The first group stage had seen some of the World Cup's most memorable moments to date with Archie Gemmill's weaving run through the Dutch defence offering arguably the competition's best goal. In a stranger story concerning France and Hungary, a mix-up with kits and both sides arriving at the Estadio José Maria Minella with white jerseys led to the French team donning the green stripes of local side Kimberley de Mar del Plata. The 1978 World Cup was only to get stranger as the second group stage began.

The controversy of the second group stage would be exemplified no more clearly than when Argentina were pitted against Peru in what is now considered to be the tournament's most infamous and debatable moment. In spite of the competition already having been overshadowed by the civil unrest on the streets of Buenos Aires, the premature whistle-blowing of Clive Thomas and the drug misuse of Scot Willie Johnston – this would transcend all. La Albiceleste, in need of a four-goal victory to seal their place in the final, would eventually defeat their South American neighbours 6-0 in order to meet the Netherlands at the Estadio Monumental. Ever since the final whistle was blown in Mendoza, reports and rumours of match-fixing and military intimidation have been rampant.[527]

The tournament and the success of the Argentine squad had helped to promote a wave of nationalism across the country.[528] For those in power, football had managed to do what the nation's corrupt policies and brutal repression couldn't do – unite. With the final and victory in touching distance, the opportunity for global triumph was too good to miss. The players had undoubtedly been used as political pawns by the Argentine government, echoing Italian use of the game in 1934 and 1938.

A delay to the kick-off did little to ruin the final itself, which was a genuinely good game. Mario Kempes opened the scoring before Dick Nanninga equalised with a powerful header eight minutes from time. With the score locked at 1-1, extra time would be needed to separate the sides. A trademark solo run by Kempes, just before half-time in extra time, was finished after a slice of good fortune. In the 115th minute, Daniel Bertoni completed the victory after capitalising on some suspect Dutch defending. For the Netherlands, it would prove to be a second World Cup Final defeat in succession, but

---

527 Jonathan Stevenson, 'The story of the 1978 World Cup', *BBC Sport*, 18 May 2010
https://www.bbc.co.uk/blogs/jonathanstevenson/2010/05/the_story_of_the_1978_world_cu.html

528 Jonathan Wilson, *Angels With Dirty Faces: A Footballing History of Argentina* (London: Orion, 2016)

without Johan Cruyff the squad could at least take some solace in their achievements.

Presenting the trophy to captain Daniel Passarella was the military leader, General Jorge Rafael Videla. The World Cup had achieved national euphoria and a cover for the atrocities which would reconvene following the final. To this day, many commentators, including players from the Argentine squads believe the 1978 World Cup should never have been played. By allowing the tournament to go ahead, FIFA had turned its back on the thousands of 'disappeared' individuals and political prisoners in the South American state. This episode of the World Cup story is sure to be endlessly scrutinised and studied by historians in the years to come.

116

Andrés Iniesta wins the
World Cup for Spain (2010)

WHEN DEBATING the greatest international sides to ever grace the beautiful game, one that must always be considered is the Spanish side of 2008 to 2012. La Roja won three successive major tournaments, the 2008 and 2012 European Championships sandwiching the crowning glory, the World Cup of 2010. In the 116th minute of the 2010 World Cup Final in South Africa, Andrés Iniesta's extra-time goal secured the well-deserved trophy and sent this Spanish team down in history.

The Spanish were first introduced to the tiki-taka style of play by Luis Aragonés after he took the reins in 2004. The Wise Man of Hortaleza, as he was known, was 'obsessed with possession football' and the new style of fast, short passing and movement led to an unbeaten 2006 World Cup qualification campaign.[529] At Euro 2008, tiki-taka would bring Spain victory, waltzing through the tournament in Austria and Switzerland before beating Germany 1-0 in the final.

Domestically, Pep Guardiola's tiki-taka Barcelona side dominated La Liga (Minute 10) and added a Champions League

---

529 Gareth Thomas, 'Luis Aragonés – The Wise Man of Hortaleza', *The Football History Boys*, 7 February 2014 https://www. thefootballhistoryboys.com/2014/02/luis-aragones-wise-man-of-hortaleza.html

in 2009 in the build-up to the 2010 World Cup, which would be played in Africa for the first time, South Africa given the honour of hosting the competition. However, for Spain, things got off to an unexpected start as Vicente del Bosque's side lost 1-0 to Switzerland.

Subsequent 2-0 and 2-1 wins against Honduras and Chile respectively made sure the Spanish were back on track in order to earn a second-round clash against Portugal. A single David Villa goal sent the Portuguese home, with the Valencia forward also netting in the 1-0 defeat of Paraguay in the quarter-finals. The last four saw a replay of the Euro 2008 final with Germany seeking to earn revenge over the Spanish in Durban. Yet again just the one goal would separate the teams, centre-back Carles Puyol smashing a bullet header in with 17 minutes to go.

The final saw del Bosque's men take on the Netherlands but the game would be remembered for a feisty performance from Oranje as they sought to prevent tiki-taka hitting its full flow. English referee Howard Webb issued 14 yellow cards and one red, nine of those bookings and the red going to the Dutch, with the most famous foul being Nigel de Jong's kung fu kick on Xabi Alonso (Minute 28). Despite Spanish domination, the scores would remain goalless after normal time.

In extra time, Spain continued to control the possession. With time running out, it seemed as though the match was heading for a penalty shootout, but in the 116th minute, Iniesta was found by Cesc Fàbregas inside the box. The Barcelona midfielder controlled the ball and finished in style past keeper Maarten Stekelenburg.

Many were disappointed by the Dutch antics, describing the final as a game so 'toxic in nature the stadium is in need of decontamination more than the regular clean-up'.[530] Spain, though, had 'completed their mission for world

530 *The Guardian*, 11 July 2010

domination',[531] and had 'punished' the Dutch for their fiery behaviour.[532]

Euro 2012 would see Spain continue their reign of footballing success. Putting away Croatia, the Republic of Ireland, France and Portugal en route to the final, the favourites faced a strong Italian team on 1 July. Spain put Italy to the sword that day, four goals decimating their opponents in Kiev.

531 James Dall, 'World domination for Spain', Sky Sports, 12 July 2010
https://www.skysports.com/football/netherlands-vs-spain/report/221760
532 *The Guardian*, 11 July 2010

117

Homare Sawa equalises for Japan in the World Cup Final (2011)

MASSIVE MOMENTS in extra time are not just limited to the men's game. Indeed, women's football has also seen a number of its most important games head to the additional 30-minute period. In 2011, at the Women's World Cup, the final would go the distance as Japan faced the USA for the game's biggest prize. Since the turn of the millennium, Japan had quietly grown as a side and recorded group-stage victories in both the 2003 and 2007 World Cups. Despite this, a failure to reach the knockout stages of any edition of the competition since 1995 meant supporters would look elsewhere for their favourites. The USWNT were, as always, tipped to triumph.

Japan had been building since the end of the 2007 World Cup. Among their ranks were world-class talents in captain Homare Sawa and midfield maestro Aya Miyama, who played her football professionally in the US. A strong performance in the 2010 Asia Cup was enough to see the Nadeshiko qualify for the following year's World Cup.[533] Defeating hosts China in the third-place play-off highlighted Japan's rise to prominence and suggested that they could be regarded as dark horses before the World Cup began in Germany.

533 Kieran Theivam and Jeff Kassouf, *The Making of the Women's World Cup: Defining Stories from a Sport's Coming of Age* (London: Robinson, 2019)

As the tournament began with an impressive number of spectators, Japan reached the knockout rounds following wins over New Zealand and Mexico. Despite impressing with 'their neat approach play and movement', defeat to Hope Powell's England would be a stark reminder as to the quality still left in the competition.[534] It would be after victory over host Germany in the quarter-finals that commentators and neutrals began to take notice of the Japanese squad. Germany, the winners of the last two tournaments, had been tipped to come close to a global treble but Karina Maruyama's extra-time winner had proven enough to see Japan reach the semi-finals for the first time.

After Sweden were comfortably beaten 3-1 in Frankfurt, the only obstacle in Japan's way to becoming world champions was the USWNT. The US had indeed looked strong throughout the tournament and were looking to seal a first World Cup in 12 years. Abby Wambach's last-gasp equaliser in the quarter-finals against Brazil had seemed to demonstrate that *this* side wouldn't let victory slip away for a third World Cup on the bounce. *The Guardian* wrote that coming back from the brink of defeat would surely mean they were favourites to win the whole tournament.[535] Furthermore, the rise of youthful talent in Alex Morgan, Megan Rapinoe and Kelly O'Hara suggested that they could dominate for years to come.

The final would see a goalless, if entertaining, first half. Wambach came closest after seeing her fierce drive come thundering off the crossbar before the match burst into life in the second 45. Morgan hit the post and Japanese goalkeeper Ayumi Kaihori would perform heroically to deny a looping Wambach header. Recovering from her earlier miss, Morgan opened the scoring in the 69th minute before Japan equalised against the run of play 12 minutes later through Aya Miyama.

534 Jonathan Stevenson, 'Women's World Cup: England 2-0 Japan', BBC
    Sport, 5 July 2011
    https://www.bbc.co.uk/sport/football/14038052
535 *The Guardian*, 10 July 2011

As the game headed into extra time, the US once more went up a gear and took the lead through Wambach just before half-time in extra time. With just three minutes to play, Japan earned a corner in the 117th minute. Swung into the near post by Miyama, the ball was met with an audacious flick from Sawa before hitting the back of the net. The Japanese bench euphorically emerged from their seats to celebrate. Sawa, a symbol of the national team for the previous decade, had scored the greatest goal in her nation's history. Heading into the shootout, the US were visibly deflated and following misses from Shannon Boxx, Tobin Heath and Carli Lloyd, the World Cup was heading to Japan.

An 'astonishing success', the victory would prove pivotal to the women's game. Japan had become the first Asian champions (men or women) of football's greatest prize.[536] Just four months after an earthquake and tsunami which had rocked the nation to its very core, the efforts of the Nadeshiko had galvanised the country into triumphant celebrations.

536 BBC, 'Women's World Cup: Japan celebrate win on penalties', BBC Sport, 18 July 2011
https://www.bbc.co.uk/sport/football/14183115

118

Marcelo helps seal La Décima for Real Madrid (2014)

WITH THE European Cup having first been played in 1955 (Minute 14), you wonder how long the founders expected it to take before a club would win it ten times. Real Madrid started off very strongly, dominating the early years of the competition by winning the first five.

For Los Blancos, the tenth title, La Décima, would finally be achieved in 2014 as Marcelo's 118th-minute strike sealed another fine continental success.

Following their flurry of early crowns, Real Madrid's conveyor belt of European trophies would slow down and their 1966 title was their only victory until 1998. Further wins in 2000 and 2002 then saw another blank spell for the Spanish giants and for them an unacceptable 12 years without a final, especially with the talent at their disposal. Under manager Carlo Ancelotti in 2013/14, though, they did reach the final where they would face city rivals Atlético Madrid at Lisbon's Estádio da Luz.

Real had marched their way through the Champions League, picking up 16 points from a possible 18 in their group before defeating three German sides in succession in the knockout stages. Schalke, Borussia Dortmund and Bayern Munich were brushed aside 9-2, 3-2 and 5-0 on aggregate, respectively. Cristiano Ronaldo led the goalscoring with a staggering 16 goals scored up to the final, Welshman Gareth Bale adding six of his own for the free-scoring Los Blancos.

Atleti themselves had also secured 16 points from 18 in their group before then overcoming the challenges of AC Milan, Barcelona and Chelsea to earn their place in the final. Atleti had only made the European Cup Final once previously, 1973/74 seeing a painful 4-0 loss in a replay to Bayern Munich that was etched into the club's records. So 2014 offered the chance to right that wrong, and in the process of doing so, prevent La Décima for their bitter El Derbi Madrileño rivals.

Pre-match, Ancelotti declared, 'I'm not thinking about what happens if we lose, only how we might win the game,'[537] but there was no doubt that Atlético Madrid's La Liga title victory the previous week had given the game an additional dimension (Minute 49). Thirty-six minutes into the final in Lisbon, Atleti took the lead, Uruguayan defender Diego Godín opening the scoring with a header. The lead was kept by Atleti for the rest of the match and Real's commemorative La Décima shirts remained on hold until, in the 93rd minute, Sergio Ramos struck.

The injury-time header brought extra time, and in the bonus half hour of football, Real asserted themselves. Ángel Di María's charging run and shot was well saved by Thibaut Courtois but the rebound found Bale's head and in the 110th minute, Los Blancos had taken the lead at last. Then, eight minutes later, left-back Marcelo put the game beyond doubt. His low drive from 18 yards out helped end the 'impassioned clash',[538] with Ronaldo wrapping up the triumph 4-1 from the penalty spot two minutes later.

La Décima was Real's, and in doing so, they became the first club to reach the feat. Barcelona would lift the famous trophy in the next campaign, but from 2016–18 Real would build a Champions League winning streak. Atlético Madrid

537 *The Independent*, 24 May 2014
538 *The Telegraph*, 25 May 2014

were again defeated, this time on penalties, in 2016, Juventus were beaten 4-1 in Cardiff in 2017 and Liverpool were sunk via a Bale stunner (Minute 64) in Kiev in 2018. Ten had quickly moved to 13 for Los Blancos, the greatest club in the history of European continental competition …

119

Fabio Grosso's late strike decides one of football's greatest ever matches (2006)

THIS IS not the first mention of the international rivalry between Italy and Germany in this book. Major tournaments have seen the two great footballing nations battle it out in some of the game's greatest ever contests. The 2006 World Cup would see both sides progress to the semi-finals after impressive runs through the earlier stages. Germany, the tournament's hosts, had reinvented themselves after a dour performance at Euro 2004 and Italy were looking for their first international success since 1982.

Staging the tournament for the first time since 1974, the competition would prove vital to Germany in more ways than one. Firstly, coach Jürgen Klinsmann had managed to totally reform the national team. Before the opening match in Munich, German faith in the side was at an all-time low with supporters determined to make the most of the World Cup, even if the side couldn't progress. The introduction of youth, however, seen clearly through Bastian Schweinsteiger, Philipp Lahm and Lukas Podolski, was integral to the nation's success. Somehow, Klinsmann had managed to build a 'young, exciting and attacking team that was ready when it counted'.[539]

539 Uli Hesse, 'World Cup 2006: When Germany learned to love its national team – and each other', *FourFourTwo*, 10 June 2014
https://www.fourfourtwo.com/features/world-cup-2006-when-germany-learned-love-its-national-team-and-each-other

Likewise Italy also entered the World Cup with an ominous cloud looming over them. The Calciopoli scandal had rocked Italian football and seen the domestic league, Serie A, embroiled in a match-fixing probe. The nation's top club sides – Juventus, Milan, Lazio and many others – had all seen their very futures under serious threat. The start of the tournament was ranked in second place, given the importance of the scandal, with some calls for Italy to be totally removed from the competition and Juventus defender Fabio Cannavaro to be stripped of his captaincy.[540]

Nevertheless, in spite of both nations' less-than-ideal preparations, the two teams would grow into the tournament. Germany scored goals for fun and Italy would rely, as they have so much in the past, on their impressive defence. When the sides eventually met in the semi-finals, the game was absolutely incredible. The list of superlatives used to describe the 'stonking' encounter goes some way to explaining the unbelievable entertainment both sides produced in Dortmund.[541] Despite a goalless 90 minutes, chances were in abundance at both ends of the pitch. Podolski, Bernd Schneider and Miroslav Klose all came close for Germany with Fabio Grosso, Andrea Pirlo and Simone Perrotta all testing Jens Lehmann before extra time.

Like it had in 1970 (Minute 111), extra time would bring the game to life. *The Guardian* wrote that with the two sides going 'at it hammer and tongs' it had been refreshing to see them 'so hell-bent on avoiding penalties'.[542] Gianluigi Buffon was in spectacular form for the Azzurri, once again denying Podolski from close range, and Italy twice struck the woodwork in the additional period.

With perhaps the finest 0-0 in history drawing towards a close, Italy earned a late corner. In the 119th minute, Alessandro Del Piero's flag kick was cleared by the German defence, but

540 John Foot, *Calcio: A History of Italian Football* (London: Harper Perennial, 2007) pp.523–4

541 *The Guardian*, 11 July 2006

542 Ibid

only as far as Pirlo. A beautiful through ball found left-back Grosso, who struck his shot sweetly with his left foot. Curling the ball beyond the reach of Lehmann and into the far corner, Italy had snatched it at the death.

Grosso's celebrations were compared to Marco Tardelli's mazy run in 1982. As he ran, shaking his head, he shouted 'non ci credo' or 'I don't believe it'.[543] To rub further salt into the German wounds, Del Piero then added Italy's second goal in the first minute of stoppage time.

German dreams had been shattered but the country was united in their heartbreak. In defeat, they had brought the reunified nation, so often suspicious of patriotism, together in a wave of national pride.[544]

Italian celebrations back home would also echo the euphoria of Grosso, with parties lasting late into the night. The Calciopoli scandal could be put to the back of people's minds for a little while and football was the clear winner on the day ...

543 John Foot, *Calcio: A History of Italian Football,* p.526

544 Uli Hesse, 'World Cup 2006: When Germany learned to love its national team – and each other', *FourFourTwo*

120

'They think it's all over... it is now!' – England win the World Cup (1966)

ENGLAND'S STUBBORN rejection of the World Cup saw them refuse to join the international competition until 1950. When they did, they received a shock, the Miracle on Grass seeing them sent packing early from the Brazilian tournament (Minute 38). Three years later another blow was dealt, this time by the Mighty Magyars of Hungary at Wembley (Minute 1). The awakening to football outside of the British Isles eventually saw 'football come home' in 1966 as in London, the World Cup was lifted.

Sixteen teams would arrive in England that summer but one of the most well-known stories in the build-up was the disappearance of the hallowed Jules Rimet Trophy. The trophy, on display at Central Hall in London, was taken by thief Edward Betchley on 20 March 1966. After Betchley's arrest, it remained missing until a dog, named Pickles, uncovered it while on his walk.

Pickles's owner, David Corbett, understandably stunned by the discovery, told journalists, 'I was about to put the lead on Pickles when I noticed he was sniffing at something near the path.'[545] The package Pickles was sniffing turned out to be the iconic prize, wrapped in newspaper. Pickles hit the headlines

---

545 *Birmingham Daily Post*, 28 March 1966

and was given many rewards, even receiving a medal from the Italian town of San Rocco di Camogli, named after the patron saint of dogs.[546]

In July 1966, manager Alf Ramsey's England opened their tournament with a 0-0 draw with Uruguay, before 2-0 wins against both Mexico and France secured a quarter-final spot. West Ham United striker Geoff Hurst scored in the 1-0 victory over Argentina and gave England a semi-final tie with a strong Portuguese side. Portugal were led by their talisman, Eusébio, but the English would have Manchester United's Bobby Charlton to thank for their victory. His brace (30 and 80), was enough to earn a place in the final, despite Eusébio's late penalty taking his tally to a Golden Boot-winning nine goals.

The World Cup Final on 30 July would see England face West Germany. The West Germans took a quick lead through Helmut Haller's sixth goal of the tournament but after 18 minutes the scores were level again, Hurst the goalscorer. In the second half, Hurst's Hammers team-mate Martin Peters gave England the lead. However, the 78th-minute strike was not enough as Wolfgang Weber equalised for the Germans with just a minute remaining and extra time beckoned.

Extra time was a 'thrill every minute' as 'England forced the pace'.[547] The hosts pushed on against the West Germans and in the 101st minute, the pressure paid off. Alan Ball fired a ball in from the right to Hurst who controlled it with a touch and unleashed his shot. The ball thundered off the crossbar and bounced down on to the line, or was it over the line? The Soviet linesman and Swiss referee Gottfried Dienst ruled that a goal had been scored, and in controversial circumstances England were 3-2 ahead.

In the 120th minute the fixture was put beyond all doubt. Picking the ball up 40 yards out, Hurst charged towards keeper Hans Tilkowski's net. Hitting it from just inside the box, the

---

546 *Daily Mirror*, 15 August 1966
547 *The People*, 31 July 1966

forward blasted home and completed the first – and so far only – men's World Cup Final hat-trick. England were 'truly heroes',[548] the greatest prize of them all was finally theirs, and they had done it at Wembley.

BBC commentator Kenneth Wolstenholme made English footballing legend of his own with his commentary of Hurst's final goal. Seeing some fans spilling on to the pitch in premature celebration he said the now-famous words, 'Some people are on the pitch, they think it's all over,' before Hurst struck the fourth, and he added, 'It is now, it's four!' Wolstenholme would later fondly remember that 1966 squad, remarking that 'it wasn't just a team, Alf Ramsey formed a football club in 1966'.[549]

The question marks about Hurst's third saw an Italian newspaper label the incident a 'scandal' and blamed 'favouritism', while a Bolivian one wrote, 'England may now be world champions but it is no longer the country of culture, of education, of gentlemen.'[550] West German boss Helmut Schön said post-match, 'It was impossible for anyone to tell, and in a match of that importance we should have been given the benefit of the doubt.'[551]

In January 2016, Sky Sports would claim to bring an end to the years of debate about Hurst's third goal. Using modern technology, the broadcaster declared that the ball did cross the line and that 'the Germans can't complain any more'.[552]

Legitimate goal or not, 1966 was England's year and has not been bettered internationally for the nation since.

548 Ibid

549 *The Guardian*, 26 March 2002

550 Kevin Moore, *What You Think You Know About Football Is Wrong* (London: Bloomsbury, 2019) pp.26–27

551 *The Independent*, 4 December 1997

552 *Daily Mirror*, 5 January 2016

Penalties

1. Antonín Panenka chips in for Czechoslovakia (1976)

This is probably one of the most famous penalty shootouts of all time, and all because Antonín Panenka of Czechoslovakia would write his name into footballing terminology. At the 1976 European Championships, Czechoslovakia had made the final and faced world champions West Germany. The fixture finished 2-2 after extra time, with West Germany having fought back from 2-0 down. In the penalty shootout, Uli Hoeneß would miss West Germany's fourth penalty, offering the Czechoslovaks the chance to win the tournament.

Up stepped Panenka. Rather than blast the ball past keeper Sepp Maier, or slot it into the corner of the net, Panenka instead ran up and chipped the ball home to win the Euros, a move unseen before. Panenka's original dink has inspired many to also attempt the cheekiness on the world stage, such as Zinedine Zidane in the 2006 World Cup Final, and Sergio Ramos v Portugal and Andrea Pirlo v England, both in Euro 2012.

2. Bruce Grobbelaar's spaghetti legs (1984)

Over the course of 120 minutes, goalkeepers are rarely in the limelight. Overshadowed by goalscorers and other outfield players, attention is rarely devoted to the number one. In a penalty shootout, however, the tables turn and those between the sticks become their side's most important player.

This was clearly the case in the 1984 European Cup Final as Liverpool faced Roma, who were playing at their home ground, the Stadio Olimpico. After the match was drawn 1-1, and following a goalless extra period, the game headed to penalties.

For eccentric and flamboyant Reds keeper Bruce Grobbelaar, the penalty area became his stage. With Liverpool scoring three of their first four kicks and Roma striker Francesco Graziani stepping up to potentially level the scores, Grobbelaar improvised his 'spaghetti legs' routine. Clearly distracting and putting Graziani off, the resulting kick flew high over the bar leaving left-back Alan Kennedy with a chance to win the cup once again with Liverpool's fifth penalty. Kennedy comfortably slotted the ball home and a fourth European Cup was heading to Anfield.

3. Chris Waddle blazes over after Gazza's tears (1990)

The penalty 'curse' is considered something as English as a Sunday roast or fish and chips, those who support the Three Lions having experienced their fair share of penalty heartbreak. In the 1990 World Cup semi-final against West Germany, talisman Paul Gascoigne famously broke down in tears after receiving a yellow card that would rule him out of a final appearance. The tie went to penalties after a 1-1 draw. West Germany put their four kicks away, with Stuart Pearce and Chris Waddle missing the decisive efforts, Waddle blasting over to send the English home. In Euro 1996, hosted in England, the Three Lions would again lose to Germany on penalties in the semi-finals, and this time Gareth Southgate was the culprit.

The idea of a penalty 'curse' was even investigated by a German university, the 2020 study finding that English footballers actually net 90 per cent of penalties awarded during matches. However, this number drops by a third when it comes to the pressure of a shootout. Germany's success, meanwhile, increases from 75 per cent in games, to 85 per cent when it comes to shootouts.

England would finally break their penalty 'curse' in the 2018 World Cup with their last-16 victory over Colombia after a shootout delighting the nation.

4. Roberto Baggio skies it over the bar (1994)

The early 1990s were dominated by Italy's Roberto Baggio. Following his emergence on the international stage at Italia 90, he was the game's most instantly recognisable figure by the time the tournament took place again in 1994. Affectionately known by the Italian fans as 'Il Divin Codino' (the Divine Ponytail), he had come to prominence in the knockout rounds, scoring a brace in the last 16 against Nigeria before breaking Spanish hearts with his late goal in the quarter-finals. A further pair against a resurgent Bulgaria secured Italy's place in the final where three-time World Cup winners Brazil awaited.

Contrary to the buccaneer spirit of the wider tournament, the final was a drab affair as both sides failed to entertain the 94,000 people packed inside the Pasadena Rose Bowl. A penalty shootout, therefore, would be required to see which nation would win their fourth global title. With the score at 3-2 in Brazil's favour, it came down to Baggio to keep Italy in the tie. He smashed the ball high over the bar, sparking wild celebrations in the Brazilian camp and leaving a lasting legacy that even those on top of the world can come crashing down in the lottery of penalties.

5. Uruguay win the first Copa América Final shootout (1995)

The Copa América, first held in 1916 as the Campeonato Sudamericano de Fútbol, has produced some spectacular moments for South American football. In 1995, the reigning world champions Brazil would face off against the hosts Uruguay in the final. This was the third time the two had met in the showpiece, with the two winning one each. This Copa

América tournament ditched extra time with matches instead going straight to spot kicks if scores were level. Following a 1-1 draw after 90 minutes, penalties would be required to decide a winner for the first time in the competition's history. Botafogo striker Túlio Maravilha missed Brazil's third kick, meaning that Uruguay's five out of five penalties earned their 14th Copa América crown.

This win continued a staggering run of home success for Uruguay. The eight-tournament run of home triumphs included the 1917, 1923, 1924, 1942, 1956 and 1967 Copa Américas, and the 1930 World Cup too.

6. Brandi Chastain wins it for women (1999)

Before the 1999 Women's World Cup Final, expectations were high. The United States, the hosts, expected the victory, but China would be a world-class opponent. Over 90,000 fans were crammed into the Pasadena Rose Bowl to witness the match and despite profiting from a tournament laden with goals (123 in total), the final would end goalless after extra time. The raucous fans, including US president Bill Clinton, had witnessed an encounter balanced on a knife edge. A penalty shootout would follow and see both teams comfortably slotting away their respective spot kicks.

The turning point came following a Briana Scurry save from Liu Ying, offering the chance for defender Brandi Chastain to send 90,000 screaming fans into utter pandemonium. Thumping the ball into the top left-hand corner, a euphoric Chastain would remove her shirt and create one of the defining images of the decade. Numerous articles have been dedicated to this moment alone as the image of the US left-back on her knees was splashed on every newspaper and magazine in the States. The tournament in 1999 had set the standard and created a platform for the women's game around the world.

7. Patrick Vieira scores to deny United in the FA Cup's first final shootout (2005)

Despite being football's oldest competition still in use today, the FA Cup Final has only ever seen two penalty shootouts. Despite being introduced to the tournament in 1982, it would take until 2005 for a final to be decided in the most dramatic fashion. With only the following year's final also heading to penalties, the lack of previous or future contests being decided this way is somewhat surprising.

The 2005 final between Arsenal and Manchester United would be the first to create genuine football history after a game dominated by the latter ended goalless. The rivalry between the two sides had been bitter and immensely competitive since the late 1990s with Arsenal's Patrick Vieira and United's Roy Keane providing the game's most volatile, yet intriguing, moments. It was Vieira who decided the shootout at Cardiff's Millennium Stadium, scoring the Gunners' fifth kick after Paul Scholes's earlier miss, to confirm his side's third FA Cup in four seasons.

The game's oldest competition had been decided by one of its more recent inventions.

8. Zambia win the Africa Cup of Nations 19 years after tragedy (2012)

In April 1993, disaster struck African football and the Zambian national team after a plane carrying the squad crashed shortly after take-off from Libreville, Gabon. All 30 people lost their lives, including 18 players, manager Godfrey Chitalu and other coaching staff. In 2012, the Africa Cup of Nations was hosted in Gabon and Equatorial Guinea. Zambia would make their third AFCON final, the opponents being 1992 champions, Ivory Coast.

A 0-0 draw after 90 minutes saw the scores remain goalless after 120 too, meaning penalties would be needed. Following seven straight penalty conversions each, Rainford Kalaba

(Zambia) and Kolo Touré and Gervinho (both Ivory Coast) all then missed for their teams. This meant that if TP Mazembe's Stophira Sunzu could score, Zambia would be AFCON winners for the first time. Defender Sunzu netted the decisive spot kick to bring joy to the Zambians. Even more poignantly, the final stadium, Stade d'Angondjé, was just a short distance away from where most of the 1993 Zambian squad had lost their lives 19 years previously.

9. Tim Krul's late introduction saves the day (2014)

It is not uncommon to see managers make late substitutions in extra time. Often, they are made in order to put one of the squad's more reliable penalty takers in place of a defender or poor finisher. What is rare, however, is seeing a coach replace the goalkeeper before what could potentially be the most important moment of their career to date.

At the 2014 World Cup in Brazil, Holland's enigmatic manager Louis van Gaal would utilise this very notion as he dramatically replaced number one Jasper Cillessen with back-up Tim Krul seconds before the quarter-final against Costa Rica ended goalless. Delighting the Dutch, Krul would make two excellent saves to keep out Bryan Ruiz and Michael Umaña. Cillessen would lead the celebrations as the Oranje once more reached the World Cup semi-finals where once again the match would end in penalties. This time they lost 4-2 to Argentina and Krul remained on the bench.

10. Chile stop Lionel Messi in the Copa América Final again (2016)

There were two 2016 South American penalty moments that could've taken this final place in our book. The first was Neymar, Brazil's modern superstar, scoring the last penalty in the Olympic gold medal match against Germany to secure a mighty home victory for the host nation. This was particularly notable for its part-redemption of the 2014 World Cup Mineirazo defeat to Germany (Minute 29). However, the moment chosen is Chile winning the 2016 Copa América against Argentina for the second year in a row.

In 2015, Chile hosted the continental tournament and after 120 goalless minutes in the final, they kept their cool to win 4-1 and disappoint Lionel Messi. A year later, the tournament would be held again, to celebrate 100 years since the first competition. Once more, Argentina and Chile met in the final and yet again it was goalless after 120 minutes. Messi stepped up but missed his country's first penalty in the shootout as Chile were victorious 4-2.

A devastated Messi would briefly retire from international duty after the game, declaring, 'I've done all I can. It hurts not to be a champion.' To this day, Messi remains trophyless on the international stage, something that quite publicly pains him.

Epilogue

THERE IS something that binds all who love the beautiful game together. The passion, heartbreak and euphoria brings together spectators regardless of who you support. Whether you get your football fix at the local stadium, cheering on your club every other week, buying a programme and eating a burger, or whether your football is consumed via the all-encompassing television, internet and social media age, this brilliant sport is about single seconds that can send an ordinary game down in history.

This book was completed during the COVID-19 coronavirus outbreak of 2020, when 'lockdown' had brought a temporary and unexpected end to sport as we knew it. Football across the globe was cancelled in a way not experienced since World War Two. That said, football still played a role in society during both world wars, whereas the infectious nature of COVID-19 meant friends, families and sports stars were forced to stay away from each other to help prevent the spread of the disease.

The separation from the sport that permeates all aspects of our modern society actually showed its importance. Much like in wartime, government minister Dominic Raab told UK citizens in May 2020 that they hoped football would 'lift the spirits of the nation' when it was allowed to return.[553] The absence of live sport led many broadcasters to fill schedules with old matches. This resurgence in the fixtures of yesteryear showed how much joy there was to be found in the stories of games gone by.

553 Foreign Secretary Dominic Raab MP, at the government's daily
     COVID-19 press briefing on 5 May 2020.

With us both working as teachers, COVID-19 has meant we have had to find a new normal and teach from home. It has been difficult, at times, to adjust but the willingness shown by both teachers and learners to pull together has been remarkable. Unfortunately, by not being able to go to school, we have been limited in our chance to see first hand the impact that football can have on the younger generation. This is of course a great pity, but with books like this, we hope that those who read it, adults and children alike, can take new lessons and inspiration from the beautiful game.

While researching this book, we spent weeks poring over some of the finest moments that football has provided from decades of domestic, international and worldwide competition. With timings not recorded as clearly in the Victorian age, perhaps this period is one under-represented. However, the inclusion of Morton Betts's winning goal in the first FA Cup Final in 1872 (Minute 15), Blackburn Olympic's FA Cup victory in 1883 (Minute 107) and Samuel Thomson's invincible double-securer in 1889 (Minute 70), proves that for a century and a half, football has been about those individual moments that write their own place in the history books.

Likewise, the many years where women's football was pushed to the sidelines and excluded from sporting conversations in the UK and across the world limited the recording of minutes to be included in this book. We felt it vitally important that the inclusion of the women's game was present here, and it is also with delight that we look forward to many more moments being written in the future with the rapid and exciting growth impacting young football fans, both boys and girls, today.

For Manchester City supporters, the number 93:20 is one ingrained in their collective memories as the moment Sergio 'Kun' Agüero sealed their dramatic 2011/12 Premier League title win (Minute 94). Visit the Etihad Stadium and you will see the time displayed everywhere, a moment that the football club can rightly be proud of and will remember for generations to come.

This will, of course, differ from club to club, but one thing is for sure, football is a deeply personal game that allows all of us to dwell and fondly remember instances where a moment in time, caused us to be lost in time.

For a Welsh fan, perhaps the moment that encapsulates their love for football is 54:34, the time on the clock when Hal Robson-Kanu Cruyff-turned the Belgians at Euro 2016 (Minute 55). As a secondary school teacher, when asked by the Maths department to post our favourite numbers and a reason on our classroom doors, this was my chosen one. Over the coming days, the poster led to many conversations with students who remembered with ecstasy that phenomenal, jaw-dropping moment when Wales were on top of the footballing world. A rarity in our nation's footballing journey.

Ask a fan from Brazil who witnessed and remembers the 1950 World Cup, and the Maracanazo defeat to Uruguay is sure to be at the forefront of their mind (Minute 79). It was a loss that helped shape the great footballing nation, leading them on to become the giants of the international scene they are today. That said, the very same fan could also lament the terrible 7-1 home World Cup defeat to Germany in 2014, Mineirazo (Minute 29) failing to banish the haunting ghosts of 64 years previous.

That is in essence the point of our book, to take you back to snippets of a match that are not just about the ball hitting the back of the net but history-defining minutes that shaped the beautiful game we know and love today. Whether it is the controversy of Manchester United's Eric Cantona delivering his own form of justice to a fan (Minute 48), Barcelona supporters welcoming Luís Figo back to the Camp Nou with a very unique gift (Minute 72), England being awoken to sporting quality from beyond their own shores (Minutes 1 and 38), or a goal that helped lead to an international war (Minute 101), we hope *The History of Football in 90 Minutes (Plus Extra Time)* has allowed you to see that football is more than just a game of scorelines.

Bibliography

Aldrich, Robert and McKenzie, Kirsten, *The Routledge History of Western Empires* (London: Routledge, 2013)

Ashton, Timothy, *Soccer in Spain: Politics, Literature and Film* (Plymouth: Scarecrow, 2013)

Banks, Gordon, *Banksy: The Autobiography of an English Football Hero* (London: Penguin, 2003)

Bassett, Dave and Downes, Wally, *The Crazy Gang* (London, Bantam, 2016)

Bellos, Alex, *Futebol: The Brazilian Way of Life* (London: Bloomsbury, 2002)

Bergkamp, Dennis, *Stillness and Speed: My Story* (London: Simon and Schuster, 2013)

Birley, Derek, *Sport and the Making of Britain* (Manchester: Manchester University Press, 1993)

Bolchover, David, *The Greatest Comeback: From Genocide to Football Glory* (London: Biteback Publishing Ltd., 2018)

Bolchover, David, and Brady, Christopher, *The 90-minute Manager: Lessons from the Sharp End of Management*, 3rd edition (London: Pearson Education Limited, 2006)

Boyle, Raymond, and Haynes, Richard, *Football in the New Media Age* (London: Routledge, 2004)

Brown, Paul, *The Victorian Football Miscellany* (Newcastle upon Tyne: Goal-post, 2013)

Butler, Bryon, *The Football League: The First 100 Years* (Guildford: Colour Library Books Ltd., 1988)

Butler, Bryon, *The Illustrated History of the FA Cup* (London: Headline Book Publishing, 1996)

Caliono, Luca, *Messi vs Ronaldo 2018: The Greatest Rivalry* (London: Icon Books Ltd., 2017)

Cavallini, Rob, *The Wanderers: Five Times FA Cup Winners* (Surrey: Dog and Duck, 2005)

Charles, John, *King John* (London: Headline Book Publishing, 2003)

Clay, Catrine, *Trautmann's Journey: From Hitler Youth to FA Cup Legend* (Liverpool: Yellow Jersey, 2011)

Cloake, Martin and Radnedge, Aidan et al, *Football The Ultimate Guide: Updated 2010 Edition* (London: DK, 2010)

Clough, Brian, *Clough: The Autobiography* (London: Corgi Books, 1995)

Constable, Nick, *Match of the Day 50 Years: Players, Goals, Matches and Memories* (London: BBC Books, 2014)

Couzens-Lake, Edward, *Mapping the Pitch: Football Coaches, Players and Formations Through The Ages* (Maidenhead: Meyer & Meyer Sport Ltd., 2015)

Cox, Richard, Russell, Dave, and Vamplew, Wray, (eds), *Encyclopedia of British Football* (Hove: Psychology Press, 2002)

Cruyff, Johan, *My Turn* (London: Pan Macmillan, 2016)

Dalglish, Kenny, *My Liverpool Home: Dyed-in-the-Wool Red* (London: Hodder and Stoughton, 2010)

Darby, Paul, *Africa, Football and FIFA: Politics, Colonialism and Resistance* (London: Frank Cass, 2002)

Dauncey, Hugh and O'Dare, Geoff, *France and the 1998 World Cup: The National Impact of a World Sporting Event* (London: Routledge, 2014)

Desbordes, Michel and Richelieu, André, (eds), *Global Sport Marketing: Contemporary Issues and Practice* (London: Routledge, 2012)

Dubois, Laurent, *Soccer Empire: The World Cup and the Future of France* (Los Angeles: University of California, 2010)

Dunmore, Tom, *Encyclopaedia of the FIFA World Cup* (Maryland: Rowman & Littlefield, 2015)

Dunmore, Thomas and Murray, Scott, *Soccer for Dummies* (Indianapolis: John Wiley & Sons Inc., 2013)

Durham, Adrian, *Is He All That? Great Footballing Myths Shattered* (London: Simon & Schuster UK Ltd., 2013)

Ferguson, Alex, *My Autobiography* (London: Hodder and Stoughton, 2013)

Foot, John, *Calcio: A History of Italian Football* (London: Harper Perennial, 2006)

Gerrard, Steven, *My Autobiography* (London: Bantam: 2006)

Gerrard, Steven, *My Story* (London: Penguin, 2015)

Gray, Daniel, *Black Boots & Football Pinks: 50 Lost Wonders of the Beautiful Game* (London: Bloomsbury, 2018)

Hampton, Janie, *The Austerity Olympics: When the Games Came to London in 1948* (London: Aurum Press Limited, 2008)

Hapgood, Eddie, *Football Ambassador* (Norfolk: GCR Books Limited, 2009)

Harrison, Paul, *Keep Fighting: The Billy Bremner Story* (Black and White Publishing, 2010)

Hesse, Ulrich, *Tor!: The Story of German Football* (London: WSC Books Ltd., 2003)

Hill, Tim, *Encyclopedia of World Football: From the Origins of the Game to 2007: The Essential Fans' Guide* (Bath: Parragon, 2007)

Hobsbawm, Eric, *Nations and Nationalism Since 1780: Programme, Myth, Reality* (Cambridge: Cambridge University, 1992)

Holt, Richard, *Sport and the British: A Modern History* (Oxford: Oxford University, 1989)

Hong, Fan, *Soccer, Women, Sexual Liberation: Kicking Off a New Era* (London: Frank Cass, 2004)

Hughson, John, *England and the 1966 World Cup* (Manchester: Manchester University, 2016)

Hunter, Graham, *Barca: The Making of the Greatest Team in the World* (Glasgow: BackPage Press, 2012)

Hurst, Geoff, *Geoff Hurst's 50 Greatest Footballers of All-Time* (London: Icon, 2016)

Jones, Ben and Thomas, Gareth, *Football's Fifty Most Important Moments* (Worthing: Pitch Publishing, 2020)

Jones, Vinnie, *It's Been Emotional* (London: Simon and Schuster, 2013)

Kelly, Stephen F., *The Kop: Liverpool's Twelfth Man* (London: Virgin Books, 2008)

Klotz, Liedy, *Sustainability Through Soccer: An Unexpected Approach to Saving Our World* (California: University of California, 2016)

Krasnoff, Lindsay Sarah, *The Making of Les Bleus: Sport in France 1958–2000* (Plymouth: Lexington, 2013)

Large, David Clay, *Nazi Games: The Olympics of 1936* (London: W.W. Norton, 2007)

Lisi, Clemente A., *A History of the World Cup: 1930–2010* (Plymouth: Scarecrow Press Inc., 2011)

Lisi, Clemente A., *The U.S. Women's Soccer Team: An American Success Story* (Plymouth: Scarecrow Press Inc., 2010)

Lowe, Sid, *Fear and Loathing in La Liga: Barcelona vs Real Madrid* (London: Yellow Jersey, 2013)

Lyttleton, Ben, (ed.), *Match of My Life: European Cup Finals* (Studley: Know The Score Books Limited, 2006)

Maconie, Stuart, *The People's Songs: The Story of Modern Britain in 50 Records* (London: Ebury Press, 2014)

Martin, Simon, *Sport Italia: The Italian Love Affair with Sport* (London: I.B. Tauris, 2011)

McTear, Euan, *Hijacking La Liga: How Atlético Madrid Broke Barcelona and Real Madrid's Duopoly on Spanish Football* (Worthing: Pitch Publishing, 2017)

Millar, Colin, *The Frying Pan of Spain: Sevilla vs Real Betis: Spain's Hottest Football Rivalry* (Worthing: Pitch Publishing, 2019)

Moore, Glenn, (ed), *The Concise Encyclopaedia of World Football* (Bath: Parragon, 1999)

Moore, Kevin, *What You Think You Know About Football Is Wrong* (London: Bloomsbury, 2019)

Mortimer, Gavin, *A History of Football in 100 Objects* (London: Serpent's Tail, 2012)

Motson, John, *Forty Years in the Commentary Box* (London: Virgin, 2009)

Murphy, Jim, *The 10 Football Matches That Changed The World: And The One That Didn't* (London: Biteback, 2014)

Murray, Scott and Walker, Rowan, *Day of the Match: A History of Football in 365 Days* (London: Boxtree, 2008)

Osgood, Peter, King, Martin, and Knight, Martin, *Ossie: King of Stamford Bridge* (London: Mainstream, 2002)

Pelé, *Pelé: The Autobiography* (London: Simon and Schuster, 2006)

Pirlo, Andrea, *I Think Therefore I Play* (London: BackPage Press, 2014)

Platt, Mark, *Cup Kings: Liverpool 1977* (Bluecoat Press, 2003)

Pozzo, Vittorio, *Campioni del Mondo: Quarant'Anni di Storia del Calcio Italiano* (Rome: Centro Editoriale Nazionale, 1960)

Rinke, Stefan and Schiller, Kay, *The FIFA World Cup 1930 – 2010: Politics, Commerce, Spectacle and Identities* (Gottingen: Wallstein Verlag, 2014)

Rush, Ian, *Rush: The Autobiography* (London: Ebury, 2008)

Sánchez, Antonio Cazorla, *Fear and Progress: Ordinary Lives in Franco's Spain, 1939–1975* (Chichester: John Wiley & Sons Ltd., 2010)

Scherer, Jay and Rowe, David, 'Sport, Public Service Media and Cultural Citizenship' in *Sport, Public Broadcasting and Cultural Citizenship: Signal Lost?* (London: Routledge, 2013)

Scraton, Phil, *Hillsborough: The Truth* (London: Mainstream, 2016)

Shaw, Duncan, *Football and Francoism* (Madrid, Alianza, 1987)

Steen, Rob, *Floodlights and Touchlines: A History of Spectator Sport* (London: Bloomsbury, 2014)

Steen, Rob, Novick, Jed and Richards, Huw, (eds.), *The Cambridge Companion to Football* (New York: Cambridge University Press, 2013)

Taylor, Matthew, *The Association Game* (London: Routledge, 2008)

Taylor, Matthew, *The Leaguers: The making of professional football in England, 1900–1939* (Liverpool: Liverpool University Press, 2005)

Theivam, Kieran and Kassouf, Jeff, *The Making of the Women's World Cup: Defining Stories from a Sport's Coming of Age* (London: Robinson, 2019)

Thompson, Dave, *Football FAQ* (Milwaukee: Backbeat Books, 2015)

Tomlinson, Alan, *Sport and Leisure Cultures* (London: University of Minnesota, 2005)

Tomlinson, Alan, and Young, Christopher, (eds.), *German Football: History, Culture, Society* (Abingdon: Routledge, 2006)

Tongue, Jo, Poole, Simon, and Hewitt, Paolo, *The League Doesn't Lie: The 606 Book of Football Lists* (London: BBC Books, 2012)

Turnbull, John, Satterlee, Thom, and Raab, Alon, (eds.), *The Global Game: Writers on Soccer* (Lincoln: University of Nebraska, 2008)

Vaizey, Hester, *Born in the GDR: Living in the Shadow of the Wall* (Oxford: Oxford University Press, 2014)

Wahl, Grant, *The Beckham Experiment* (New York: Three Rivers Press, 2010)

Webb, Howard, *The Man in the Middle* (London: Simon and Schuster, 2016)

Wesson, John, *The Science of Soccer* (Bristol: Institute of Physics, 2002)

Wilson, Jonathan, *Inverting the Pyramid: The History of Football Tactics* (London: Orion, 2010)

Wilson, Jonathan, *The Outsider: A History of the Goalkeeper* (London: Orion, 2012)

Wilson, Jonathan, *Angels With Dirty Faces: A Footballing History of Argentina* (London: Orion, 2016)

Wilson, Jonathan, *The Names Heard Long Ago* (New York: Bold Type Books, 2019)

Wilson, Steve, *Glad All Over* (London: Lulu, 2014)

Witzig, Richard, *The Global Art of Soccer* (New Orleans: CusiBoy Publishing, 2006)

Wise, Dennis, *The Autobiography* (London: Boxtree, 2012)

Newspapers

Aberdeen Evening Express
Aberdeen Press and Journal
Athletic News
Belfast Telegraph
Birmingham Daily Gazette
Birmingham Daily Post
Birmingham Mail
Blackburn Standard
Burnley News
Coventry Evening Telegraph
Daily Express
Daily Herald
Daily Mail

Daily Mirror
Daily Post
Daily Record
Derbyshire Courier
Derby Daily Telegraph
Dublin Evening Herald
The Field
Glasgow Herald
Grimsby Daily Telegraph
The Guardian
Hartlepool Northern Daily Mail
The Independent
Irish Independent
Irish Times
L'Equipe
Liverpool Echo
London Evening Standard
Manchester Courier
Manchester Evening News
Manchester Guardian
Metro
Morning Post
Newcastle Journal
New York Times
North British Daily Mail
Northern Whig
Nottingham Evening Post
Nottinghamshire Guardian
Nottingham Journal
The People
Preston Herald
Reading Evening Post
Sandwell Evening Mail
The Scotsman
Sheffield Independent
Sheffield Telegraph
Shields Daily News
Shropshire Star

Sports Argus
Sporting Life
The Sportsman
Staffordshire Sentinel
Sunday Life
Sunday Times
Sunderland Daily Echo and Shipping Gazette
Sussex Agricultural Express
The Telegraph
The Times
Torbay Express and South Devon Echo
Washington Post
Watford Observer
West London Observer
Western Mail
Yorkshire Post
Yorkshire Post and Leeds Intelligencer

Websites with named authors

Adams, Tom, 'Best and Worst of Euro 2016: The tournament in review', Eurosport, 11 July 2016 https://www.eurosport.co.uk/football/euro-2016/2016/best-and-worst-of-euro-2016-the-tournament-in-review_sto5683581/story.shtml

Bate, Adam, 'Battle of Bramall Lane: Sheffield United and West Brom have history', Sky Sports, 14 December 2018 https://www.skysports.com/football/news/11688/11579928/battle-of-bramall-lane-sheffield-united-and-west-brom-have-history

Begley, Emlyn, 'Champions League 2018-19: The Greatest Tournament Ever?', BBC Sport, 2 June 2019 https://www.bbc.co.uk/sport/football/48354681

Bevan, Chris, 'Netherlands 2-1 Brazil', BBC Sport, 02 July 2010 http://news.bbc.co.uk/sport1/hi/football/world_cup_2010/matches/match_57/default.stm

Brandstatter, Kevin and Merkens, Paul, 'Attendances: England', European Football Statistics, 2018 https://www.european-football-statistics.co.uk/attn/nav/attnengleague.htm

Freddie Campion, 'David Beckham Picks Infamous World Cup Red Card as One of His "Top Career Moments"', GQ, 18 March 2016 https://www.gq.com/story/david-beckham-red-card

Dall, James, 'World domination for Spain', Sky Sports, 12 July 2010 https://www.skysports.com/football/netherlands-vs-spain/report/221760

Dawkes, Phil, '1970 FA Cup Final: The most brutal game in English football history', BBC Sport, 27 April 2020 https://www.bbc.co.uk/sport/football/52416192

Dean, Lewis, 'England v Iceland preview: Roy Hodgson to ring changes', Sky Sports, 27 June 2016 https://www.skysports.com/football/england-vs-iceland/preview/353099

DelGallo, Alicia, 'U.S. star Megan Rapinoe: Love, not hate motivated World Cup win over France', ProSoccerUSA, 29 June 2019 https://www.prosoccerusa.com/us-soccer/united-states-womens-national-team/u-s-star-megan-rapinoe-love-not-hate-motivated-world-cup-win-over-france/

Djazmi, Mani, 'World Cup whisky and the Cold War: When East & West Germany met', BBC, 07 March 2019 https://www.bbc.co.uk/sport/football/47456049

Glass, Alana, 'FIFA Women's World Cup Breaks Viewership Records', Forbes, 21 October 2019 https://www.forbes.com/sites/alanaglass/2019/10/21/fifa-womens-world-cup-breaks-viewership-records/#31c926be1884

Grez, Matias, 'France's 'Rainbow Team' looks back at historic World Cup triumph', CNN, 06 July 2018 https://edition.cnn.com/2018/06/08/football/france-1998-world-cup-win-anniversary/index.html

Hansen, Alan, 'Dalglish is perfect fit for Liverpool', BBC Sport, 12 May 2011 https://www.bbc.co.uk/sport/football/13381711

Hansen, Alan, 'Hansen: Dellas Made the Difference', BBC Sport, 4 July 2004 http://news.bbc.co.uk/sport1/hi/football/euro_2004/3865371.stm

Hayward, Joshua, 'Lionel Messi: Xavi is the best player in the history of Spanish football', Eurosport, 2 June 2015 https://www.eurosport.co.uk/football/liga/2014-2015/lionel-messi-

xavi-is-the-best-player-in-the-history-of-spanish-football_
sto4764080/story.shtml

Hesse, Uli, 'World Cup 2006: When Germany learned to love
its national team – and each other', FourFourTwo, 10 June
2014 https://www.fourfourtwo.com/features/world-cup-2006-
when-germany-learned-love-its-national-team-and-each-other

Jones, Ben, 'The 1982 World Cup: The Best Ever?', The
Football History Boys, 9 April 2019 https://www.
thefootballhistoryboys.com/2019/04/the-1982-world-cup-
best-ever.html

Lara, Miguel Ángel, 'Barcelona's 6-2 win over Real Madrid,
Guardiola's masterpiece', Marca, 17 August 2018 https://
www.marca.com/en/football/spanish-football/2018/08/17/5
b768c7dca4741bb0f8b4635.html

Lewis, Tim, '1982: Why Brazil V Italy Was One Of Football's
Greatest Ever Matches', Esquire, 11 July 2014 https://www.
esquire.com/uk/culture/news/a6396/1982-why-brazil-v-
italy-was-one-of-footballs-greatest-ever-matches/

Livie, Alex, 'Zidane announces retirement', Sky Sports,
January 2006 https://www.skysports.com/football/
news/11835/2374656/zidane-announces-retirement

Marcotti, Gabriele, 'Best teams never to win a World Cup:
Brazil 1982, ESPN, 9 May 2014 https://www.espn.com/
soccer/blog/name/93/post/1845214/headline

Massarella, Louis, 'Football's greatest-ever title finish?
Arsenal's 1989 triumph over Liverpool, told by the players',
FourFourTwo, 3 March 2017 https://www.fourfourtwo.
com/features/footballs-greatest-ever-title-finish-arsenals-
1989-triumph-over-liverpool-told-players

McNulty, Phil, 'Barcelona 3-0 Liverpool: How Lionel Messi
Proved a Force Too Powerful for Liverpool', BBC Sport, 1
May 2019 https://www.bbc.co.uk/sport/football/48129168

McNulty, Phil, Euro 2016: Cristiano Ronaldo becomes true
great with Portugal win, BBC Sport, 11 July 2016 https://
www.bbc.co.uk/sport/football/36761007

McNulty, Phil, 'Euro 2016: England Disappoint, Iceland
Impress, Portugal Come Good', BBC Sport, 12 July 2016
https://www.bbc.co.uk/sport/football/36763052

McNulty, Phil, 'Man Utd 1 – 6 Man City', BBC Sport, 23 October 2011 https://www.bbc.co.uk/sport/football/15325536

McNulty, Phil, 'Scolari Remains Upbeat', BBC Sport, 5 July 2004 http://news.bbc.co.uk/sport1/hi/football/euro_2004/portugal/3865787.stm

McParlan, Paul, 'The Unbreakable Goalscoring Records of Dixie Dean', These Football Times, 11 February 2019 https://thesefootballtimes.co/2019/02/11/the-unbreakable-goalscoring-records-of-dixie-dean/

McTear, Euan, 'How a Baque Derby brought about the legalisation of the Basque flag', These Football Times, 19 February 2016 https://thesefootballtimes.co/2016/02/19/how-a-basque-derby-brought-about-the-legalisation-of-the-basque-flag/

Mitten, Andy, 'Eric Cantona's kick, 25 years on', FourFourTwo , 25 January 2020 https://www.fourfourtwo.com/features/eric-cantona-crystal-palace-fan-i-didnt-punch-strong-enough

Moore, Joe, 'Former England goalkeeper David Seaman on THAT 2002 World Cup goal', TalkSport, 22 February 2019 https://talksport.com/football/497485/we-didnt-know-how-good-ronaldinho-was-former-england-goalkeeper-david-seaman-on-that-2002-world-cup-goal/

Murray, Andrew 'Roberto on THAT goal in 1997', FourFourTwo, 10 April 2018 https://www.fourfourtwo.com/features/roberto-carlos-goal-1997-i-was-aiming-a-la-poste-it-went-miles-away

O'Connor, Robert, 'The Golden Goal: Remembering Football's Failed Attempt at Self-Improvement', Vice, 28 October 2015 https://www.vice.com/en_uk/article/z4djnj/the-golden-goal-remembering-footballs-failed-attempt-at-self-improvement

Ornstein, David, 'Spain 1-5 Netherlands', BBC Sport, 13 June 2014 https://www.bbc.co.uk/sport/football/25285043

Parrish, Rob, 'Messi magic inspires Barca', Sky Sports, 27 April 2011 https://www.skysports.com/football/r-madrid-vs-barcelona/report/234365

Portley, Jack, 'Why Preston North End are football's greatest invincibles', These Football Times, 23 November 2016 https://thesefootballtimes.co/2016/11/23/why-preston-north-end-are-footballs-greatest-invincibles/

Petrone, Nilton, 'Ronaldo's knee cap exploded, it was by his thigh', FourFourTwo https://www.fourfourtwo.com/performance/training/ronaldos-kneecap-exploded-it-was-his-thigh

Pritchard, Dafydd, 'Wales 3-1 Belgium, BBC Sport, 1 July 2016 https://www.bbc.co.uk/sport/football/36613679

Riach, James, 'Dutch courage stuns Brazil', Sky Sports, 2 July 2010 https://www.skysports.com/football/netherlands-vs-brazil/report/218453

Ramsey, George, 'Christine Sinclair breaks all-time international goalscoring record', CNN, 30 January 2020 https://edition.cnn.com/2020/01/30/football/christine-sinclair-goal-record-canada-football-spt-intl/index.html

Rice-Coates, Callum, 'Lucien Laurent: France's forgotten World Cup pioneer', Tifo Football, June 4 2018 https://www.tifofootball.com/features/lucien-laurent-frances-forgotten-world-cup-pioneer/

Sanders, Emma, 'Ada Hegerberg: Lyon striker breaks Women's Champions League goalscoring record', BBC Sport, 30 October 2019 https://www.bbc.co.uk/sport/football/49746194

Scragg, Steven, 'Building and destroying a legacy: Luís Figo at Barcelona', These Football Times, 14 September 2018 https://thesefootballtimes.co/2018/09/14/building-and-destroying-a-legacy-luis-figo-at-barcelona/

Scholten, Bernd, 'Michels – a total footballing legend', UEFA, 03 March 2005 https://www.uefa.com/insideuefa/about-uefa/history/obituaries/newsid=285010.html?redirectFromOrg=true

Stevenson, Jonathan, 'The story of the 1978 World Cup', BBC Sport, 18 May 2010 https://www.bbc.co.uk/blogs/jonathanstevenson/2010/05/the_story_of_the_1978_world_cu.html

Stevenson, Jonathan, 'Turkey 3-2 Czech Republic as it happened', BBC Sport, 15 June 2008 http://news.bbc.co.uk/sport1/hi/football/euro_2008/7363029.stm

Stevenson, Jonathan, 'Women's World Cup: England 2-0 Japan', BBC Sport, 5 July 2011 https://www.bbc.co.uk/sport/football/14038052

Surlis, Patrick, 'El Clásico moments: Luis Figo's return to the Nou Camp and the pig's head', Sky Sports, 21 November 2015 https://www.skysports.com/football/news/11828/10070994/el-clasico-moments-figos-pig-head

Thacker, Gary, 'Benfica and the Curse of Béla Guttmann', These Football Times, 29 June 2015 https://thesefootballtimes.co/2015/06/29/benfica-and-the-curse-of-bela-guttmann/

Thomas, Gareth, 'Luis Aragonés – The Wise Man of Hortaleza', The Football History Boys, 7 February 2014 https://www.thefootballhistoryboys.com/2014/02/luis-aragones-wise-man-of-hortaleza.html

Whelan, Greg, 'Brian Deane: The story of the first Premier League goal', Sky Sports, 23 November 2019 https://www.skysports.com/football/news/11095/11867410/brian-deane-the-story-of-the-first-premier-league-goal

Winter, Simon, 'The story of Giuseppe Savoldi, football's first million pound player', These Football Times, 23 February 2016 https://thesefootballtimes.co/2016/02/23/the-story-of-giuseppe-savoldi-footballs-first-million-pound-player/

Websites without named authors
Arsenal club website: https://www.arsenal.com/
BBC Sport: https://www.bbc.co.uk/sport
Bundesliga: https://www.bundesliga.com/en/bundesliga
Cardiff City club website: https://www.cardiffcityfc.co.uk/
CNN: https://edition.cnn.com/
FourFourTwo: https://www.fourfourtwo.com/
FIFA: https://www.fifa.com/
The Football Association: http://www.thefa.com/
Get French Football News: https://www.getfootballnewsfrance.com/

Also available at all good book stores

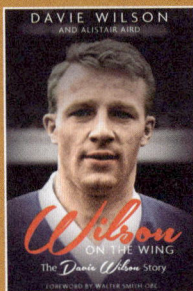

9781785316333

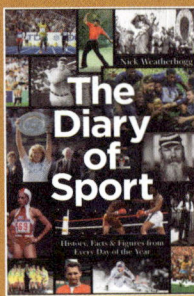

9781785316289

9781785315510

9781785316388

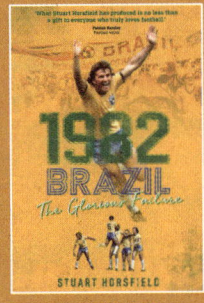

9781785316869

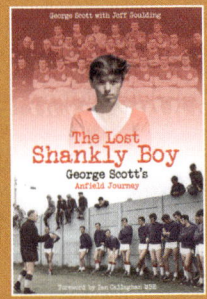

9781785316784

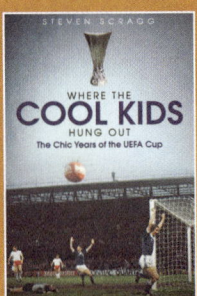

9781785316838

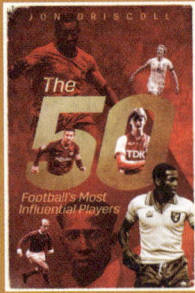

9781785316906

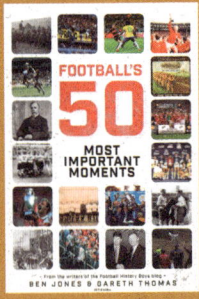

9781785316326

Stafford-Bloor, Sebb, 'The Story of Don Revie & "Dirty Leeds", Tifo Football on YouTube, 10 Feburary 2020, Available at: https://www.youtube.com/watch?v=f2nmgf_z60k

National Football Museum: https://www.
nationalfootballmuseum.com/
Real Sociedad club website: https://www.realsociedad.eus/
UEFA: https://www.uefa.com/
WalesOnline news: https://www.walesonline.co.uk/
West Ham United club website: https://www.whufc.com/

Documents

IFAB, 'Minutes of Annual General Meeting', International
Football Association Board, 1897, Available at: https://
theifab.com/home

IFAB, 'Laws of the Game', International Football Association
Board, Available at: https://www.theifab.com/laws/chapter/4

Play Fair!, 'The IFAB strategy to develop the Laws of the
Game to improve football 2017–2022', IFAB, 2017,
Available at: https://www.play-fair.com/

UEFA Publication, 'UEFA's Euro: 60 years on', UEFA Direct,
Issue 179, 1 July 2018, Available at: https://www.uefa.com/

Women's Sport and Fitness Foundation, 'Football
Factsheet', Sport England, March 2011, Available at:
https://sportengland-production-files.s3.eu-west-2.
amazonaws.com/s3fs-public/case-study-female-team-v-
individual-sports.pdf

Journals

Johnes, Martin, 'Fred Keenor: A Welsh Soccer Hero', *The
Sports Historian,* Vol. 17, Issue 1 (May 1998)

Baller, Susann, Miescher, Giorgio, and Rassool, Ciraj, 'Global
Perspectives on Football in Africa: Visualising the Game',
Soccer and Society, Vol. 13, Issue 2 (March 2012)

Referenced videos

FIFATV, 'Brazil in 1970: Football's most beautiful team',
FIFA on YouTube, 15 May 2014, Available at: https://www.
youtube.com/watch?v=rbSgpuwVEok

FIFATV, 'When France ruled the world', FIFA on YouTube,
13 September 2012, Available at: https://www.youtube.
com/watch?v=lFeRvBPdssU